MICHAE

LIVING PROOF

MY
TRUE LOVE STORY
UNINTERRUPTED
BY DEATH

Filament
Publishing

Published by
Filament Publishing Ltd
16, Croydon Road, Beddington,
Croydon, Surrey, CR0 4PA UK

Living Proof by Michael Ayers
ISBN 978-1-911425-50-2

Printed by IngramSpark

LIVING PROOF IS FOR YOU IF

- If you have ever lost your loved one to cancer

- If in your despair you asked God to take her from you

- If you have ever received a divine answer to your prayer

- If your received a clear message from your beloved

- If you became certain that she continues to live in the next dimension

- If you know that she still loves you

- If you believe that the spirit continues after physical death

- If you know that you are blessed and receive proof and guidance through your life

- If your beloved shows you another to share your life with because she loves you

- If by dying your beloved changed your life and your belief system

- If you know that there is a Spirit World of unconditional love

- If you want to find your way there by living a happy and worthy life

Michael Ayers
Wednesday, 5th October 2016

DEDICATION

First and foremost I want to dedicate this book to my wife Libby. She gave me so much, her love, her help, her being in this world and the next. She also gave me my son, John. I wait to be reunited with her when my time comes.

Secondly, I must thank Marie for acting as a personal guide to me in the beginning and acting, on occasions, as an intermediary between Libby and me. I wish to thank Ron Gilkes for opening the door to mediumship and Alan House who at the age of ninety-two invited me into his home to learn and discuss the World of Spirit. He also introduced me to Doreen, a wonderful and natural medium.

I am grateful to my mother-in-law, Joan and all our friends for their help and support.

I have been blessed in many ways and Libby has brought to me the greatest and most precious gift that a loving wife can give her husband – the love of another woman.

I must also thank David Hatton for keeping my computer running and all his help and hard work with the graphics and setting the type and photographs in the way I wanted them. Without his input it would have been a much less professional job.

I wish to thank Ron Denney for his interest in this book and his writing of the Preface. I would also like to thank Jane for reading the manuscript through and for her valuable and constructive suggestions.

I wish to thank my beloved wife, Jenny for painting the beautiful pictures in oils of my guide Red Cloud - an expression of sincere love. I also wish to thank her for her love and support throughout the difficult paths that we have walked together as we work unashamedly for the Spirit Realms. I wait for all three of us, Libby, Jenny and myself to be united together in the Spirit World.

Michael R. L. W. Ayers

CONTENTS

Preface...7

Introduction...9

Chapter 1   The Meeting...13

Chapter 2   The Passing...27

Chapter 3   The Understanding..37

Chapter 4   The Sittings...71

Photographs..117

Chapter 5   The Birthday Present......................................123

Chapter 6   The New Century..171

Chapter 7   The Vision...208

Chapter 8   The Waiting...226

Chapter 9   The August..277

Chapter 10   The Preparation..316

Chapter 11   The Wedding...337

Appendix   Bibliograhy...343

PHOTOGRAPHS

Libby in thoughtful appreciation   117

Libby in reflective mood on a visit to Cambridge   117

The prize winning combination of Forest King and
Libby at the Hurst Horse Show   118

Libby presenting the Forest King Trophy at the
Hurst Horse Show   118

Angela, my guide who prepared me for the coming of my
new beloved   119

Barn Owls had always fascinated me so that flying a Barn
Owl in Gloucestershire was a dream come true   119

The Rollright Stone Circle in Oxfordshire that played a large
part in my spiritual life   120

The road junction near Orpington in Kent that was to change
my life - and for the better   120

The vision becomes a reality as Jenny and Michael are
married at the Sanctuary, Arthur Findley College, Stansted
Hall in Essex on Saturday, 30th March 2002   121

Jenny and Michael on Honeymoon in Egypt   121

Jenny's portrait of my guide Red Cloud   122

PREFACE

Occasionally in life we come across something that is different and quite exceptional. 'Living Proof' comes in that category. It is not often that a mature male opens his heart and mind to the world in order that other people can feel and follow the traumas he has gone through seeing his wife die.

The difference in this book is the way Michael Ayers' wife, Libby, has been able to reach back to him from the Spirit World in order to help him overcome the depression following her death and to develop his own spiritual gifts that serve to guide and comfort others.

Michael Ayers has the openness to talk about life after death and direct communication with the dead. This is something few people will admit to, but some experience and many hope will occur when their loved ones depart this Earth.

Michael Ayers is a retired agronomist who was born in Chislehurst, Kent in 1940. He was educated at Christ's Hospital, Horsham, England and later studied fruit growing and bee-keeping. He worked at East Malling Research Station and later for Ciba Laboratories Ltd and Rank, Hovis, McDougall. His first marriage was dissolved in 1982 and most of what he reports in this book relates to the period during and after his second marriage to Elizabeth (Libby) Saunders from 1985 until her death in 1999.

It was nearly two years before he met spiritual healer and clairvoyant Jenny Eales whom he married in March 2002. During that intervening period Michael was supported and guided by the spiritual presence of his former wife as he progressed through dejection and despair before becoming spiritually enlightened with the development of his own healing gifts channelled by his spirit guides.

This book will challenge the beliefs of many readers and will encourage those who have been bereaved but believe that they will meet their loved ones again when their own life in this world is over.

Ron Denney

INTRODUCTION

Before you read the events described in this book I feel I should explain I had no previous personal experience of the Spirit World, clairvoyants, mediums or the reading of books about the 'Afterlife' prior to what is described here. I certainly had no thoughts about writing a book on this subject until the various incidents, events and situations related here occurred.

I loved my wife, Libby, very dearly. During her illness I honestly believed that she would beat cancer and live with me for many years to come. I believed that at fifty-two years old she still had a life in front of her and that she had so much to give to the world that she would continue to work for those who needed her. I thought that she would be helping people by telling them what it was like to have breast cancer and how she was able to overcome it.

When I learned that she was going to die, in what turned out to be within a week, I somehow managed to carry on with her nursing. It was something I had to do – something I wanted and needed to do. I became concerned that she didn't suffer more than she had to. I was totally involved in her welfare at that time. I prayed to God not to let Libby suffer and to take her into his care.

I was looked after during this time, although I didn't understand it then, by the Spirit World, as well as those wonderful nurses and doctors at the Sue Ryder Palliative Care Home at Nettlebed in Oxfordshire, England. Our friends and relatives helped my mother-in-law, Joan and me as much as they could. Everybody loved Libby. She was one of those wonderful people that one couldn't help loving in one form or another.

When Libby died at twenty to five in the afternoon on Thursday, 7th October 1999 I felt relief, pain and great loss. I did what had to be done. I registered her death the following day with the Henley-on-Thames Registrar and returned to thank the nurses and doctors at the Sue Ryder Home and to visit the remains of Libby in their Chapel of Rest. I was crying as I left.

When Libby first spoke to me in the car park at the Registry Office and suggested that I went to Sue Ryder Home to thank the doctors and nurses and to check the body in the chapel, it was as though I had the idea myself.

"That's a good idea," I thought and did just that.

Later in the gardens Libby spoke to me again. It came to me as thought transference and I 'heard' in my mind as if it was my own voice only it was much clearer, but it was certainly her manner of speaking.

The first time I wasn't expecting anything but the second time, after I had received God's words, I was far more receptive and recognised her 'voice print' so to speak. In those early days Libby had to come very close to communicate and this used a lot of energy as she had to come from the lighter vibrations of the Spirit Realms into the heavier vibrations of the earth plane.

Later on she learned to send her thought waves from much greater distances to save energy and then we could talk for longer. The guides 'talk' to us in a similar way. After a time we recognise their manner of communication and sometimes they give a physical warning that they wish to communicate. My guide Red Cloud gives me a tingling sensation in my right hand if he wishes to give me my daily sitting and I am busy doing something else.

During my walk in the gardens I had two very clear messages. The first was from God Himself and the second was from Libby. I was amazed and strangely at peace. I had never expected anything like this to happen!

Up to the time of her funeral on Monday, 18th October, I was kept busy with the arrangements. I felt as if Libby was about me keeping an eye on things and everything had to be done just right. She was a perfectionist and I wasn't going to have any slip ups.

For the first three nights after her passing I closed my bedroom curtains as usual, although I had the strong impression that I should leave them open so Libby could come to me. I felt that if she was there, a spirit could certainly find a way in! However on the fourth day I distinctly felt that I should not close the curtains. That night I felt Libby's presence very strongly and very near to me before I went to sleep.

I could accept that the dead could be around for a while to say goodbye or to put right any unfinished discord with anybody in their lives. That was as far as I could imagine. I knew that Libby would do anything she could to spare me pain, but what could she do that she hadn't already done? She had told me in the gardens in Nettlebed that she was at peace, that everything was alright and that I wasn't to worry.

At first I doubted everything. I was no Spiritualist. I have been amazed and shattered by everything that has happened. I have done nothing here except write down a record of the events that have occurred. This book is a record of those events.

I have been told by Libby that they should be recorded and that I must publish them in order to help other people who are not as well looked after as I had been. I was fortunate because Libby and I had a very special relationship that continued on after her death. I have learned that death is not something to be feared. I have been told much about the Spirit World. It was not Libby who had more work to do on Earth. That job had been entrusted to me. I have received much help in order for me to do this.

All I ask the readers of this book to do is to have a completely open mind. There is absolutely no doubt in <u>my</u> mind that these events recorded here have truly happened. I have been blessed with a wonderful gift. A gift of great magnitude that I thank God for, my wife Libby and all those in the Spirit World who have made this possible.

I believe that I have been spared some of the grief of losing my wife and given support and guidance in a way that may be considered somewhat unusual. I believe that if we are open and don't protect our emotions there is help available to us from the Spirit Realms. I received continuous contact and daily help.

In thanks for this I believe that I must share these events and help others who aren't so fortunate. Much of this journal could be described as very personal. Yes, it is very personal, but as Libby has said to me, *"We have nothing to be ashamed of!"* I make no apology for revealing my emotions and feelings, however sensitive these may be.

To make it easier to read, I have shown the words of my beloved Libby in italics. It is after all her words and her teachings to me that are the most important and not my comments, although I have tried to put down my reactions as I walked this incredible pathway of learning and love. I hope that the reader therefore finds it easier to follow.

If this book can help other people, I am happy that the journey of the life and death of Libby and I should be shared.

Michael Ayers
2008

Chapter 1

THE MEETING

I was divorced in 1982 at the age of forty-two and following the break-up of this, first marriage and I decided to move from the Devon/Somerset borders to Hungerford in Berkshire. I was unhappy about what had happened after fourteen years and I just wanted to start a new life in a new area. Because of this I joined a company based in Hungerford and eventually bought a house on the edge of the town.

After a while I felt that it was no good just staying at home. I had to make new friends and find another partner if possible. The first move was to go to a singles pub night, but I am sorry to say that was definitely not for me. It was ghastly! Next I tried computer dating. I met some very nice ladies and some that were not so interesting.

It wasn't leading me anywhere but then somebody mentioned a magazine called Singles. I duly bought a copy and found it to contained advertisements for boyfriends from women in one half and advertisements for girlfriends from men in the other half. People were seeking friendship from the ages of eighteen to ninety-five!

I answered about ten advertisements and from the replies went out to meet prospective friends. Some of the ladies were very nice but some were, I must say, pretty grim! I did not find anyone who really suited me so I decided to put an advertisement in myself and was rather surprised to receive some twenty replies. One of them was from a lady named Libby Saunders. I telephoned her and we arranged to meet one evening on Monday, 7th February 1983 and then I found that Libby was an abbreviated form of Elizabeth. On that first evening I just took her out to the local pub for a drink and we had an enjoyable evening. We continued meeting and had meals together and we started to go to the theatre and the ballet.

One day I asked her how many advertisements she had replied to from the Singles magazine. I had previously found that many ladies answered a dozen a month hoping that one of them would turn out to be Mr Right.

"Only one," Libby replied.

Apparently someone at her place of work had given her a copy of the magazine and told her to find herself somebody! That just happened to be the one with my advertisement in it and Libby just happened to choose it.

After my marital break up and the trauma of the divorce I had suffered from depression. I'm not proud to say it but I even tried to commit suicide.

A short time after we had come to know each other Libby and I had spent a weekend on the Isle of Wight. It was a super weekend but as we drove back to Berkshire the depression started to come back. Libby saw it happen. She said that it was like a curtain coming down.

"If that's what it's doing to you you'd better pack up your job and come and live with me," she said. *"You won't have to do much – just stroke my cat and cuddle my pony."*

Now I must admit that at this time of my life I had a particular opinion about horses. They are very large with big teeth and large metal shod hooves. If I was going for a walk and there was a horse in the field I would certainly take a detour!

But the depression was becoming overpowering at times and I had gained so much confidence from this exceptional woman that I took Libby up on her offer.

I moved to Betty Grove Farm and sold my house in Hungerford. I filled my time trying to be useful while I rebuilt my life. I re-fenced the farm and did jobs around there, fed the horses and got to love them, despite the teeth and hooves. Libby and I had been together long enough to know that we were in love with each other. We had also made an incredible discovery. We were driving somewhere, I forget where, when Libby said to me,

"When's your birthday?"

"Twenty-seventh of December," I replied automatically.

"So is mine!" she said.

It took a few moments for the significance of this to sink in. I was born in 1940. Libby was born in 1946. We then discovered that with Leap Year we were both born on a Friday! We asked our mothers at what time we were born. I was born at ten past six in the morning and Libby was born at ten past six in the evening! It is not perhaps surprising that we later got married on Friday, 27th December 1985, but not at ten past six!

There were many other 'coincidences' in our lives. My grandfather had worked for the same company, British Oil and Cake Mills, as her grandfather – my grandfather was in Kent and hers in Somerset. I had won a scholarship to Christ's Hospital boys' school near Horsham in West Sussex and I was educated there. Libby had the chance to go Christ's Hospital girls' school at Hertford, but she chose not to go there in the end. Instead she went to Kendrick girls' school in Reading where her mother was educated. Both our fathers had gone off with other women leaving our mothers to bring up their only child.

Libby had a very good job with Ferranti International in Bracknell, not far away. She was the Personal Assistant to the sales Director, Harry Johnson. I spent my time on the eight-acre farm where she kept her horses doing fencing and did it need doing! All credit to Libby because she kept down a high-powered job as well as keeping her horses. There were times in the past when she had had to phone Harry to say, *"I may not be in until nine-thirty or ten this morning because my horses have got into next door's maize!"*

Harry thought it was a great joke but Libby always made up for it and never went home before the day's work was done whatever that time was. She was so conscientious that on several occasions I would telephone her at work and say, "It's one o'clock – go to lunch!" In the evenings I would cook a meal and open a bottle of wine. If she wasn't home by seven-thirty I would telephone her at the office and tell her the wine was getting warm! She would stop work and be home in twenty minutes. I'd meet her in the farm car park with a glass of vino.

Libby loved her horses and I learned to love them too. Libby also loved cats. A tabby and white cat had adopted her. Opposite the farm were two cottages and Libby was visiting her friendly neighbour Jill one morning. As Libby walked down the drive she found this tomcat on the lawn. It was impossible for Libby not to make friends with any cat and she was about to pick him up when suddenly she heard Jill call, "Don't touch him! He's very wild. I leave food out for him but I can't get near him."

The tabby followed Libby home and moved in! She told me that he was the ugliest cat she had ever seen. He was cross-eyed, had a wound in his chest, was as thin as the proverbial rake and hadn't been doctored. She took him to the vet who asked the cat's name and Libby thought about it and then said, *"He's a tabby cat so put him down as TC."*

And so TC he became and Libby looked after him. By the time I arrived he was the most beautiful and intelligent cat I had ever seen. On the first morning after I had stayed the night, he jumped up on the bed, lay on my chest and purred. It was his way of saying, "You're okay. You're staying!" I did.

Libby told me that when TC arrived after fending for himself he had a ravenous appetite. One evening Libby had made herself a ham sandwich. She had sat down and raised the sandwich to her mouth when, as quick as lightening a paw shot out and neatly removed the ham without touching the bread on either side of it!

Over the years of looking after himself, his constitution wasn't as good as it could have been and his kidneys started to fail. I eventually had the awful job of taking him to the vet to be put down. I shall never forget the look in his eyes as I held him while he had that fatal injection. "Judas," it said and I can see it even now.

Libby had eight acres where she kept her horses. I decided, while I was recovering from depression, to do a bit of the Good Life. We kept free-range chickens and ducks, got our milk from goats and we grew a fair amount of vegetables.

There were some weedy patches in the field where the horses used to deposit their recycled grass. Initially I treated them with weed killer until it dawned on me that some sheep would do the job just as well. Besides they would help to manure the soil and would provide us with some joints for the freezer. I bought four orphan lambs. They came from ewes that had triplets but could only suckle two and so I bottle reared them every four hours. That's six feeds a day including getting up through the night.

They thrived and did well. The following year I bought some more and again raised them using powdered milk. Unfortunately, in their enthusiasm to get at the bottle of warm milk, one of them gashed my finger and I contracted a disease called Orf. This was in 1984 and I was left with a condition known as M.E. (Myalgic Encephalomyelitis). It is also known as yuppie flu but my condition was better understood as Chronic Fatigue Syndrome (CFS).

I was working as a Consultant Agronomist at this time but I found that after a little exertion I was completely worn out and had to go to bed and sleep. I suffered from physical and mental exhaustion, hyperventilation, giddiness, aching limbs and flatulence. I was unable to cope with physical or mental stress. Libby was wonderful and managed to keep sane while I frankly became a liability. I had to give up my consultancy business as well as the vegetables but we continued to keep the animals.

For many years I had been interested in cricket and I used to go to watch Berkshire play Minor County Cricket. I used to sit near the score box with my scorebook and record the play. I found this relaxing and definitely therapeutic. It helped my recovery from the CFS. This eventually led to an offer in 1988 to tour New Zealand for five weeks as their scorer. I went back to the farm and decided not to tell Libby until there was a suitable moment.

As soon as I walked in she said, *"What's happened?"*

"Why nothing?" I said.

"Come on," she said, *"I know something has happened!"*

"Nothing really, I've been asked to go to New Zealand with Berkshire for five weeks. That's all."

"What did you say?" she asked.

"Oh, I said I couldn't possible leave you with the farm and a full time job."

"Nonsense!" she said. *"You must go. It's a wonderful opportunity."*

So I did and it was a wonderful experience. Libby looked after the farm and did an exacting full-time job while

I was away. On the way back I met Libby and her mother in Florida and we spent a week there.

A good friend of mine, Len Cross who was the official Berkshire Scorer told me that the Surrey scorer, Tom Billston had died and so why didn't I write to Surrey County Cricket Club for the job. "Hey, that's professional and serious!" I said, but after a while I thought they could only say no! So I wrote and Geoff Arnold, the Surrey Coach, took me on.

I spent five and a half years scoring for Surrey from 1989-95, doing the statistics and even scoring for England when they played at the Oval. Libby was very enthusiastic. She came to games whenever she could and always came to the Test Matches and One-Day Internationals when I was scoring them. She even took the scorers' examinations.

On one occasion when I was detained at the Oval because the BBC was recording a television programme and I had to explain about the new system of computer scoring. Libby went down to Southampton and scored for Surrey with Tony Weld, the Hampshire Scorer.

On another day Stan Tracey, the Derbyshire scorer, asked Libby to score for him in a Surrey v Derbyshire County Championship match at the Oval as he had to go back home for a funeral. So that was a splendid day with husband and wife officially scoring a first class match together. She did incredibly well too! She helped me write a statistical book about Surrey CCC and to edit a scorers' magazine. She entered into every new interest with enthusiasm, skill and dedication. She was always my better half in every respect.

My mother died in 1991. We decided not to sell her lovely cottage in North Oxfordshire but to rent it out as a holiday cottage with English Country Cottages. Libby busied herself with getting the cottage into a suitable condition to let and in 1995 we had our first visitors. It was a foursome from London who wanted a weekend away from the "Smoke". It has been a highly successful venture and up to the time of Libby's death we had over two hundred bookings and visitors from around the world.

One of the hardest things I had to do after Libby died was to take her name off everything to do with the cottage. I always sent a welcome letter to every booking that came our way and I also did a welcome note for when our visitors arrived at the cottage. Just writing them from me became very sad and not natural in some way. Libby had as much, if not more, to do with the success of the venture and I hated just sending these things from just "Michael".

Libby had taken early redundancy from Ferranti in 1991. One day I remember saying to Libby, "You know if we had only met when we were younger we could have spent so much more time together!"

She replied, *"We should be grateful to Graham and Christine* (our former partners) *because without them we would probably have never met!"*

How right she was! As I write this, I know that we wouldn't have been ready for each other, even if we had met sooner. She was a very bright lady, my Libby.

After taking early retirement from Ferranti she took a job with the Arborfield and Newland Parish Council, which she did well and conscientiously for nearly six years. It was impossible for Libby not to be always busy. She loved the work and was very good at it. She was only paid for eleven hours a week but there were times when she put in eleven hours in a single day!

I feel that this is as good a place as any to mention my feelings about spiritualism before Libby died. Adrian, Libby's cousin, had lost a loved one called Carolyn. She had also died of breast cancer. Adrian had told me that Carolyn had spoken to him and that he had received messages through a medium.

In retrospect I am rather ashamed of my reactions at that time to this news. However I must be completely honest and say that, although I listened politely, my private thoughts were, "Good Lord! What has he got himself involved in?" I felt that if it helped him all well and good, but my thoughts about mediums were, to say the least, rather unkind!

After the break-up of Libby's first marriage she had seen a clairvoyant. She had told me about it one day and added, *"You must listen to the tape. He described you and knew all about your coming into my life!"* He had also predicted that she would give up her job with Ferranti International and go into social work. *"No way,"* Libby had said to me. If being a Parish Clerk isn't social work I don't know what is!

In 1990 Libby told me she was pregnant. She had a full time job that she didn't want to give up and I was scoring for Surrey CCC, which I didn't want to give up. Neither of us wanted the other to give up their work. After a great deal of discussion we decided that Libby would have an abortion. She did so in September 1990.

In 1996 Libby had a pain in her left breast after Folly, her grey mare, had playfully knocked it with her muzzle. Following a visit to her doctor she went to the Royal Berkshire Hospital in Reading and they subsequently diagnosed breast cancer. First she suffered the beastly chemotherapy, then surgery and after that radiotherapy. Then she was put on a course of Tamoxifen and for two years everything went well.

We had moved in with Libby's mother, Joan, in Melton Cottage, just a few hundred yards from the farm and Libby was outside the cottage with the farrier one morning. I had just taken them coffee and returned to continue some work on my computer when suddenly Libby rushed in. *"Feel that,"* she commanded, *"Come on, I'm serious!"* There was a small lump in her neck. It was later diagnosed as active. They changed the Tamoxifen for another newer drug called Arimidex.

Libby and I had had a week's holiday near Ludlow in Shropshire. While we were in the shop at Ludlow Castle Libby came over to me.

"I don't want you to buy it," she said, *"but I've seen the most beautiful bronze of a horse's head."*

I went and looked at it with her. It was extremely well done and I bought it for her. She was thrilled with it and loved it dearly.

Some time later Libby's New Forest pony, Forest King, died and Libby wanted to present a trophy at Hurst Park where he had won many times. She made contact with the sculptor and acquired another bronze head on a special plinth. At the Hurst Show 1999 Libby presented the trophy for the first time. I was very proud of her. Unfortunately the weather was atrocious and it pelted with rain before and during the presentation.

Gradually Libby developed more pain, first in her chest and then in her legs. On Thursday, 5th August 1999 we went in for one of her regular check ups at the Royal Berkshire Hospital in Reading. They wanted to do a bone scan.

"That can't be the problem," Libby said, *"I had one done last October!"*

"Nevertheless," said the doctor firmly, "it's over six months and I'd like to see the results of another one before we go any further."

At eleven o'clock on the Wednesday, 11th August 1999 while the world was watching the eclipse of the sun, live or on television, I was with Libby while she had an injection four hours before the bone scan! Six days later she was to return to discuss the results.

Martin Stubbs, a friend and colleague in as much as they both worked for the council (Martin was the District Councillor for Wokingham), died on Tuesday 3rd August. They both fought against cancer, which they both lost. They supported each other and so it was a great blow when Martin died. Libby attended his funeral on Friday, 13th August. It was to be her last public appearance.

On Tuesday, 17th August, Libby and I attended the Cancer Clinic at the Royal Berkshire Hospital. They wanted to keep Libby in there and then. They feared that the cancer was encircling the vertebrae in her spine. If she tripped or jarred her back she might never walk again. *"I want to go home first,"* she insisted but they begged her to stay in hospital.

"What you're not telling these good people," I said, "is that we live down a potholed lane and no matter how carefully I drive we now know that there is a big risk."

I drove back alone and collected the things that she would need immediately. She never came home again.

I visited her every day and stayed as long as possible. I helped with her nursing, washing, going to the toilet and acting as one of the porters when she went down for treatment or X-ray. One evening I was later back than usual. Libby was particularly clinging that night and didn't want me to go. Her mother and I discussed what had happened during the day and we didn't eat our meal until nine o'clock.

She had nearly finished her supper when she suddenly passed out. "Help," I thought, "she's gone this time!" I called for an ambulance and while they were coming I was told to get her off the chair and lay her out on the floor. I put my arm round her and she opened her eyes and grinned at me.

"Are you alright," I said with much relief. She assured me that she was and then the ambulance arrived from Wokingham. After checking her over they took us both into Reading so she could have a further check up.

So at about eleven forty-five on Thursday, 23rd September 1999, I was sitting in the Accident and Emergency Department at the Royal Berkshire Hospital thinking, "My wife's upstairs with cancer. My mother-in-law, Joan, is beside me being checked after her turn earlier and Libby's father, Charles, was in that Britannia aircraft that went off the runway at Gerona airport in Spain!"

The accident happened in the early hours of Monday, 20th September. I had received a phone call from Charles on the Wednesday morning saying that he was alright and that he was going to continue with his holiday. Later that morning I told Libby that Charles had been in a plane crash, but that I had heard from him and he was alright.

The next day, Thursday, I was driving along as usual to the hospital to see Libby and I was told, the message just arrived in my head, to put the car radio on! Now I rarely have it on while I'm driving and almost never on short journeys. However I switched it on. The station was in the middle of the eleven-thirty news and the first words I heard were, "A survivor of Monday's Spanish air crash, Charles Bryant of Cardiff has died of a heart attack."

I turned the radio off and stopped the car. I was bewildered! I telephoned my mother-in-law, Joan and told her the news before driving on to the hospital. I was met in the ward by one of the nurses. "Was that Libby's father who died?" she asked. "We haven't told her but we are afraid that someone might mention it to her." I went to her bed to see her. She smiled as she always did when I came.

"How do you feel?" I asked.

"Not very good," she said. *"I didn't sleep well last night. Will you take those cards away and those roses too? They had demons coming out of them last night."*

I took down the "Get Well" and "Thinking of You" cards that were up on a string above the end of her bed. I also took away the dozen red roses that I had brought her a few days before. I discussed the matter of her father's death with the nurse in charge of the ward.

"I think you should tell her," she told me.

I still had my doubts. I didn't want to do anything that would upset her. I kept her television turned off and when the Macmillan nurse came I discussed the matter with her. She was of the opinion that I should tell Libby.

So with an uneasy heart I went and told her that I had some bad news for her. When I told her that her father had died she said, *"Thank God!"* She went very quiet. I am sure she knew more than she was going to tell me.

It transpired later that Charles had been released from the Spanish hospital after just two hours. The Spanish inquest confirmed that he had died of a heart attack. They apparently went on to say that his heart attack had been brought on by a ruptured spleen that was caused by the air crash. In this country he would have been kept in for at least twenty-four hours for observation. Charles was eighty-four. As I typed these words I had the unmistakable feeling that Charles was there with me.

Over the next few weeks Libby had more radiotherapy to her breast, hips and back. She was in a great deal of pain. I stayed with her each day. She hated it when it was time for me to go but she knew I had to. She seemed to be responding well to treatment before the MRI found that between T2 and T3, the second and third vertebrae of her back, had collapsed. I was told that evening that surgery would do no good and that my wife would never walk again. I cried unashamedly.

We prepared for life with a wheel chair. Libby was due to go to the Sue Ryder Home at Nettlebed in Oxfordshire to learn how to sit up. She had been lying pretty flat to save damage to her back and now she had to learn to use a wheel chair. However she suffered a bladder infection and had to go to Battle Hospital in Reading for treatment.

At last, at the third attempt, we got Libby to the Sue Ryder Home. Whenever we were ready to go Libby had developed further symptoms that needed investigating —pains in her hip, the collapsed vertebrae in her neck and then the bladder infection. It was there at the Sue Ryder Home that I learned a few days later that Libby had a tumour in her bladder and that she would die.

Not in years, not in months, probably not in weeks but very soon. The doctor had given her an opportunity to talk about the future but she said, *"No, thank you."* She must have known already and would have wanted to spare my feelings. I followed the doctor out and asked if I could speak to him. He took me into a small private room and there I learned the truth. I went back to Libby. We always shared everything but she never asked me what he had said. She already knew.

I now believe that she knew a long time before this. I remember one afternoon when she was in the Royal Berkshire Hospital and she looked me straight in the eyes and said, *"Oh Bear, I do love you."* I think she knew then. Libby had always called me 'Bear' virtually from the time we first met.

Libby died at twenty to five in the afternoon on Thursday, 7th October 1999.

Chapter 2

THE PASSING

Monday, 4ᵗʰ October 1999

In the afternoon a few days before Libby died, I was walking towards the lake at the Sue Ryder Home approaching it from the right. I was praying to God to take Libby and not let her suffer. I felt absolutely nothing. I became cross and called out, "Are you listening God?"

At that precise moment from a heavy grey cloudy sky, a bright shaft of golden light came through the clouds to the ground. It was not the sunlight breaking through it was solid gold. There was no doubt in my mind that God had answered my prayer because the timing was absolutely perfect.

Elise, one of the Sue Ryder nurses who had sat with me in the evenings by Libby's bed and always asked if she could sit with her if I went out of the ward for any reason, has since told me that she too had prayed to God. She had also asked Him to take Libby so she wouldn't suffer.

Tuesday, 5ᵗʰ October 1999

Today I drove up to the Sue Ryder Home for the last time to see Libby. I had been invited to stay there each night now so that I could be with her. I was very grateful for all their kindness and consideration. Elise had told me that I would know when the time was right for me to stay. I had told Libby's mother that I wouldn't telephone her when Libby died. If I had she'd have jumped every time the phone rang and it would mean that I couldn't call her from Nettlebed just to keep in touch. We agreed that I would come home and she'd then know without me having to tell her.

Paul and Trish, long-standing friends of Libby, visited to say their farewells. As they were standing by her bed, Libby looked a little puzzled and Paul said, "It's not a dream. We are really here!" Libby's face lit up into a wonderful smile. She was so happy to see them and to know that they were really there beside her bed.

Wednesday, 6th October 1999

I had invited Graham, Libby's first husband, to come and say his final farewell to Libby. He came up after lunch and we went in to see her. She was asleep and heavily sedated with diamorphine (opium) to relieve the pain. She was not able to speak at this time but I am sure she could hear what was said to her.

After a while I suggested that we took a walk round the grounds. There are twenty-six acres of garden at the palliative home and we walked right round. When we returned the nurses were making Libby comfortable and seeing to her toilet so we waited outside in the front of the house. Elise came out to us.

"I think you should come in now," she said. "I don't think she will last much longer."

"How soon?" I asked. I always wanted some idea so I was prepared as much as I could be.

"I can't be sure but perhaps twenty minutes."

Everything was so unreal. It was as though I was in a play and soon I would be able to walk off the stage and come back into reality. Libby was certainly very close to dying. Her pulse was weak. I could see a point at the top of her nightdress, which rose and fell. Twice her pulse became so weak that I thought, "This is it." I had sat by my mother's bedside when she died. The breathing changes. It becomes shallower and then deeper and deeper. The breath can then be held for up to a minute before it starts again. I'm told that it's called Cheyne-Stoking. There are deep breaths taken in and agonising waits before another breath is taken.

I found myself wondering if the last breath was her last, but Libby rallied and Graham eventually had to leave. In all I sat holding her hand for two and half-hours before I decided that her pulse was strong enough for me to get up and go round to the other side of the bed. As I sat there I felt an incredible feeling in the circumstances. I felt absolutely normal. It was as though the dreadful strain of the last few weeks had been lifted off me. I had my supper and a couple of glasses of red wine. I was at peace that evening and later I went up to the room they had kindly lent me and I slept really well.

Thursday, 7th October 1999

After lunch I had an unexpected visitor. Sally, a friend, had come on a surprise visit because she wanted to say goodbye to Libby. I had a routine now. I sat down with Sally in the big hall and warned her of what to expect. Then I took her into the ward. After a while I suggested a walk in the garden. We walked round the whole of the gardens and came back to the lake. I saw the white uniform of one of the nurses coming down from the house and I said to Sally, "Either she's on her way home or she's coming for me."

The nurse came down to the lake and said, "I'm sorry Michael your wife has just died."

Libby had died at four-forty that afternoon at the Sue Ryder Home. She had slipped away while we were in the garden. She knew my routine and she knew that I would walk round the gardens with Sally. I have been told that they could choose when they were ready to go. I believe

Libby deliberately went without me being present to save the pain of what I would certainly have felt by seeing her die.

Friday, 8th October 1999

I registered Libby's death at Henley-on-Thames. Afterwards I drove to the Sue Ryder Home to thank the doctors and nurses for their help and kindness. I visited Libby's body in the chapel. Her eyes were half open and her lips were parted. If her body hadn't been so cold I would have thought she was asleep. I told her that I loved her and that I would look after her mother, the animals and her farm. I cried.

As I left, the nurse who had taken me to the chapel asked if I was alright. I said that I was and that I would walk down to the lake and back to the car park and then go.

I stood on the top of the steps overlooking the lake. It was a still morning and there was no wind at all. Suddenly I was aware of a very warm breeze coming up from the lake. It blew over and through me and as it did I felt the warmth and love that it contained. It was healing and just as I was thinking, "That feels wonderful", I heard from the left side of my mind and I understood clear words.

"I heard you. She is at peace with me. She is at rest." I thanked God.

I walked round the lake and up the path towards the house. It was the same path that I had been walking when I had seen the shaft of bright gold. Before reaching the steps near the house I felt distinctly that I was being told exactly what to do.

"Walk up the steps. Stop at the top and turn and face the lake. Don't just look over your shoulder. Walk up the steps and face the lake."

I walked up the steps and turned and faced the lake as I had been told to do. Above it, as wide as the lake and up in the sky above the treetops, there was a presence. It was oval, white and contained a number of very small different coloured lights. From the left-hand side of my mind I heard words again. They were clear and unmistakable

"I'm not there in the chapel. I'm here. I'm at peace. Everything is alright. You don't have to worry about anything."

I too was at peace. I walked to the car and drove back.

Thursday, 14th October 1999

I went to see Libby in the Chapel of Rest at the undertakers. I closed her eyes and told her that I loved her. She wasn't there in her body but I felt her near me.

Later I went on into Anthony Blay Menswear in Wokingham and collected a hired grey suit, a white shirt and a black and white small chequered tie. I wanted to look my best at Libby's funeral on Monday.

Friday, 15th October 1999

I went to the undertakers again to see her in her coffin. I wanted to see that everything was alright on each step of the journey. I knew she wasn't in her body but I needed to know that everything had been done properly. There was certainly no presence of Libby there at all. It all felt like an empty room. Somehow I had a feeling that she was cross with me for coming to see her body in the coffin, but I loved her body too and I am glad I saw that things were in order.

I spoke to Libby's cousin, Adrian, by telephone about the arrangements for Libby's funeral on Monday. He was due to come up from Worcestershire with his then girl friend, Marie. She had worked as a medium up to two years before but had given it up because of the jealousies and backstabbing between the other mediums. Suddenly Adrian said, "Just a minute, Marie is saying something. Did you and Libby ever have a disagreement about a tie?"

I thought and then replied. "No," I said, "I can't remember anything like that."

"She's getting something very strongly about a tie and it being the wrong one or something like that!"

"I can't think of anything," I said, "but I'll see if I can remember anything about a tie."

Monday, 18ᵗʰ October 1999

I had decided against wearing the black and white chequered tie and reverted to my usual black funeral tie. I always hated black at funerals because I felt that if you believed that your loved one had left this life in order to be with God in Heaven, it was something to be happy about. After all God is Light not Darkness. Our grief was natural but there was no need to go over the top with it with Victorian overload.

Before we left for Barkham Church, Marie used her psychic powers to relax me in the bedroom. I was facing the window but my eyes were closed. She told me that Libby was pleased with the arrangements and that she would be attending the forthcoming Thanksgiving Service on horseback. I would know which one – her New Forest pony Forest King of course – in casual clothes and the horse would be wearing his rosettes. This I found difficult to take on board because Libby was no show off and didn't believe in flaunting rosettes to say that she had won.

Marie also told me that Libby had said that the front room, where I had tidied up the office and laid out the drinks, cards and letters etc was fine, but it shouldn't stay like that. Marie also told me that Libby had said the tie was fine!

Libby's Thanksgiving Service for her life was held at Barkham Church and then we held the Committal at the Easthampstead Park Crematorium. Libby's mother, Joan and I drew great strength from knowing that Libby was in God's hands. More than a hundred people came to the Thanksgiving Service, fifty to the Crematorium and about forty came back to Melton Cottage.

That night as I closed the bedroom curtains I felt that I was shutting Libby out. I said, "Come on, Libby, you can come through a set of curtains." But she didn't.

Tuesday, 19th October 1999

That night as I closed the bedroom curtains I again felt that I was shutting Libby out. Again I said, "Come on, Libby, you can come through the curtains."

Wednesday, 20th October 1999

I took the hired suit, shirt and tie back to Anthony Blay's hire shop in Wokingham. After I had left I suddenly remembered that I hadn't worn the tie with the small black and white squares. I had decided to wear my own black one that I had worn at previous funerals Libby and I had attended, so it was clear that she would have approved of it! It was also clear that she didn't want me to wear the hired tie, which fortunately for me I had decided not to use.

That night as I closed the bedroom curtains I still felt that I was shutting Libby out. Yet again I said, "Come on Libby, you can come through a set of curtains."

Thursday, 21st October 1999

During the day the feeling about the bedroom curtains returned to me. I was made to understand that I must not close them. I resolved to find out if I was being silly or if I really was shutting Libby out.

I wrote several letters that day, thanking the ministers as well as the staff of the Berkshire Hospitals and the Sue Ryder Home for the kindness and treatment. I showed the letters to my mother-in-law after I had written each one.

She approved. I read through the letter to Dr Charlton at the Berkshire Cancer Centre to check it once more.

As I folded it ready to put it in the envelope I heard, in my mind, Libby say in a slightly bored way, *"Read it again!"* I read it through to the last paragraph and thought, "This is alright", but there in the very last paragraph the mistake leapt out at me. There was a split infinitive! Libby would never let that letter go out in that state and she wouldn't let me send it either.

So by bedtime I had decided to leave the bedroom curtains open. As usual I turned off the light to go to sleep and settled down. I felt Libby's presence. I didn't hear words in my mind but I understood. I was not to open my eyes or she would be gone. I felt her presence and I could feel a warmth from her. Later I couldn't remember what had passed between us, but when she had gone I knew that I must learn to be able to receive and understand her.

I didn't sleep well that night. Each time I settled down to sleep she wasn't there.

Friday, 22ⁿᵈ October 1999

The curtains were left open. I settled down to sleep. I felt Libby's presence and we communicated. I asked if I should write down my experiences so I wouldn't forget them. She said that I should. *"Would you like me to come with you?"* she asked. I said that I would like her to and she came. Without thinking I typed onto the computer screen in the dark. When I had nearly finished the telephone rang and I put the light on. She was gone.

I went into the darkness of the bedroom. Her presence was there, but far away. We didn't communicate but we knew of each other's presence there. I didn't think Libby would come back again that night but she would have been welcomed if she had.

Saturday, 23rd October 1999

Coming back from my late mother's Oxfordshire cottage and turning left over Henley Bridge, Libby said, *"Well done Bear!"* I understood that if I wanted her presence in the car I had to have the roof or the window open. Subsequently she has come to talk to me without this being necessary.

While I was watching a film I was told "Libby is waiting for you" but I waited, selfishly until the film had finished before I turned out the light. I was wrong. I shouldn't have waited. I wondered who came for her at Nettlebed to take her to the Spirit World. She couldn't or wouldn't tell me.

I asked her if I should read a book that Marie had left me and she said I should. It was called Life in the World Unseen by Anthony Borgia. Libby seemed quite insistent and when I read it, in my slow ponderous way, she became frustrated at my progress. She was a very fast reader. I slept well that night and at peace with what I'd read.

Libby showed me an image of three sets of three black horses abreast each pulling flat field rollers coming down the road from Wokingham to the Woosehill roundabout where they turned round and went back to Wokingham. The horse nearest the curb was leading and the right-hand set pulled in behind the middle set as it came over to the offside.

When I had added the above collection of images in what I called the journal on the computer she said, *"You've done well Bear. You can go to bed."*

Tuesday, 26th October 1999

I was lying on the bed doing the crossword when I was suddenly aware of being touched in a way that Libby used to touch me sometimes out of affection. I do not propose to describe it here even though this is my personal journal. I know what it was and it felt exactly as she used to do it. I took no notice of it because Libby was dead and I was convinced that there was no way that she could have been responsible for doing that.

I felt sure it had happened. I just thought that it was one of those things! It wasn't until sometime later when Libby and I were chatting that I asked her if that had been her. She said, *"Yes, of course it was! Who else did you think it was?"* There was, of course, no answer to that!

Saturday, 30th October 1999

I was preparing to go to sleep when Libby told me to ring Marie. We had a long conversation including a discussion about another two books that Marie was going to bring me to read. Libby clearly wanted me to read them. Marie also told me about a stone that she had given Libby that Marie said would now be suitable for me to carry.

Chapter 3

THE UNDERSTANDING

Tuesday, 2nd November 1999

I was working with the computer on NVD (Honeysuckle Cottage's code with English Country Cottages) records and I suddenly felt nervous as I always do when someone is standing behind me. Libby watched for a while and then said, *"Go to bed Bear, you're too tired."* I did.

Thursday, 4th November 1999

We had a long talk before I went to sleep about many things that had been causing me some concern. However I needn't have worried. Libby put my mind at rest and I felt much relief at her answers. I have been apparently doing things correctly, apart from some of my spelling and grammar errors and I knew she would let me know if I got things wrong. She was able to tell if corrections were needed and I was doing alright.

We discussed much that I had been trying to understand about the Spirit World and I could now believe that I have got things into perspective. I thanked her for preparing me so well, but she explained that it was God as well as her that had helped me so much at Nettlebed to understand what was happening. After writing this she told me to go to bed as I had done enough for tonight.

Saturday, 6ᵗʰ November 1999

Marie was talking about stones and their power. Libby said to me, *"Go to bed, Bear, it's a load of rubbish!"*

Sunday, 7ᵗʰ November 1999

Marie was asked in the middle of the night if the 8ᵗʰ September meant anything to me. She was told to remember to tell me.

Tuesday, 9ᵗʰ November 1999

In B&Q, a store that offered DIY for home and gardens, I was buying a stepladder for use at Betty Grove Farm. I chose the tallest but Libby clearly told me, *"Not that one, the next one down."*

"You always need that extra foot," I said and I tried to get the longer ladder out of the rack but the top stuck on the pallet above.

"Alright," I said, "I'll have the smaller one."

When I got the ladder out to the Range Rover I found that it only just fitted in and the longer one wouldn't have travelled safely because the back window would have had to be left open.

Wednesday, 10ᵗʰ November 1999

Libby's presence was strong in the bedroom tonight when I was ready for sleep after working late on the records of Honeysuckle Cottage. I knew she was there but talking was difficult as if I couldn't get on the right wavelength. After the resting because of her illness I wondered if she has become more spiritual and therefore it is more difficult for me to be on her wavelength. I have read that it requires a lot of energy

Thursday, 11ᵗʰ November 1999

After I had finished watching a film I put out the light to go to sleep. Libby came to me. I knew that she had finished her period of rest and was ready to do her work. I told her that I loved her but I knew that her love was greater than mine was. I said that she was good and that I would try and be as good as she had been on Earth. I knew that she must go and I said a prayer and when I had finished she was gone.

I knew that I must get up and record this and I did so with tears in my eyes, because I now knew that she had indeed gone. It was thirty-five days or just five weeks after she died and she had gone to do her new work.

Friday, 12ᵗʰ November 1999

It was quite clear that Libby had gone away. I felt empty and alone without her. I missed her terribly and I now know that I had started to grieve.

I spoke with Libby! Before I went to sleep I was able to "speak" with her. It was really a matter of thought transference. I couldn't feel her presence, that was gone, but I could understand her better.

I asked her about her work and she told me that she was seeking out and looking after horses. Many had been abused on Earth and she was helping to restore their spirit. She told me about a foal, which had been beaten with an iron bar while on Earth. She was with Forest King and all her horses that had passed into the Spirit World. I could see the heads of three horses that were in a field while I was talking to her, but I didn't see her.

I spoke to her about Betty Grove Farm and asked her if what I had been doing pleased her. She said it was my farm now and I must do what I wanted to do with it. She said that she had no connection with it as in the Spirit World you owned nothing on Earth. I must do what I liked with it. It was mine now. I asked if I was doing things alright. I was referring to the admin jobs here on Earth and she said that I was doing well and that she was proud of me. Her presence was gone, but I could always talk to her by thought transference whenever I wanted to. I felt much better knowing that I hadn't lost her all together. I slept happily.

Sunday, 14ᵗʰ November 1999

On the way up to Honeysuckle Cottage in Shenington I spoke to Libby. She told me that I must stop loving her and lead a new life without her. She had moved on. I felt gutted that I had to stop loving her. I could never stop loving her, but she was of course right that I must leave her to do her work and get on with my new life without her.

Trish, a close friend of Libby's, telephoned to say that she and her husband Paul would be coming up on Wednesday to help scatter Libby's ashes over Betty Grove Farm. I now felt empty about the task but Libby has moved on however I felt about it. The job must be done. Not for Libby but for those of us who are left behind, it is an earthly duty.

Monday, 15ᵗʰ November 1999

It was horrible and empty. It felt as though Libby and I had had a row. I suppose we had. I didn't seek her out and in any case when my thoughts did find themselves there, she wasn't. I saw the space where I had seen the three horses and it was empty. No doubt this was a lesson to me to let go but I couldn't help feeling that after all the help and support that I'd had it was a bit abrupt and cruel. Damn it, she'd only been dead for five and a half weeks!

Trying to look on the bright side, maybe we'd been too close since she died and she'd been advised it was best for me or else perhaps I'd learned too much, but whatever the case it hurt and it didn't seem to add up with her being in a place of love and happiness.

Perhaps I'd been fortunate that I hadn't grieved and been through the normal process. I believed that grieving was an earthly thing and was selfish if you believed that your loved one had gone to a better place, but I thought that it could have waited until we had scattered her ashes at the farm.

Whatever the case I was grieving now and felt very much alone. I felt that nothing really mattered and it had shaken my belief in things that I have learned about the Spirit World. I resolved to use this journal to relieve my feelings to some extent. I felt that I'd come back to earth with a bump!

I didn't look forward to going to bed now. Perhaps she would come and talk to me again and explain what had happened. I couldn't believe that I had misunderstood. I found it difficult to get on with earthly jobs.

When I was ready for sleep Libby was waiting for me. She said she didn't want to hurt me but it was best for me to get on with my life without her. She came close and I could feel her presence near me for the first time since she left. She told me she had her work to do and she couldn't spend all her time watching over me.

My deceased Uncle Teddy and Auntie Myra came and tried to make me understand that I could still love Libby and grieve for her without her having to be near me. I saw them very clearly. I understood that Libby has her work to do and I must live my life without her.

Tuesday, 16th November 1999

To be frank with myself I feel as though I have been spurned, given up and pushed aside. I feel angry because I don't think that I've been pushy or demanded any time with Libby that she wasn't prepared to give. I was the one that felt her near. She didn't have to be there at all. I can't see anything wrong with loving and caring about my wife and wanting to do things as we would have done them together. Perhaps I do go on a bit sometimes but I feel very hurt and I know Libby wouldn't hurt anybody on purpose, let alone me with all my faults.

The only thing I can believe in now is that I have got my own work to do on Earth and I must do it without Libby's guidance. Perhaps I must put right mistakes that I've made or sins I've committed. Perhaps where Libby was wasn't where I would be going.

Perhaps she just can't help me through the next phase of my life and whatever it holds was just round the corner. Things that I was doing, such as the farm, didn't seem to be so important. Perhaps I must take a rest and let my Chronic Fatigue Syndrome catch up with its demands. I've certainly been protected during the last three months and I have been able to cope. Whatever was ahead of me I shall take time and try and see where I'm going. One lesson I learned while Libby was ill was patience – a difficult thing to learn for me at any rate.

Wednesday, 17th November 1999

From about one-thirty onwards Libby's and King's ashes were scattered over Betty Grove Farm. Libby's mother, Trish, Paul, Graham and I did the honours. Libby was present but in the distance. A Weeping Willow was planted on the farm in memory of Libby.

I've found a lump in my upper leg – is that significant?

Thursday, 18th November 1999

"We have to say "Goodbye" to say "Hello" to whatever passes."

I ordered the three Anthony Borgia books suggested by Marie (*Life in the World Unseen, More About Life in the World Unseen* and *Here and Hereafter*).

At last I understand! Libby was concerned that I was making Betty Grove Farm too much of a memorial to her. She felt that by doing it all in her name I was holding her back. Hence she warned me previously that the farm was mine now and I must do whatever I like with it! It's a terrific relief to have cleared up this misunderstanding. There was no way I could have stopped loving her.

Friday, 19ᵗʰ November 1999

Today I ordered three more Anthony Borgia books (*More Light, Heaven and Earth* and *Facts*).

Because Libby had told me to let her go and stop loving her as it was keeping her from her work, I had started closing the bedroom curtains again as a sign that I was content to let her go. At twelve-thirty this morning I was still reading a book when I was told to pull the curtains back in the bedroom.

I saw that my mother-in-law's sitting room light was still on and so I went to her to see if she was alright. She was sitting in front of the television sound asleep!

I called to try and wake her up. I had to shout from the door very loudly before she awoke and I could send her to bed. I couldn't go in and shake her because my night attire was not sufficiently decent! After writing in this journal I passed her bedroom door and she was sound asleep in bed.

During that day, while reading *A Venture in Immortality* by David Kennedy, I came across the marked passage,

> **"Whatever our views on the nature of the life hereafter, it appears that our loved ones may also feel a sense of shock and trauma, at first. For this reason they need**

our prayers. However, I must sadly admit that I have been sorry for myself a great deal of the time. Perhaps if we looked more honestly at the element of self pity in bereavement, it might have a cathartic effect on us. My advice to those who have lost a love one is – observe how often such thoughts as "I can't go on", etc., occur. Notice the number of times that this ego – self – I, dominates your field of thought and accept that the Buddhist may be right; suffering is attachment to selfhood. <u>This process also causes suffering for the loved one on the other side, of this I am certain. It delays the progress of the soul whom we claim to love. We hold back our loved ones by not being willing to let them go "in love".</u>"

Later I was told it was time I went to sleep. *"Close your eyes and settle down."* I did so. *"You can open your eyes now."* This was unusual because I was normally told to keep my eyes closed. I could see nothing out of the ordinary. The clock said it was nine thirty-five. I then felt her presence very strongly and quite near.

Libby said, *"Bear, I want you to do something for me."* I felt a bit excited wondering what it was. *"Go and see the doctor,"* she said. I hadn't done anything about that lump I had found on my upper leg and I was wondering if I should mention the pain I had in the other leg to the doctor. I felt that I should.

Then I saw Libby far off standing in the countryside. The land was sloping away and the view was for many miles. It reminded me of Dorset where I had once stopped to take a photograph when I was out with my first wife. Libby went through a gap in the hedge where a gate might have been, but there was neither gate nor gateposts. Then Libby went to the left and she climbed the hedge on the far side and jumped down towards me. The field she was now in was one of combined straw.

"What do you need straw for?" I asked.

"For the horses," she said.

"As it's always day there, they don't need to go to bed," I replied.

"Why must you always question things and not just take them as read?" she replied as I tried to work it out. Then I saw a Claas combine harvester come from out behind the hedge in the nearest part of the field and continue round the corner of the field and off to my right. It was quite close to me. I had the distinct feeling that this was in the future.

Saturday, 20th November 1999

At about three forty-five in the morning I was reading in David Kennedy's book that one should pray for the dead. I put out the light and prayed to God for all the dead who had left this Earth that they may continue their good work and rise closer to him. I then said a prayer for Libby and finally a prayer for my mother. Afterwards I distinctly felt her presence near me although I didn't receive any word or message.

On the way up to Shenington for the Saturday change over of visitors, I said a prayer for Libby. When I had finished I heard Libby say, *"Thank you Bear."* I felt her presence with me most of the way up.

Sunday, 21st November 1999

I still haven't found any significance in the message "Remember the 8th September" from Marie.

I was working at the computer when I was told to put the television on Sky. I did so and found a programme about spirits coming for the dead, ghosts and mediums – surely a message from Libby. Strangely it wasn't shown on Libby's mother's Discovery Channel – only on mine!)

Monday, 22nd November 1999

The three books that I had ordered from London arrived. They were More Light, Heaven and Earth and Facts. They had been received spiritually from Monsignor Benson and recorded by Anthony Borgia. I found it interesting to note that they were first published just after World War II when people really needed a great deal of help and guidance.

I telephoned Marie to tell her that the books had arrived and that they had been written earlier than the two she had lent to me. Marie told me that Adrian had noticed that when she was talking to me on the telephone she sometimes appeared to be talking in trance without taking breath as though the words were not from her but from somebody else. Libby must be talking through Marie to me – what an interesting thought! Clearly Libby is doing a lot to keep in touch with me and prepare me for the time when I shall join her.

Marie keeps telling me that I must write down my experiences in a journal as I am doing here. Today she told me that I must keep a printed copy so that I couldn't lose it if the computer went down. Was this just good advice or was it Libby telling me to do what she clearly would have told me if she had still been here.

Marie also told me that she found that my mother-in-law's Melton Cottage had an aura of peace about it. She wanted to spend Christmas here but she knew that she had responsibilities towards her own mother and that she couldn't come. I told her that perhaps things would work out and that her mother might be away for Christmas and that she and Adrian could come up to Melton Cottage.

After I had finished talking to Marie and while I was entering details about my new books on the computer list of spiritual books that I was acquiring, I felt Libby close to me. She was behind me as if she was watching what I was doing on the computer. I wanted to finish the page so I could keep a print of it. *"Patience, Bear!"* she said. I then added the bit above about keeping a printed copy and low and behold I had finished the page.

Before going to sleep I prayed to God for those who had passed on, for Libby and my mother and for those of us on Earth including my mother-in-law. I felt there was a crowd of many souls waiting to greet me, but I didn't hear any words or messages that I could be sure about. I think that Libby came out of the crowd and blessed me but I couldn't feel her presence.

Later I saw an image of a child with his back to me sitting on the grass playing and a child's spade was there beside him. He was wearing a white shirt and blue trousers with straps over his shoulders. He had straight hair. A shadow came up to him from the right. This person, wearing a long white dress, caused the child to look up and smile. He waved his arms and hands in happiness.

Then I realised that I was the child. This discovery caused the crowd standing some way off to the right to clap and cheer as if approving of my discovery. Also I realised that the figure was my mother. Again the crowd cheered my discovery. Behind the child, over the green grass, was a town and I saw coming from that direction but some distance behind the child, a figure was approaching. As he drew near he seemed tall and was dressed in a pale blue and white striped blazer with white flannel trousers. It was my father.

The visibility was clear and it was a beautiful summer's day. I felt that this scene was not from the Earth. The picture persisted in my mind even after I had turned over in bed. I believe that it was my mother telling me that when I was young my father, mother and I were very happy. She had to divorce my father when I was seven, but she always loved him.

Tuesday, 23rd November 1999

I am feeling unsettled today as though I don't want to get on with things. It's a busy week, which I don't enjoy because of my CFS. I was labelling a file Libby in Her Memory and it was sticking incorrectly.

"More haste less speed," I said.

Libby replied, *"Patience Bear, you must learn patience!"*

At two-thirty Margaret Boys from the Sue Ryder Home visited my mother-in-law and me. She gave counselling and help to people who had been recently bereaved. I gave her an envelope containing cheques for £610.00 for the home. She spoke to Libby's Mum for an hour and then we drove down to Betty Grove Farm and talked. Margaret told me that in her experience the things that I had experienced with Libby were very common although people didn't talk about it in case they were laughed at. I lent her Anthony Borgia's book More about Life in the World Unseen.

During this visit Margaret read the vicar's address from the Cremation, the memorial article in the Wokingham Times and my journal to date. I gave Margaret these to read in order to help her understand how I was coping with Libby's death.

While she was reading the journal, "That bit about the curtains," she said. "A lady told me that she couldn't close her curtains because she felt she was shutting her dead husband out!" This lady couldn't explain to others because they wouldn't understand.

When Margaret had finished reading she said, "You ought to publish your experiences because there is very little that has been written by men for men. The only other book I know for men is CS Lewis's A Grief Observed. Margaret said she would lend me a copy that she has at the Sue Ryder Home. She also told me about a film called Truly, Madly, Deeply she had seen that gave a very good account of bereavement and ghosts. Clearly someone who had known the loss of a loved one had produced it. Could it be used as a training video?

I offered to help anyone that she thought I could with his or her bereavement. She told me that she organised group meetings at the Sue Ryder Home to help people and that perhaps I would come to one of them.

I must confess that I had not been looking forward to Margaret's visit. I didn't know how she would respond to my experiences and what attitude she would adopt over Libby's death.

After she left I felt deeply encouraged and I wanted to help by going to her group meeting and publishing my experiences. I had a mission!

"Thank you Libby. I know without you telling me that this is what you want me to do and I shall undertake it. I shall of course need your guidance but if you're up to it so am I."

I had no contact with Libby that night. I think she was leaving me to get on with my reading.

Wednesday, 24th November 1999

I saw Dr Weekes this morning. The lump was caused by a hair follicle that had grown into the skin on the top of my leg – not uncommon! The aching in my right thigh was not caused by a serious problem. Anyway I'm alright, so why did Libby, who must know if I have any problems ahead, tell me to go. One of two reasons perhaps, firstly I would have made her go and she may be getting her own back and secondly she would know that it would put my mind at rest to know that the lump wasn't a problem. When I returned Libby's mother and I invited Marie and Adrian to visit us over Christmas.

I finished the third part of *On the Death of my Son* by Jasper Swain. It was very technical and I shall have to read it more than once to fully understand it. He was describing how his son Michael told him about the three eternal laws – Law of Love, the Law of the Group and the Law of the Land. He talks of the seven planes of existence in the Spirit World and discussed the question of sex in modern life on Earth and how in the Spirit World people have no sexual organs anymore because they're not needed.

He went on to tell his father, Jasper, that there are several important phases to life. From birth to seven years old the incarnate soul is learning how to live in his body, how to gain attention to himself and use his limbs. From seven to fourteen he starts to develop emotions and temperament. At fourteen he faces the crisis of adolescence when the emotional body takes control of the physical body and the intensity increases until at twenty-one his mind awakens. From twenty-one to twenty-eight the mind advances until he realises that there is more to life than he thought. By the time he is a thirty-five year old man, if he is ever going to be, he is mentally orientated.

Further stages are from thirty-five to forty-two he is aware of something else in life, which is his soul trying to control his mind. From forty-two to forty-nine he becomes aware of the presence of his soul. From forty-nine to fifty-six he wonders if he has achieved anything in life. From fifty-six to sixty-three the conclusion is reached when he decides whether to just serve out the remainder of his life or try and elevate himself to the Golden Plane of the Spirit World. Whatever happens, we are told, the pattern will always fall into these seven-year cycles.

Michael then went on to explain about how the finite world is divided into kingdoms, the mineral, the vegetable, the animal and the human kingdoms. "God", he tells us, "created everything out of a vast sea of thought and matter is developed through the four kingdoms". Michael then explains how one can follow the Path to prepare oneself for life in God's Kingdom.

I put the light out and hoped Libby would be able to talk to me. All I got was, *"Bussssy!"*

"Shall I go away," I said.

"No!" came her reply very quickly. Then, *"I need your love and strength."*

After a while she said, *"Go and put some Ralgex on your leg!"*

I went and found the aerosol in the bathroom and sprayed some on my aching right thigh.

Thursday, 25th November 1999

An hour or so later I put out the light. I was aware of my heart warming and filling. Libby was there. I held my breath waiting for her to put her thoughts into my mind.

"I love you Bear," she said.

"I love you too."

"I know."

"What were you doing before?"

"Working."

"With the horses?"

"Yes."

"How are they?"

"King is very well. The others are well too."

"Why did you want me to see the doctor?"

"I didn't want you to worry. You won't die of cancer,"
she said. *"You won't die for a long time yet."*

"You will come for me, won't you?" I asked.

"Perhaps," she said. *"There's a lot more to happen
yet – a lot more water to flow under the bridge."*

I really didn't know how to respond to all that so I
changed the subject.

"I don't hear your voice," I said. "Your thoughts come
into my mind using my voice."

"That's normal," she said.

"There's so much I'd like to ask you and talk to you
about. When you're with me I just want to feel your presence.
I wish I could touch you. I want to kiss you."

"I know."

"But you're no longer a woman," I said. "You're a
person. You aren't men and women there anymore."

"True," she said.

There was another long pause. I felt her presence,
which was constant. I knew she could tell what I was
thinking about but I couldn't read her mind.

"I'm going now," she said.

But I could still feel her presence just as before. I
waited for a while knowing that she was going but sensing
that she was still with me. After a while I said, "I thought you
were going."

"I like being with you."

"I'm not holding you back? I have let you go?"

"Yes," she said. *"I like coming and being with you."*

"I'm glad," I replied.

There was a long pause while I felt her presence
wavering just a little.

Then she said, *"I'm going."*

She went and as she said it her voice was in a white
ball of light that went rather like the centre of an old

television screen when it is turned off disappearing very quickly away from me. Somehow the feeling of her presence lingered for a while but I knew she had gone.

Then I got up from my bed and recorded what had happened in this journal. After I had written it all down I had doubts as to whether she had really been. Have I imagined it or have my thought questions been answered by my own subconscious?

Usually when I ask Libby a question the answer comes back almost before I have finished the question. In that case I would argue that I haven't had time to dream up the answer. At other times when we are chatting or exchanging our emotions to each other, the contact is full of long pauses.

At the time I have no doubt that she is there. Certainly there are many times when I know for certain that she isn't there. There are times when I really want her to come to me because there are questions that I want to ask or I feel particularly lonely. I can't believe in these doubts, but they do occur to me. What is worrying me now, as I go to bed, is why did Libby stay so long after she said she had to go? Why did she not leave when she said she was going as she had before? Was she just really happy to be with me or does she know that we will not be together for some while? It is exactly seven weeks today that Libby died. Time alone will tell.

Friday, 26th November 1999

I felt Libby come to me quite soon after I had put the light out. My heart becomes strong and big. I felt her presence, but it was weaker than usual as though she was really far away but she was still able to transmit her thoughts and she spoke to me in my mind. She told me that she had come because she missed me.

"I miss you too," I said. "I hope you will keep coming and then I won't grieve. Do you grieve on your side?"

"I miss you."

"What have you been doing today?"

"I've been with the horses. We had a new horse in today. He's very beautiful."

"Are they all doing well?"

"Yes."

"And how is King?"

"He's very happy. He can eat as much grass as he likes and not get Laminitis!"

"Are there any doughnuts there?" I asked because we had a private joke about him and doughnuts. We had been shopping and when we returned I had left the car boot open. We had come back to find him with his head in the boot helping himself to a bag of doughnuts.

"No," she said with a chuckle."

"That's a pity," I replied. "What do you do when you're not with the horses?"

"I'm learning Greek." Libby had been a good linguist on Earth.

"Why? What will you use it for?"

"Many of the horses here are from Grecian times. They had a lot of horses then."

"They must have been there in the Spirit World for a long time?"

"Yes."

"Do others help with the horses?"

"Yes, a few. You've been to the dentist in Newbury today and to the garage."

"Yes."

"I'm worried about Mum's chest. It's getting worse."

"She won't die yet will she?"

"No." I got the impression she would live to be 89. The number kept sticking in my head but Libby didn't say it.

"I can't feel your presence so strongly tonight."

"I am here," she said quietly. *"As I get stronger and learn more the longer I can stay."*

"I've got a busy day tomorrow." I said.

"I know. It will go alright but be careful on Saturday."

"Why on Saturday?"

"You are going to put up the gate in the new fence. The gateposts are heavy. Take care. The lane verges will look good when they've been trimmed. They haven't been done for a long while."

I had a man coming to do some hedging and ditching on the following day.

I felt her fading away, but in my heart I could still feel the strength of her love. Our talk tonight was very conversational. Somehow I felt that she didn't have to be close for us to communicate. It was just like an ordinary conversation between husband and wife and not from a spirit to a mortal.

Later I had a vision of Libby dressed in white. She was much younger and with her was a bearded man in a white full length robe tied with a golden rope. His hood was up but Libby's wasn't. They came towards me, but my concentration was lost and when it returned they were walking away! I called them back. They turned and looked at me. I called them back in love and they walked back towards me, but my concentration went again. This happened three times. They walked towards me, my concentration going and I calling them back before the picture faded.

Saturday, 27th November 1999

I was playing a relaxation tape in the car on my way up to Shenington. These tapes are very good but don't try and carry them out in full when you're driving! Unmistakably I heard Libby sighing and saying phrases of love for me. I have wondered how she could love me so much. We loved each other a great deal on Earth and we were very close, but I wondered how she could love me so much when she was in such a perfect place and I wasn't really a part of that life. Today I realised that however perfect it was, it was still new to her and that it seemed sensible that she would miss me.

I also realised something else that hadn't occurred to me last night. The bearded man that Libby was walking with – it was me! I thought that it was my concentration that had let me down but when they walked back towards me, they couldn't have reached me because the time scale was different. I was being shown, once and for all, that I would one day be with Libby in the Spirit World. That has made me very happy!

I have a strong feeling that this vision was not created by Libby. Certainly I didn't feel her presence during my experience. I believe that Libby asked for help because I was worried that I may not be good enough to join her on her plane in the Spirit World. I believe that the vision was projected to me by someone far more experienced who wanted me to work out that it was me that was with her and that we would be together eventually. I also believe that if I had misinterpreted this I would be told so.

I have expressed my doubts lately in this journal as to whether I was ever to be with Libby in the Spirit World. This had arisen because of her answer to my question "Will you come and meet me?"

She had said, *"Perhaps."*

She had also told me that I was going to live for some time yet and that there was a lot of water to flow under the bridge. I confess that I can't believe that I am good enough to be on the same plane as she is. Presumably I have a lot of work to do to catch up with her but it will certainly be worth it if I can.

Tonight I spoke to Adrian. He too had lost a loved one and he confirmed how Carolyn came through to him. I didn't lead him but he described exactly the same way that Libby comes through to me. That was very comforting to know because it's natural to have doubts in your own mind, but to be told by another without having told him how Libby's thoughts come into my head and to realise that he had exactly the same experiences was truly wonderful.

So I had had my doubts but not anymore!

The questions that I had asked Adrian were these. "When Carolyn spoke to you, did you ever wonder if your own mind was answering your own question?"

"Yes," said Adrian, "but sometimes the answers came back so quickly that I hadn't had time to take them in and the words were repeated back by my own mind."

"Did you hear the words in Carolyn's voice?"

"No," he said, "they had her mannerisms but they came to me as I hear my own voice."

Now that was exactly how Libby spoke to me! If I asked her a question sometimes the answer came back so fast that I had barely finished asking the question and then, in my mind, the words were repeated back more slowly so that I could take in their meaning. I could tell it was Libby speaking to me by the way she said things but the words came to me as I hear my own voice.

As I have been experiencing these conversations from the Spirit World for the first time, it was mighty reassuring to know that somebody else has had these experiences and received them in exactly the same way. I am not trying to prove anything. I am simply recording what has happened since my wife died. I feel that I would want to remember what she had said to me and that if I didn't write these things down immediately I should forget.

I settled down in bed after the film that I had been watching finished. I said a prayer to God for all the people in the Spirit World, especially Libby and my Mother and for those on Earth. I thanked Him for hearing my prayer in the gardens at Nettlebed and for telling me that He had heard it.

Afterwards Libby thanked me and said she loved me. I asked her if she always would and she said that she would. That was very reassuring because it's one thing to ask that question of your wife on Earth, but I thought quite a different matter to ask one's wife in the Spirit World. I knew that it was impossible to tell lies there but I didn't know if the love between husband and wife would continue into infinity. Perhaps not everybody's love is strong enough to do this. Some marriages aren't based on true love and some people marry again. Personally I can see no reason why the first and second wives can't get on together on the spiritual plane if they want to and also get on with the husband as well – friendship blossoming with love. After all there is no sex in Spirit and certainly no jealousy.

I asked her how the horses were and she told me they were all well. I asked after King and Libby said that he was fine.

"No cameras there to frighten him!" I said. He hadn't like the click of my camera when I photographed him and he would gallop round the field if I took casual photographs of him.

"No," she said, "there are no cameras here!"

"Did you really ride him at the Thanksgiving Service?" I asked.

"Yes," she replied.

"And was he wearing rosettes?" I asked.

"Only the more important ones!"

"Did you like the service?"

"Yes and I especially liked Michael".

(Michael Crowther-Green led the prayers and gave the address.)

"He's a good man."

"Yes he is," Libby said. *"Give my love to Mum and tell her to look after her leg."*

"Yes I will," I said. "How's the Greek going? Your mother told me that you had always wanted to learn Greek. I didn't know about that"

"It's going very well," she said. *"Did you read about that horse that had its stable set on fire?"* A horse near Tidworth had its stable set on fire while it was still in it.

"Yes I did."

"Well, she's here with me now."

"That was terribly cruel. How can people be so cruel? Is the soul of the horse lifted out so it doesn't suffer?" I asked.

"Yes it is," she replied. *"Well I'm going now. You'd better go and help Mum to bed. Good night Bear."*

"Good night my darling," I said.

Tonight I hadn't felt her presence come, but I felt my heart filling as I prayed so I knew that she was there. I didn't feel her go either. It was as though we were just carrying on a normal conversation. I think that the absence of a physical presence is explained by the fact that Libby, who is a very intelligent woman, has learned to talk to me without having to transport herself onto this earthly plane. She was always a hard worker and learned new things very quickly. The other possibility is that I have reached the stage that it is not necessary for me to feel her presence in order to know that she was with me. In practice it is more than likely that both these deductions are true and valid.

When I have prayed to God for the people in the Spirit World and especially Libby and my mother, Libby has always been there and has always thanked me. This tells me that it is right and necessary as I have read elsewhere for us on Earth to pray for those that have passed onto the spiritual plane.

I am no expert in all this. Libby died fifty-one days ago so my knowledge is limited to that amount of time. I have read books on other peoples' experiences A Venture in Immortality by David Kennedy and On the Death of My Son by Jasper Swain. I have spoken to friends about Libby and I have heard about some things that have happened to others. I am also reading the recorded messages by Anthony Borgia from a Monsignor Benson, who died, went to the Spirit World and found that his books and teachings on Earth were wrong. He was determined to put matters right and came to Anthony Borgia and asked him to record the true state of affairs.

It has occurred to me while writing this that some people might ask why I don't prepare questions for Libby and be able to learn more about the Spirit World and get more proof on its existence. The answer to that is simple. I don't need proof of its existence. Libby's conversations with me are all the proof I need that she does exist spiritually. I am not interested in asking loaded questions to prove to others that there is life after death.

My reasons for keeping this journal are simply to record what we have talked about to safeguard my own memory and if others can derive any comfort from my journal then all well and good. As I began this section I wish to repeat that I am no expert. What I am putting down here are simply my memories of our conversations and happenings and also my personal thoughts about any explanations that occur to me.

I do not profess to be a Spiritualist nor do I consider to that I am into Spiritualism! Before Libby died I had little knowledge on the subject and even less experience. If anything I was a sceptic! I just happen to have had a wife whom I loved very dearly, who has recently died and I am trying to record, mainly for my own use what has happened to us.

Sunday, 28ᵗʰ November 1999

There is one thing that I am certain about. There is no need to fear death. Death is simply the end of our period on Earth when we shape our future and determine where we live in the Spirit World. I have been thinking about people who have violent deaths. Some die in car accidents, some are murdered and some drown. The horse from Tidworth in Hampshire, whose stable was set on fire by some brainless unfeeling idiots had been lifted clear of the torment and is now in Libby's care.

To those who may doubt I would say this, "Why should their soul or spirit be put through unimaginable agonies on death only to be taken up to the spiritual plane and be put through a long period of convalescence to repair the damage?"

Some would perhaps take this argument further and ask why some people suffer through illness, as Libby did with cancer only to die and then be rested and repaired. My response would be that I believe that God would not let His children suffer more than they can bear. Suffering is a state of mind and it may well be that one is judged by how well one behaves through affliction. I certainly believe that if the suffering becomes too great that person will levitate out of their body. If it is not their time to die they will return to it.

I believe that Libby died twenty-five hours before her heart stopped beating. One of the very experienced Sue Ryder nurses, Elise told me later that she was convinced that Libby would die within twenty minutes when she called us in. The nurses had been making Libby comfortable and we had stepped outside for a breath of fresh air. Graham, her first husband and I sat either side of her bed each holding one of her hands, while her pulse slowed and so nearly stopped. It quickened again for a few minutes and then again almost stopped. She would have gone happily I know in that situation with the two men that she loved beside her bed each holding her hand and wishing her well on her journey. I am certain she was ready to go, but her young heart had not finished beating and I see no reason why she shouldn't have left her body then and escaped from her mortal remains into a life of happiness and relief.

Graham eventually had to go and I continued to hold Libby's hand for some two and half-hours before I got up and moved round to the other side of the bed. When I did so I felt a burden lifted from me. Somehow or other I felt completely normal, almost as though I hadn't a care in the world. I am sure now that Libby had gone and that, although I didn't understand at the time she was already at peace.

When she did 'die' the following evening of course I cried and found it unbearable that I had lost her. There was also relief that she was free of the cancer that had caused her so much pain and suffering. Several times she had said to me, *"I'm sorry I'm not brave."* But she was. She was frightened but she never complained. She suffered in silence and was wonderfully brave all through this tragic illness.

It has taken me seven weeks to get to the point that I can write about Libby's death in the Sue Ryder Home in Oxfordshire. I definitely couldn't have done it before and even now I do so with tears on my face. I heard Libby say, *"Don't cry."*

But I need to cry and it's good for me to cry because it releases the tension. If anybody is reading this later on – don't be afraid of crying. It's a bodily gift for releasing pent up sadness. I don't subscribe to the "It's not manly" or "You must keep a stiff upper lip". It's right to cry. I know for a fact that Libby is alive and in good hands. I couldn't wish for better! But when I re-live her death surely it's only human to cry?

Tonight I prayed to God for the souls in the Spirit World and those of us on Earth and asked Him to let Libby still come to me. I was concerned because this evening I felt that Libby wasn't about. I felt empty and hollow. I have a dread of her not coming to talk to me. I worry that without her coming I shall lapse into grief and not be able to cope, but she came and we talked.

I said that I hadn't felt her presence about at all this evening and I felt that she wouldn't come to me. She said she had been busy and I sensed rather than hearing anything that it was caused partly by the horses but more especially the Greek! I asked after the horse from Tidworth and she told me that she was doing well, but she would need a lot of rest and love because although she had been taken out of the stable before the fire could affect her, she had been badly frightened before they set fire to the stables.

I asked her if it was full of flowers and fields and trees where she was and she told me clearly that it was so. She said, *"Oh you would love it here. There's so much you can do and you won't have your fatigue syndrome so you could be busy all the time."* I asked her if it was always day and full of light. She told me it was.

I spoke to her about the journal that I'm writing and asked if it should be used to help others. She said it was a good thing to do and I must do everything I could to help other people. I told her that her mother's leg was better and that she had lit up when I gave her the message last night. Libby said she had tried to get through to her but that her mother had put a protective shield round herself and Libby couldn't get through to give her any messages.

I asked Libby if she knew about the vision I had had that showed her walking with a bearded man. I said, "Was I right to interpret it as being me and I shall be with you there one day?"

She said that I had been meant to realise that one day we would be together, but it wouldn't be yet because I had a lot of work to do here first.

"I don't feel your presence anymore when you come to talk to me," I said. "Is it because I don't need to because I know you're there, or is it because you are more skilled and practised in being able to come?"

"It's just because it's easier to send you my thoughts straight from my mind to yours rather than having to bodily transport myself down to the earth plane. To do the latter is very tiring and if I do it the easier way I can talk to you longer."

I sensed that our time was running out so I said, "Are you going now?"

"Yes," she said. *"I must go now. I've a lot to do, but I do love you Bear and I miss not having you with me. You need your sleep and you haven't been having enough lately. You've been very busy. Good night my love"*

"Good night my darling."

Libby had been talking to me for a little over twenty minutes.

Monday, 29th November 1999

It had been a very wet day. I settled down in bed and said a little prayer to God. I heard Libby say, *"That was nice, Bear."*

"How are you today," I asked.

"I'm good today!"

"You sound very happy."

"I am," she said. *"Oh, you'd love it here, Bear. It's so fresh and clean and there are flowers and fields and trees everywhere."*

"I imagine you look like the photograph that I took of you with King after the Hurst Show. Do you look like that now?"

"Yes, a bit," she said. *"Those pictures were very good of him."*

"I've had some of them enlarged," I said. "You're very happy."

"Yes, I am."

"Why are you so especially happy today?"

"Oh, I think it's because I've been here long enough to know what I'm doing and where I'm going."

"I wish I knew what I was doing and where I'm going," I said a little mournfully.

"Oh, you're doing alright," she laughed. I could see her more than before but not entirely clearly. Part of it was sense and part was seeing.

"Yes, but it was better when you were here."

"Oh, I don't know," she said, *"You can please yourself what you do now."*

"Up to a point, but it's not the same without you. Will you always come to me?"

"Yes, if you want me to," she said laughing again.

"Why shouldn't I want you to come?"

"Well, you might have somebody with you and not want to bother about me."

"I can't imagine that. Do you want me to find somebody else?"

"Well," she appeared to need to think about this one. *"Yes and no,"* she said finally.

"Well, you can tell what's in the future," I said.

"Y-yes," she said hesitatingly. I waited for more, but she said nothing further.

"This is getting us nowhere!" I said and then, changing the subject, "Do you often ride King?"

"Sometimes."

"Won't it be wonderful when I can come up and we can ride together? I have been thinking about when we used to go for a ride at five in the morning."

"Oh yes," she said happily, *"when we used to see the deer."* She was smiling. *"Well, I'm going now,"* she said suddenly. *"Goodbye."*

She half ran and half floated away into the distance, across the lush green grass toward a huge lone tree. I could see she was dressed in a white robe. "Goodbye my darling," I said as she went further away from me. We had only been together for ten minutes.

I was delighted to see her so happy. She had not shown much emotion before except when she sighed and said, *"Oh Bear, I do love you."* I felt that somehow she was managing very well without me and it hurt a little bit, although it was tremendously good to see her in such good spirits. It seemed that something had occurred up there to put her in such a wonderful mood. It was clearly something that she couldn't tell me about because we never had any secrets from each other.

It occurred to me later on after writing the above that when Libby spoke to me I didn't feel her presence, but that's not new. I didn't find that my heart filled as it usually did before she came to me. I finished my prayer and Libby was there, straight away, saying, *"That was nice, Bear."*

I wondered if she has reached an easier stage of communication that made it more comfortable to talk with me. She certainly was very happy. Has she learned or perfected a better way that doesn't cause her as much difficulty as in the earlier days? Perhaps if she had told me about it I would have pestered her for the technical details and maybe she wouldn't have been able to explain. I probably wouldn't understand!

Tuesday, 30th November 1999

Libby came with me all the way up to the cottage and back today. We had a long chat on the way up and I hope I can remember all that we talked about. Her mother was going to come up with me but she was fast asleep when I left and I let her stay that way. Libby's presence was definitely with me both there and back.

First of all, as I drove away, I heard her say, *"Hello Bear."*

"Hello my darling. How are you today?"

"Oh I'm fine," she said.

"You were very happy last night."

"Yes I was."

"And you still are."

"Yes I am," she said.

"Can you tell me why you're so happy," I asked. "I wondered if you had found it easier to contact me and it didn't present such a problem anymore. You seem to be able to come and talk to me without your presence being so strong."

"I find it easier to come to you now as I get a lot of help from my friends here. I've met Martin Stubbs (the Wokingham District Councillor who also ran the Barkham Post Office and

the local store). *My father is here and Ron* (Adrian's father) *has been very helpful. Jerry* (Adrian's mother) *will be joining us soon."*

"But why were you so happy last night?" I asked.

"Well, something wonderful is going to happen."

"To me or to you," I asked.

"Oh to you."

"Is it going to be in the distant future or soon?"

"Oh quite soon."

"Good," I said. "I shall look forward to it."

As I drove past a house along the road from Walgrave to Henley, where Libby and I had seen flowers put out on the fence for over a year, she said, *"You could go and see them if you like. Their daughter was killed in a car accident as she pulled out on to the road. They need help because they are very distraught about her death. They have shut themselves off and can't be contacted."*

There was a long pause while I wondered if I had the gall to knock on a stranger's door to discuss their daughter's death. I started to ask her about her illness.

"It wasn't so bad," she said. *"I spent long periods in the Spirit World before I died so I was ready for death when it came."*

"But you were in a lot of pain?"

"At times, yes, but I was taken away when it was too great."

"You said to me several times that you wished you were braver?"

"Yes," she said, *"but that was before I understood about death. You remember when I asked you to take away the cards and the roses you had brought me, because at night devils came out of them? Well, that was before I could be taken up to the spiritual plane and "coached" about what was going to happen. I had to go through that stage before I*

68

was fit and receptive enough to be helped. I was helped so much. It was because of this that I was able to help you."

"I couldn't have coped without your help," I said. "I should have been totally distraught without knowing that you were in God's hands and that you were able to come and talk to me."

"If only people would open themselves up to be receptive they could be comforted."

"What happens at Christmas? Do you know yet?" I asked.

"Well," she said, *"I understand that there is such a feeling of bon ami on the Earth that we cannot fail to notice it. The Spirit World rejoices too because they celebrate God's making of the Universe and we thank him for our lives, firstly on Earth and then in the Spirit World."*

"What about the 27th?" I asked. It was our birthdays and also our Wedding Anniversary on 27th December.

"I don't think the Spirit World will celebrate that!" she said.

"I wondered whether you will remember it and that we will be able to celebrate it together?"

"We'll have to see about that, but I expect we'll be able to do something," she said.

We then went on to discuss something very personal, so I shall leave it out, even of my journal but I shall not forget what she said.

"How's the Greek going?" I asked.

"Very well. It's much easier in the Halls of Learning as you can't forget anything and the people are so kind and patient."

She made several comments about me being so tired and she said that she would stay with me until the end of the journey. I remarked that as she could see into the future she would know what might happen, but she said, *"I'm staying with you just to be on the safe side!"*

As I drove into the garage at the end of the return journey and while I was concentrating on getting the car in far enough to be able to shut the doors, I heard her say, *"Okay, Bear, I'm off now."* And she was gone.

Libby was there when I tried to sleep. I had had a severe headache all evening despite taking two painkillers.

"Hello my Bear, you have got a bad headache. I'm going to stay with you until you go to sleep."

She did and shortly afterwards I went to sleep.

Chapter 4

THE SITTINGS

Wednesday, 1ˢᵗ December 1999

I awoke this morning without my headache! In the post was a very pleasant letter from the Sue Ryder Home thanking me for the cheques that we had collected in Libby's memory. They totalled £681.00. I had decided that it was better to send a contribution to the Home rather than to have flowers everywhere at the funeral. It was much more touching to see Libby's coffin carried with a single wreath of carnations, roses and country flowers than to see a flower shop on legs! The money could be put to better use. I was certain that Libby would have agreed.

The letter was from the Matron, Heather Aldridge and I wish to quote from it,

"We all felt it was our great privilege to have been able to care for Libby when she needed us and to offer our support to you at this time. We do hope you derived some comfort in the knowledge that these gifts help us to continue providing our patients with that same care and attention."

It was the money of many other people that had provided the care that Libby received. I felt strongly that it was very important for us all to choose the charities that we wanted to help and to give as generously as possible to them rather than giving a few shillings here and there when asked. I had three charities that were important to me. They were, in alphabetical order, Cancer Research, Macmillan Nurses and the Sue Ryder Homes. All of them had played a very important part in Libby's life and death. It was through her efforts and with help of friends from Arborfield, that she was able to present the Macmillan Nurses with a cheque for £3,000. We should always do more than we do, but I had decided that I was going to do more.

Libby has been with me today. Bless her. She seemed to be about most of the time! Perhaps I should say that it seemed much easier to talk to her than at first. Is this because she has had more practice now in talking to me? Am I more receptive to receiving her? Just to prove me wrong I sat back and asked her if these points were somewhere near the truth, but she wasn't there! She was definitely able to talk to me when I settled down for the night and when I was driving gently along and under no pressure from traffic conditions. These were times when my mind was most relaxed.

This morning, as I drove the Range Rover back from delivering a load of horse manure to the Woodley Allotments, she told me that she was glad that my headache had gone. She also spoke to me when I was down at Betty Grove Farm. I had finished mending the lock on the Feed Store door and I was ready to drive back for lunch. As I was getting into the Range Rover she suddenly said that she liked it when I was doing jobs on the farm but she missed not being able to be there and share in the doing of them. I knew exactly what she meant! We were practically inseparable and we did almost everything together. She can be with me in spirit and I appreciate that, but it's not the same as physically doing jobs together.

Thursday, 2nd December 1999

I said my prayer and Libby was there.

"That was good," she said.

She usually began by commenting on my prayer. It was a short one tonight because I knew she was waiting. She had told me that I was smoking too much, but it helped me to relax before going to sleep.

"Oh, I do miss you."

"Yes, I miss you to."

"I wish I could kiss you," I said.

I moistened my lips and pouted them out! I expected her to say something like, *"Don't be silly Bear."* But instead I felt her presence very strongly and it was somehow as though she had kissed me, but I couldn't feel the pressure of her lips although I felt her presence through them somehow. I can't explain it!

"Kiss me again," I said and she did.

"How are you going to put that in your journal!" she laughed. I was so pleased that she was so happy and I certainly was!

"That was absolutely wonderful," I said. "It was unbelievable!" I felt so happy that I found that I was smiling and my heart was full.

"I wish you could be here," she said. Then there was a pause. *"Now then we must talk seriously. Some people up here* (and I had the feeling that it was the higher placed ones) *are very keen that you should publish your journal. It can help a lot of people on Earth. I'm going to make arrangements for you to get it published."*

"It's your journal really," I said.

"No!" she said, very firmly. *"It's yours. Do you want me to go?"* she suddenly asked rather crossly. She had clearly picked up my thoughts.

"No, no I don't," I said. "I was only hoping that I could remember everything so I can write it down correctly."

"Alright," she said. *"But I think I should go really."*

"No," I said, "Please don't go yet."

"Well, alright, but I must go soon. I don't want you to forget anything." There was a pause and then she said, *"Something good is going to happen at Christmas, but you mustn't tell anybody."*

"Alright," I said.

"Drive carefully to Newbury tomorrow. I'm going now. Goodbye Bear."

And then I could see her half-running and half-floating again away from me across the grass towards that tree. The image was a bit mistier than it had been before, but it was clear enough to see.

"Good night my darling."

I was pleased that she was still very happy. Our time together was a very happy one but as usual after she had gone and I had written it all down, I thought of things that I would have liked to ask her, but now I was really glad that I didn't have prepared questions to ask. If I had, then these incredible things would probably not have happened. It's much more exciting leaving Libby to tell me what she wants to and hang it all, we've never had a dull moment!

They say that truth is stranger than fiction. Certainly if I was writing a fictional story I would never have put this in. However the thought occurs to me, is anybody going to believe all this? I hope so because it's true! It's incredible but true! I can see the headline, "Deranged Husband Kissed by Ghost" – heaven forbid! In case you're wondering – no, I hadn't had a drink since lunchtime yesterday!

I've been reflecting on Libby kissing me and why not! Some years ago I can remember my mother telling me that shortly after her father had died she woke up one night and he was standing there near her bed. She told me that he had leant over and kissed her. "I knew it was your grandfather," she had said, "because only he kissed me like that." She always slept with a light on in her bedroom after that.

There was another thing that came back to me a few weeks after Libby died. I recalled that I had been driving back from the Oval in London where I had been scoring a County Championship match. My mother had died a few weeks previously. I was relaxed and the sun was beginning to set. Ahead of me I saw something in the sky. It was large, oval in shape and had very small coloured lights inside it. In my thoughts I heard my mother saying, "Everything's alright. I'm in good hands. I'm going now."

Now it wasn't until some time after Libby had died that I thought about this again. The shape in the sky looked exactly the same as I had seen over the lake at the Sue Ryder Home when Libby had spoken to me for the first time. That was on Friday, 8th October 1999. The similarities between the two presences certainly weren't coincidental and to me it was proof that after death the spirit can be seen by those whom the departed wished to see it.

I had a long chat with Adrian on the telephone tonight. It was amazing although perhaps it shouldn't be so, that when we discussed our experiences with Libby and Carolyn we found that we had had almost exactly similar experiences. I find it impossible to believe that we are the only two people on Earth that have had so much help and information from our loved ones.

For people who haven't known such comfort I would simply say, "Don't put a shell round yourself to protect yourself from your grief. Relax, have an open mind and be prepared to except what does happen. If something does occur and it can, don't just say, "That's odd! What a coincidence! Did that really happen?" The answer is, "Yes, it did!"

Perhaps it is easier for me to say this, but if you talk about your experiences to friends, counsellors or family you may find that they have had similar experiences or have knowledge of other people who have. I would suggest that you don't blurt it all out at once until you know if the person that you are talking to is receptive. Not everybody is, but I have found that about eighty percent of people that I have spoken to do understand and the rest just look at me as though I'm crackers!

I would also say that if you have a loved one whom you feel is nearby after they have died, just go and rest quietly somewhere and be ready to receive them. Give them a chance. They have to learn how to communicate with you just as you have to learn to be receptive to them. It has taken eight weeks for Libby and me to be able to pick up a conversation at will. She has done the hard work with the help of her friends in the Spirit World. I believe that our love was so great spiritually that she has been able and willing to help me with my grief.

Physical love on Earth was so much easier to demonstrate. Holding hands, an unexpected kiss, the little things one does for the one we love were all done to show your partner that you did love them. Without these it was more difficult to confirm ones affection. So after death it was harder to prove that one continued in love. Remember that ones loved one who had gone knew what you were thinking and therefore, I believe, that if one could only be receptive to them they would come and share the love that you both felt. I believe that they want to come and tell you that they were alive and well in the Spirit World. I believe that they wanted to help you. I believe that they wanted to make life easier for you. I believe that they wanted to prepare you for what will ultimately come to pass. Death was nothing to be afraid of. God is good. That was where the word came from. He couldn't possibly do anything bad.

If what we have been taught by the Church is true then death can be a terrible experience. Judgement Day is a terrible thing to contemplate. Hell fire is a monstrous invention. I believe that God is incapable of these terrible things. He wants us to be good, lead good lives and to help one another. How can we possibly believe that death is final? How can we believe that we are not to go into a world that reflects our life on Earth, where we will be happy and have the chance to be together with those who we love?

God loves us all and only wants our happiness. How can we blame Him for the bad things that happen on Earth that are caused by the natural laws of the universe or mankind's folly? I said my prayer.

"That's good," said Libby. *"Now I want to talk seriously to you. Your journal is a record of your experiences, which will help others. It's not your job to preach sermons. You can express your opinions, of course, but remember what other people whom you are trying to help will think. Don't preach sermons. You are writing it to help others.*

"You had a long talk with Adrian tonight. That was good. Don't worry about Jerry (Adrian's mother) *she's in good hands and Ron* (Jerry's late husband) *is there to help her and Adrian."*

"Okay."

"Now you need a good night's sleep because you're going up to the cottage tomorrow. Don't stay up all night doing the crossword. I shall not be with you all the time tomorrow. I've got a lot to do but call me if you want me. Oh Bear," she said, *"I must go now. Take care."*

"Good night my darling."

Friday, 3rd December 1999

No contact with Libby at all today. I drove up to the cottage and back alone. I felt very hollow and very lonely. I now realise to some extent what it is like for other people who aren't as fortunate as I have been. I have been privileged to have had so much communication with Libby that I found myself feeling bitterly alone. When I went to bed tonight I said my prayer as usual but Libby didn't come to me. I went to sleep. When I woke up about an hour later Libby came. I was a bit sleepy and I heard her ask me what was wrong. I told her nothing was wrong, but of course she knew differently.

She could always tell on Earth so why should she not still be able to tell now that she is in the Spirit World. I was in the wrong and I knew it, but I was upset because she had not been to me all day and so I had expected her to be there before I went to sleep. I was sulking like a child and I knew that I was in the wrong. We were having our first spiritual row and quite rightly she left me. I was ashamed of myself. This of course only made me feel worse. I went to sleep wondering if she would ever come to me again. Certainly she was entitled to let me sulk it out of my system – and serve me right!

Saturday, 4th December 1999

I woke up at five o'clock and wrote up my journal. There was a Tawny Owl hooting outside as though mocking me. He was calling out to a mate and getting no answer. I made myself a mug of coffee and went back to bed. I tried to do the Daily Telegraph crossword but it was Friday's, which was always more difficult and I couldn't concentrate.

I prayed to God that she would forgive me and come back to talk to me. I waited and after a few minutes she came. I said that I was sorry and that I had been very selfish. She forgave me.

"Where were you anyway?"

"We had a visitation from some people from the Higher Realms," she explained.

"Can you tell me about it?" I asked.

"No," she said, *"I will later, but you're not ready yet to understand."*

"Can you speak to Martin Stubbs?" I asked. "I saw Pam (his wife) yesterday and I asked her how she was. She said she was so-so. I have lent her *Life in the World Unseen*. I asked her if she had heard from Martin and she said, "No, she hadn't." I said that you had mentioned seeing him and she told me that I was the fourth person who had said something similar. She could feel that he was about but had made no real contact."

"Alright," Libby said, *"I'll talk to him, but he was extremely ill and he may not be strong enough to get through to her."*

"I understand that," I said, "but I know that it would make her very happy if he could. I asked her if she would like to read my journal and she said she would so I'm going to ask her round one evening."

"I think that's a good idea," Libby said. *"I like Pam, but no sermons!"*

"Alright," I said. "I've learned that lesson."

I don't remember Libby going. Perhaps I fell asleep.

I did some jobs on the farm this morning and after lunch I had a little nap. I then had a long telephone conversation with Pam Stubbs. She was so brave to come to Libby's funeral so soon after Martin died. The service was held in the same church as Libby's Thanksgiving Service too. I hadn't realised it was also their Wedding Anniversary. How she coped I shall never know.

She told me that Martin has been in touch with her through somebody in Canada who is a medium and she had written down precisely what Martin said. Apparently he had said things that only Pam and Martin would know about. Pam also said that she was finding the Post Office rather stressful to run and so it is quite possible that that is the reason why Martin hasn't been able to get through to her directly.

Libby's mother started reading my journal today while I was down at the farm. I'm glad she had. Apart from checking the facts about our lives on Earth I thought it was good for her to know all that has happened since Libby died. She belongs to the stiff upper lip school and I hoped that it would break down the protective barrier a little bit.

Libby hasn't been about today. It's now late and I'm going to bed in the hope that she will be there to talk to me.

I settled straight down and said my prayer. When I had finished I heard Libby say, *"You're coming on Bear. You're learning a lot. Now I've got a lot to talk to you about. I haven't been with you today but I was aware of what you were doing. I've had a lot to do.*

"Martin has been in touch with Pam in other ways. He's there to help her and everything's alright so you needn't worry. I'm glad Pam is coming round to read your journal. Perhaps she can correct your spelling mistakes and grammar!"

"Perhaps," I mumbled.

"I've been making arrangements to get your book published. I know you've only just started writing it but it still needs to be organised so that there aren't any difficulties later on. You won't have any problems publishing it and you'll know what to do when the time comes. Don't worry about it. It'll be alright. I'll be with you to help you."

"Thank you," I said quickly as it was difficult to get a word in at all. "Will you just be there while I'm writing the book or will you be there to help me afterwards?"

"I'll be there to help you for a long time to come," she said. *There are going to be some difficult periods but not for a while yet. Everything will be fairly straight forward for some time to come, so you don't have to worry about anything.*

"Now Portia (our late Golden Retriever) *is here with me. She can't find any shoes to carry about but she wags her tail a lot to make up for it. Sam and Dougal* (previous dogs) *are here too and so are all my ponies. King sends you his love and says he's glad that you have put in so much about him. He always thought a lot about himself that pony! I think you should put in some more about the other horses though. You haven't said enough about them. Settle* (nickname for TC the tabby cat) *is here and is very happy.*

"You have been wondering if I had a house here. Well, no I don't. I could have one but as there's so much to do I don't have much need of one. I visit friends here and sometimes I stay with them for a while, but I'm always busy doing something as you know and I've lots to do here. There are the horses; my languages and you take up a lot of my time too. There are people here, mainly in the Higher Realms, who are very interested in you and me and our communications. Some of them take a special interest in you and keep an eye on you.

"Now tomorrow (she meant in the morning as it was already tomorrow!) *I want you to go down to the farm. I know that it is worming day but you don't have to get involved because the others can do that, but I want you to be seen about the farm and it's important that you're about. The farm's coming on quite well but you must remember that you're doing it for you and not for me. You never wanted it when I was there because you said it was too much trouble!"*

Yes, that was quite true! I used to tease her by saying that it was her farm. She'd then say, *"Do you want me to put it in our joint names?"* and I'd always reply, "No thank you, it is always too much trouble, mending broken fences all the time!"

"Well," Libby went on, *"it's yours now and it's up to you to look after it and do whatever you want with it."*

"I've been looking at the photograph that I took of you at Hurst," I said. "You look so very beautiful."

"Well, I happen to know better!" she replied. *"That's enough for tonight. It's quite late and you need your sleep. Goodbye Bear. I'll see you again soon."*

"Yes, my darling" I replied. "See you soon."

It was wonderful to be back to normal conversation again. Admittedly Libby was doing most of the talking in her business-like way, but that meant that she was happy and enjoying her work. She was always at her best when she had got her teeth well and truly into something! She was clearly enjoying herself and that was good.

Sunday, 5th December 1999

I had been meaning to look for an audio tape that Libby had once played me a part. It was made in 1981 when she had gone to see a clairvoyant. He had described our future relationship. I had left a note to remind myself to look for it when I went down to the farm. When I had parked the Range Rover something in my head said, "Go and look for it now before you forget!" I did.

A couple of years previously I had put all our tapes together in drawers and tape boxes. I now searched through them all without success. I didn't remember what it looked like because Libby had just played me the relevant piece one evening some dozen years ago. I was about to give up when I noticed some old tapes that I had put there to use again. Right on top of the pile was one that I didn't recognise. I played it and to my delight it was Libby's clairvoyant's tape.

I spent the afternoon and evening transcribing it. The tape was of poor quality and I wanted to make sure I had a complete copy should anything happen to it. When I heard what he had said to Libby about our future relationship, he was right! Absolutely right!

"I don't know if you're married my love but in three to five years time you'll be in the middle of a really dynamo relationship. It's the sort of relationship that it would make no difference whether people are male or female, or anything else that man might like to discover. It is a two-people relationship, who will get on like a house on fire, who will have implicit faith, implicit trust and implicit trust for each other. I am very strongly led to believe that this is a male and female relationship that I'm looking at, but the sex, or the gender is the right word, the gender of the participants sort of far removed. Can you follow?"

"Yes, I think so," **said Libby laughing excitedly.**

"It's where you get to, what you get up to, etc., as I've been trying to say to you, your free will at that time will be quite golden. You can make what you like of it, but from the point of view of depth of companionship, someone to help, someone indeed to shelter you from time to time from things that have been going on around you. You'll have what you need in the way of a relationship on the go with somebody.

It's an unusual one here – a picture shown here of a love affair in the pure sense of the word. If there in the pure sense of the word of two people who virtually exist for each other, but if it turns into the romantic love affair that's a bonus on the thing of this one. The basis of it, the foundation of it is deeper than exists between most people."

"Really," says Libby.

"Male to female and everything that goes with that, all of which keeps life extremely enjoyable, that's built up on top of the relationship. Much better, much more flamboyant, I think that's the word. It's one of those relationships that everyone else around you would wish to be involved in. We'd wish to God that we could be like you, sort of thing. The strong, very, very strong, (pause) very, very strong spiritual involvement, man or woman is a secondary consideration."

"Helpmates then."

"Umm. I'd have to say, if you've got a husband tucked away somewhere, he's got nothing to worry about, it's, it's to – it is very, very deep. It's certainly very fulfilling for you. If you have got a husband tucked away somewhere this could develop into that but it would be both of you there knowing, <u>knowing</u>, each other. If it got itself to a church or everybody else is happy with it they would only be agreeing to what you two already knew. This is one of those – it's there.

"Oh," **said Libby in what sounds like**
wonderment.
"Support you for the rest of your life
that one. And that's it."

Well, that is what the clairvoyant medium said. We
had all that and more and now we have the very spiritual
involvement developing through this journal and beyond.

I had said my prayer for those in the Spirit World, for
those on Earth and thanked God for giving me such a
wonderful person in Libby. I heard Libby say, *"Oh Bear you*
do go on!"

"Well," I said, "It's true."

"What have you been doing today?" we both asked at
the same time!

"I know what you've been doing," she said. *"I'm glad*
you found the tape so interesting. He got things pretty spot
on!"

"Yes he did, but you haven't told me what you've been
doing today!"

"Well, I won't tell you the details but I've been doing
some organising."

"Oh dear," I said, "you haven't been reorganising the
Spirit World?" I wouldn't have put it past her to try!

"No, of course I haven't! It doesn't need organising.
It's wonderful here. No, I've been organising pony rides for
the children here. Some of them are very young when they
come here and very often their parents don't come here for a
very long time. Of course by then they hardly know them and
so there are many people here who are needed to look after
them and teach them.   It's so important to give them
confidence."

"I think it's a wonderful idea," I said.

"If they don't want to learn to ride then I hope I can teach them about looking after horses and learning to love them."

I think that I must have fallen asleep here, because I had been working very late and it was nearly three o'clock when I went to bed. I know that I had a dream and it was about nothing important. Certainly it had nothing to do with Libby, children or horses and when I woke up she had gone.

I wrote up the journal and went back to bed and settled down to sleep. I heard Libby say, *"So you went to sleep on me, eh!"*

"Yes," I said, "I'm so sorry. It was late and I was so very tired."

"I know you were. You go to sleep now and don't bother to write this bit down in your journal."

"Oh I shall," I said.

"Good night my Bear," she said.

"Good night my darling.

I got out of bed to add this to my journal before I forgot it and as I passed the end of the bed I distinctly heard her say, *"Silly old Bear!"* She's right as usual.

Monday, 6ᵗʰ December 1999

Sharon, who was an old friend of Libby and her mother, called round this morning. I gave her the transcript of the clairvoyant's tape to read. She and Libby had discussed broken relationships about this time and I was eager to know what she thought about it. Sharon said, "That's uncanny. He's got Libby to a tee!"

I felt that a great deal was happening all of a sudden. I must try and keep up! I have looked at some old photographs of Libby and have begun a small collection. I went to bed early because I was very tired after all the typing that I had done yesterday. I said a short prayer but Libby didn't come to me and I went to sleep for a while. I woke up after about an hour and than went to sleep again. I rarely sleep for more than a few hours these days.

Later I woke again and when I settled down after a while, Libby was there.

"Hello Bear," she said.

"Hello my darling. Are you really there? Have you been giving rides to the children today?" I asked.

"No," she said.

"What have you been doing then?"

"Well, I've been walking about thinking."

"That doesn't sound like you! What have you been thinking about?"

"It's not all as simple as you may think. I've been thinking about you. You must understand that it's not so simple. You see, I want the best for you."

"Thank you."

"No, don't be silly Bear. This is important. What I want for you may upset others."

"Well, we have free will," I said.

"Yes, but you can't go around doing just what you want. If I want something for you, it may have effects on others and upset what they want. It has to be thought out. You have free will and if you don't want to do something then you don't have to. If what you want to do upsets others then that's down to you, but if I want to look after your interests, so to speak, I can't allow things to happen, even if they're for your good if they upset other people's plans. Do you see?"

"Yes I see that," I replied. "Do you think that I should go and see this clairvoyant lady that Sharon has told me about?"

"That's up to you."

"Well, do you think it's a good idea?"

"Yes, if you want to, but you'll find that it will open things up considerably. At the moment you are focusing on

our life together. She will tell you about your life. Are you ready for that?"

"I'm very impressed with the tape of your clairvoyant."

"Yes, he was pretty good. He got everything quite spot on."

"Now that's what I have been thinking about. He said that if you didn't remove a rock in your hearth you would inevitably dash yourself on it. I quote,

**If we remove it now it would lead to
a much more fuller happier run at the next
fifty to sixty years.**

"I have been wondering if that rock was the emotional state of your first marriage and that by finishing it you were then free to find future happiness. If you hadn't removed it you would have been very unhappy for life."

Libby seemed reluctant to talk about it and to be fair I don't blame her. We never had any secrets from each other but this was before our time together. If she had told me to mind my own business it would have served me right, but the point that I was really interested in concerned the reference to fifty or sixty years of happiness. At the time of the visit to the clairvoyant Libby was thirty-five. Another fifty years would have meant that she would have been eighty-five and I'd be ninety-one!

"He got everything else so right that I'm wondering if our relationship, which is still continuing even though I'm here on Earth and you're in the Spirit World, was what he was referring to. When I die that will be the end to our earthly relationship because I will join you in the Spirit Realms. I've already been shown that this is so. He also points out,

The strong, very, very strong, (pause) very, very strong spiritual involvement.

"I've lost the physical involvement but the spiritual one is going on now! You must agree that our spiritual love is certainly very, very strong. It will surely go on until I die and we are together once more and free to hold hands in the Spirit World."

"I think you may be right Bear but I'm not clear about everything. I know there is a lot of water to go under the bridge yet!"

"I want to ask you about something else."

"No Bear, I don't want to talk about <u>that</u> – at least, not yet. Anyway I must be going."

What I wanted to ask her about was something very personal and private that happened during our life together. It was a crisis that we weathered together and I don't believe that has any bearing on this journal at least not now.

"One thing more," I said, "You remember some weeks ago you told me to let you go because you had moved on?"

"Yes," she said, *"I remember."*

"Well I want to know if I'm holding you back at all?"

"No Bear, you're not. You've let me go and it is me who comes to you when I want to. I keep an eye on what you're doing but I can come to you when it doesn't interfere with my work. We can talk together in my time off, so to speak. No, you don't have to worry about that! I know that it's difficult to understand, but when I was newly arrived here and I was starting my work with the horses and it was difficult to be in two places at once. You see in order to concentrate on my work I needed all my faculties. In order to come to you I needed all my faculties. I couldn't be using them for two different things at the same time.

"Now I am learning how to talk to you without the great effort of actually being there with you. I am able to transmit my thoughts to you and to pick up your thoughts without the need of a "physical" presence. You have already noticed that you don't feel me so strongly when we are talking, but you also know that I can be there if required. You remember when I kissed you. You must also remember always that if you do need me I can be there with you, but you are right to wait for me to come to you – even if you do keep me waiting sometimes!"

This is quite true. When I go to bed sometimes I know that Libby is there, waiting to talk to me. In order to be sure that I am fully receptive I make sure that I am completely relaxed. This may involve finishing the crossword, having a smoke or finishing the page of a book I'm reading. Whatever it takes! I then settle down comfortably, say my prayer and I'm ready to talk to Libby.

"Well, I'm going now Bear. Good night."

"Good night my darling," I said.

I'm feeling very happy as I go back to bed after typing up my journal. The chats that Libby and I are having seem to me to be getting more meaningful. We're not just glad to be together and cementing our love and our relationship. Those things are taken as read as they were on Earth. We knew that we loved each other almost from the time we first met to the time Libby died, but when we talked across the divide we needed to feel that it was still possible to love and love just as deeply as we had before. We needed to know that because we were separated our love hadn't changed. It hadn't. I also feel that we have both learned a lot about our new life together. Certainly I understand more about her life in the Spirit World and I think that Libby knows how I'm coping with my continued existence on Earth. It is two months since Libby died. It seems much longer! If time is the measure of events then, as so much has happened since then, no wonder it seems to me to be so much longer.

Another worry has been lifted off my shoulders. I can accept that Libby is a good and wonderful person and that she richly deserves her place in the Spirit Realms, but I found it very difficult to accept that I was good enough to be given this wonderful support of continued contact with her. After hearing her clairvoyant's words about our love on Earth I now realise just how special it is. It is <u>that</u> that is supporting me now. It is <u>that</u> that cannot be ended by Libby's death. It was <u>that</u> that showed me how I got through those awful days of her illness. I'm so fortunate to have had and still have, this wonderful relationship with such a wonderful person. Our time together on Earth was comparatively short but our time together, all in all, is perhaps more than most people can manage in a full lifetime together.

Tuesday, 7th December 1999

One thing I have realised is the seemingly unimportance of things that were important to me before Libby became terminally ill. Things like television programmes, sport, hobbies, shopping, material things and urgent jobs! One mustn't cut oneself off from reality but I find now that perhaps as I am more at peace the lesser things aren't so important. I'm certainly more relaxed and I can cope with things that crop up better than I could because I'm beginning to understand what is really important and what only seems important at the time.

After a late lunch I decided to telephone the clairvoyant who Sharon had mentioned. She answered the telephone and I asked if I could come and see her.

"Yes," she said, "Do you want to come now?"

"Yes," I said, rather surprised. "I can be with you in about half an hour."

I had never consulted anybody in this sort of field before and so I didn't really know what to expect. However in the car on the way over Libby told me not to worry."

"Just be relaxed and patient. Remember patience Bear."

"Will you be with me?" I asked.

"Of course I will be," she said in such a way that I felt that all the hounds of hell won't keep her out!

Well, I must be quite honest about the whole session. She had apparently, according to her, been a famous medium, but I am very sorry to say that she had lost it. She even assumed that Libby and I were still alive together. She asked for my watch and later for something of Libby's. I gave Libby's wedding ring that I now always wear with my signet ring. Five minutes after I had sat down, by complete coincidence, it was two months to the minute that Libby had died. I had expected her to pick up something. It was very sad that she didn't.

When she had finished I told her a bit about Libby and I think she then realised that she had missed all the important points. Finally she said, "I'm not going to charge you anything for this. You'll be my last customer. I think I'm too tired out and I can't do it anymore." I gave her a tenner anyway and thanked her for her time."

Libby didn't talk to me on the way back. The traffic was horrendous in Bracknell. It was about six-twenty when I left. She seemed a kind lady and I wondered if I had been sent to her to make her realise that it was time to stop. She said she had a book coming out so perhaps now is a good time for her to hang up her optics. She can bask in the glories of her past achievements. She told me she was seventy-three. I don't think I shall do anything off my own bat again. I have tried twice and both times my efforts have been unsuccessful.

I spoke to Marie by telephone tonight. She was of the opinion that the clairvoyant had found me a difficult subject because I wanted a professional session. She thought that I knew so much about it all already that she had found it very difficult. I had rightly given nothing away. I told her about Libby's remarks to me in the car on the way over and Marie thought that Libby might have been doing the blocking! If you work on the premise that Libby was there and was doing the blocking for a bit of fun, then the following thoughts certainly come to mind. Libby would certainly have got her to tell me to lose weight and give up smoking. There was one taboo subject that came up that I know Libby doesn't want to talk about and that was dismissed very quickly! I feel that many of the comments made about Libby's mother could refer to Jerry, Adrian's mother. Libby would have been very amused at me being told that I should learn to dance, especially when she told me that I should take Libby dancing! We both hated dancing. She would have enjoyed this joke and she would know that I would too.

She would have enjoyed the joke too about me being told that I should tell Libby to cuddle her mother. She is not the cuddling type of mother. The comment about not eating butter or spread (Libby's Mum loves butter and cream) but to use olive oil must have been another joke because we only use spread that is made from olive oil! Another joke, although slightly sick, would be to tell Libby's mother that Charles, her divorced husband of some thirty-three years, will come for her. He is the last person Joan Bryant would want to come for her! I was told that she is highly sensitive at the moment and I should treat her like a child! (Anybody knowing her would get that joke! She's a very strong-minded lady.)

I was told to eat lots of salads and Libby knows that I hated salads! There were several references to me playing cricket. Libby knows that I am not a player of cricket. I was a scorer of cricket matches and since I packed up with Surrey

CCC I had lost all interest in the game! When my mother-in-law dies will I be able to live in the house means that Libby is having another joke. Mother-in-law's house is to be knocked down and the area is to be built on in the next six months!

I should write a book! I am writing a book about our spiritual life together! I see a farm I was told. Well, as I spent most of my life on various farms giving advice to farmers that's not surprising but to miss out on the most important farm in our lives at Betty Grove is surely another joke! Have we a cat in the house I was asked. He's Joan's cat. Our cats are at Betty Grove Farm!

Then there was a very clear message from Libby right under the nose of the clairvoyant. "Don't be afraid of being left on your own because you won't be!" Of course I won't be alone because I've got Libby with me, looking after me and seeing that no harm comes to me. Unfortunately the clairvoyant wasn't able to see that Libby had died! I don't like Greyhounds although I love dogs, as Libby well knows. Do you gamble? I hate gambling. It's a complete waste of money! Libby knows that I shall never win the lottery because I have never bought a ticket and never will!

These are some of the things that have occurred to me since I got the message, or should I say, joke! Marie was quite right but she didn't go far enough. Libby was there alright. Libby was having a great deal of fun at the medium's expense. It wasn't until I had finished doing my typing and I added the bit about Marie's comments that I started to see the joke. Well done Libby! You did a great job!

The joke is also on me, because why should I go and see a clairvoyant medium when I have got all I could possibly want with Libby. Well done! That's the smartest bit of sleight of hand I'm ever likely to see. It was even better in retrospect because Libby would know that by being so non-committal last night when I asked her if I should go, I would want to go all the more!

Did she do all that off her own bat or did she have a little help from her friends? I was rather apprehensive about what she was going to say about my visit today. Now I'm looking forward to talking to her about it. Either my imagination has gone completely astray or I could hear chuckling as I wrote these comments!

To be fair the clairvoyant did get one thing right when she said "I can see you being very happy!"

Wednesday, 8ᵗʰ December 1999

I went to bed after midnight and despite all the revelations of the above I managed to say a serious prayer to God.

I heard Libby say, *"Well Bear!"*

"Well, my darling," I said. We were both laughing and happy. "Was that the great set up that I imagined it was?" I asked.

"Yes," she said, *"and you were right; I did have some help from my friends. They were delighted to get their own back on some of the twaddle some of the mediums put about."*

"Some time ago," I said, "you were very happy about something and you said that something good was going to happen. Was that it?"

"Yes my Bear," she said, *"that was it! Good wasn't it?"*

"Yes," I replied, "it certainly was! Now then you must tell me if you knew about it that long ago. Have I been completely stitched up too?"

"Yes my Bear, I'm afraid you have, but you were wonderful. If you had known about the rubbish that she was being fed and then passed on to you, you wouldn't have been able to act your part. You wouldn't have been able to keep a straight face and allow it to go on. When she lost her cool in

the middle and accused you of blocking her – that was brilliant. Then she accused you of not wanting to pay her – you were superb. You stood and threw the money down on the table in front of her. We were laughing our heads off."

While Libby was telling me all this I could hear her finding it difficult to talk for laughing.

"So I was set up some time ago!"

"Yes Bear, I'm afraid you were!"

"You knew all about it that day when you appeared so happy?" (My journal shows that this day was on Monday, 29th November, see page 65 – over a week ago!)

"Yes," she said, *"I knew!"*

"When I was told to go down to the farm and look for your tape that was part of the plan?"

"Yes my good Bear!" She was chuckling all the time!

"And when I spent all that time searching for it, through all the boxes and cupboards and not finding it, you had the tape put on the very top of those that were lying above the cupboard?"

"Yes," she said simply, but still enjoying the merriment of it all.

"I then spent all that time typing out the contents of that tape. When I asked you if I should go and see this clairvoyant you were so non-committal that you knew I would want to go and see her all the more!"

"Yes," she said, *"but we knew and I was certain, that you would enjoy the joke."*

"You're right there!" I said. "The whole thing was absolutely brilliant!"

"I'm so glad you enjoyed it. We certainly have and you played your part superbly well."

"Why hasn't this been done before?" I asked.

"It has been tried before but it hasn't worked so well. You see it is very important to have two people who are as

close as we are who can communicate from a distance by thought transference. If there had been too much "presence" about, the medium would have detected it. We were able to feed her just enough. We were able to lead her up to a certain point and then turn her away so that she completely missed the obvious point of connection. Several times you thought, "Now she's beginning to get somewhere." For example she asked if October meant anything to you. Well of course it did, but you said, "Do you mean in the past or the next?" We were able to feed her the wrong information and she directed you away from last October into next October! How could next October mean anything to you? It hasn't happened yet!

"There were a number of times when she was about to make a link and she was turned away from it and missed the point. A lot of the information that she received about Mum, as you correctly guessed later was about Jerry. You should have seen your face when she told you that Mum was going to die in a few weeks!"

"Don't you think that it was rather cruel though to the old lady?" I asked.

"No," said Libby, *"she had it coming to her."*

"Well," I said, "you must give my congratulations to all concerned. It was brilliant!"

"I will," Libby replied. *"Now you've got something else for your book, although whether you put her name and address in it I'll have to leave up to you! I'm going to go now Bear. We can't discuss anything serious tonight because we'll only burst out laughing in the middle. Good night my Bear."*

She had already started to go and I said, "Good night my darling."

Not surprisingly we were very happy tonight. The Spirit World, as I had read, certainly enjoys a good joke and they nailed one down today. Libby and I have had some very serious conversations. We have had some very happy moments together and shared some intimate times, but never in my wildest dreams have I imagined that anything like this would happen. I don't know if I'll get much sleep tonight. As my mother-in-law said, "You're not going to be good for anything tomorrow!"

My reply was, "Who cares!"

Something has just occurred to me. Today was the end of second month after Libby died. What a way to celebrate the anniversary? There must be more wonderful days ahead if the last two months are anything to go by! Something else has occurred to me. If anybody reading this has the slightest doubts about the truthfulness of the above – think again. Nobody could possibly have made that up. I doubt whether she's going to put this in her book. I'm certainly going to put it in mine!

Later that evening I said my prayer. An image came to me of Libby with a hoe in her hands scuffling up the soil along a row of plants. There were several rows. The ground was clean and dry. There were no weeds. The soil looked of average colour, just a light medium brown. The field or plot disappeared into some dead ground behind her so I couldn't judge how big it was. Beyond the land rose up again showing some unspoilt grassland and trees.

"What on earth are you doing?" I asked. "You can't have weeds there!"

"Oh," she said, "sometimes old habits die hard! I'm just helping a friend with his nursery. Have you recovered from yesterday's little show?"

"Yes, it was very good. By the way your mother wants to go and see her!"

"Well, it can't do any harm, but you're not to go."

"No of course not. Perhaps Marie will take her in January when she's got some time off."

"Okay. It might be interesting. It is also possible that Marie won't have as much time as she thinks because of Jerry. Don't say anything about that though."

"Yes I understand. Marie and I were going up to a bookshop in Oxford."

"Don't buy too many books!"

"That's what I wanted to ask you. Can you guide me to those books that I would find interesting and helpful?"

"Yes, I can do that certainly," she said. *"But really you've got a lot of experience yourself now. You have visited a medium so you're into that side of it as well!"*

"Marie wondered what the old lady had done to deserve yesterday's joke."

"Well, that will become apparent to her if she goes with Mum."

"Marie wants to take something of yours with them, something that was entirely yours and not something that you were given. It needs to be something that you've had for a long time that's very personal."

"Well, there are all my clothes still in the wardrobe. You must get rid of them Bear they could be useful to other people. Then you've still got my glasses beside the bed and my clogs on the floor."

"Yes, I know but I'm not having your bedside table cleared of everything telling me that you're not there anymore. That would hurt too much!"

"Alright but you must let go of things."

"We spent many happy years in that bed and you can't expect me to clear them away just like that!"

"Okay, but you can't leave things there forever. We didn't spend as much time in that bed as you think because we only bought it a couple of years ago!"

"That is true," I said, "but you know perfectly well what I mean. If I took everything out of the bedroom that was personal to you I wouldn't be able to bear to go in – let alone sleep there."

"How is Mum?" she asked.

"You know perfectly well how she is," I replied. "You don't have to ask."

"Oh I know. It was only conversational. Tell her I think about her."

"Of course I will."

I had this picture of the field in my mind's eye as it were, but if I tried to peer into it too closely it disappeared from my mind. I couldn't see Libby's face – I never can. I just know it's her.

"It's a good job you can't get any dirt on your robe doing that!"

"Yes it is," she said, *"there are no washing machines up here!"*

"Your sense of humour seems to have improved since you went there!" I said.

"Well, yes," Libby admitted, *"there is always a great sense of fun here. You'd be very happy here."*

"Don't you mean that I <u>will</u> be very happy there?"

"Don't pick on words! You know exactly what I meant," she said laughing. *"You're not here now and I wasn't implying that you wouldn't be."*

"Oh Libby, I do love you so much."

"I love you too Bear. I wish that I could come to bed and lie beside you."

I suddenly felt my eyes filling with tears. My heart was full. I could remember how good it was to have the comfort of knowing that she was there.

"I'm sorry Bear I didn't mean to upset you."

My eyes began to release their tears and they ran down my cheeks uncontrollably.

"Oh I'm so sorry Bear. I didn't mean to upset you."

"I know but I could just feel you beside me – your warmth, your smell, your being there! You'd better go. I can't carry on talking."

I opened my eyes and got out of bed and tried to pull myself together. I saw the clock. We had been together for twenty-five minutes.

Thursday, 9th December 1999

As soon as I settled down again Libby asked,

"Are you alright Bear?"

"Yes, I'm alright. I'm sorry it was just the thought of my Bat lying there beside me again." (I used to call her Bat because without her glasses she was as blind as one!)

"I know. I'm sorry I upset you."

"You didn't upset me I just felt emotional about it and I cried. I think its good that I do cry. It takes the stress out of not having you there to love and to hold. I'm fine. How are those potatoes doing?"

"Oh, they're fine."

"What happens to them? You don't need to eat them?"

"No, of course not, they go to the animals. They like them. He just likes growing things. They're really of no use except for seed for the next crop. You can plant at any time of the year here because there are no seasons."

"Your Mum said that she wished that you'd give some clue about the situation here."

"Well what does she want to know? I can tell her what house you're going to move to and where it is, but it really isn't time for that yet. You won't have to worry about that for six months."

"I was talking about the farm to a chap today. He doesn't foresee much likelihood of building down there either for us or on the whole site."

"Remember – patience. I've spoken about this to you before. You must be patient. Let things come to you. They'll come when the time is right. Just be patient. Now you must get some sleep. You need it."

"Okay. Good night my love."

"Good night Bear."

I took my mother-in-law to the post office and for a big shop in the local Sainsbury's supermarket. We were completely exhausted! As I was unloading the car I felt that Christmas, which I had been dreading without Libby, was going to be okay. Marie and Adrian were coming to stay from Christmas evening to our birthdays and Wedding Anniversary day. I felt that January was going to be more difficult. That is when all the *bon ami* is over and it is quiet with very little happening except the bills arriving! I suddenly felt very lonely at the prospect and I shouted out across the front lawn, "Libby I miss you. God, how I miss you."

I went to bed early and put the television on. I was looking for a film to occupy me. I flicked down the list on the digital screen. I came to one called I'll be home for Christmas. I didn't fancy it but I heard Libby say, *"Watch it and I'll be home for Christmas."* So I watched it. It was about an American family who received a telegram on Christmas Eve telling them that their son Michael had been killed in action. It made me cry a lot. Perhaps I was being told that I wasn't the only one who had lost a loved one. Afterwards I settled down to sleep but I heard Libby say, *"I'm making you cry a lot lately."*

"Yes but I expect it's good for me. At times I miss you so much."

"Of course you do! Don't you think that I miss you? Because our love is so great," she was crying as she spoke, *"we are bound to have times when our physical feelings take*

*over even though we know that our spiritual feelings are
bigger, more important and correct."*

"You're not meant to cry in the Spirit World," I said.

"Oh we can cry too," she replied, *"but our tears are
different somehow. We are not crying because we are
unhappy. We are crying because we feel some emotion very
strongly. When you were watching that film, you were crying
because you shared the emotions that they were going
through. You understood them. You weren't unhappy. You
were sharing, understanding. Last night you were crying
because you were unhappy that I wasn't in the bed beside you."*

"Yes," I said, "I understand the difference."

I went to sleep. I didn't sleep for long, about three-
quarters of an hour. I wish I had been able to sleep for a lot
longer! My sleep patterns are terrible now! I can't sleep for
more than two or three hours at a time. I don't know why but
I'd be grateful for a solid eight hours without interruption! I
can't believe that it is anything to do with Libby except that
instead of going straight off to sleep after her visit I get up
and write my journal. I ought to sleep like a rock after that.
I'm relaxed but tired.

"That was very nice Bear," she said after I had finished
my prayer.

"Hello my darling, are you there?"

"Yes Bear, I'm here."

"What have you been doing today?" I asked although
I was conscious of the fact that there is no night in the Spirit
Realms where Libby is, so it's rather silly to ask someone
what they have been doing today!

"Oh I've been with the horses," she said. *"They're all
fine. They're all doing well. Some of them still need more
reassurance but I'm pleased to say that most of them have
come to love me."*

"I wish I was a horse!" I said.

"Oh Bear," I could hear her chuckling with laughter. *"I can't see my Bear as a horse!"*

I sneezed.

"Oh I'm sorry," I said. "Are you still there?"

"It'll take more than a sneeze to blow me away," she replied. *"You must take Cracker to see Heike."*

I had been meaning to get an appointment to take our Golden Retriever to see the vet. Her eye infection hadn't properly cleared up.

"Yes," I said, "I will do that, but the week seems to have gone rather quickly,"

"You've had some busy periods. When the farrier comes tomorrow you will be down there, won't you?"

"Of course," I said. "He'll want paying!"

"Yes of course he will," said Libby. *"I didn't mean just that. Be down there most of the time he's there. Don't let the girls take over. You're in charge of the farm you know and you must be seen to be in charge."*

"Yes dear," I said. "I'm doing my best."

"I know and you're doing well."

"Thank you." I said. "I thought I was getting a picture then, like I had of you in the potatoes last night, but it went too quickly before I could pick it up."

"Remember what I've been telling you – patience. Don't be too eager. You must learn patience."

"I'm trying to," I said.

"Yes and you're doing very well."

I couldn't help yawning. "I'm sorry," I said.

"That's alright. I know you're very tired. I must go now."

"Must you go?"

"Yes, I must. You're very tired. Good night my Bear. I hope you sleep well."

"Thank you my love. Good night."

She was right as usual. Now I had typed up the journal I was very tired. Perhaps I shall sleep well tonight.

Friday, 10th December 1999

Libby was right. I must spend more time on the farm or find further help. Some of the girls are not dovetailing as well as they should. I have reorganised the horses in each paddock and they have all been moved round. I heard two good things from the girls at the farm today. One said that she missed Libby because she was always so welcoming and friendly and you always learned something from her. That was so true. She was always kind and good-natured and she had a wealth of knowledge about horses. Another said that she always spoke to Libby when she was at the farm. "If I slam a gate I always say, "Sorry Libby!"

It wasn't so easy to talk to Libby tonight. I felt she was about but somehow we "had a bad line". Two attempts failed but then I heard Libby calling,

"Bear, Bear, can you hear me Bear?"

"Yes, I can hear you," I said, "but you appear to be shouting from far off."

"I'm finding it difficult to get through to you."

"Do you want to go and we'll talk again another time?" I asked.

"No, but I can't keep this up for long."

"Do you think it's a good idea to take Sharon on at the farm?"

"As long as everybody gets on it'll be okay," she said. *"She's certainly got some of the experience that you lack. Oh this is hopeless. I'm going."*

"Alright my darling. Good night. We'll talk again soon." I called but she had gone.

I had felt rather tired and depressed all day. It was the fatigue syndrome catching up on me. I have had these symptoms many times before so I recognised it for what it is! I don't see that that could have made any difference but I want to record everything in case I need to refer this situation again.

Saturday, 11ᵗʰ December 1999

I said my prayers and when I had finished I heard Libby say in the usual way, *"You got a bit lost towards the end. You should think it through a lot more before you start. God hasn't time to wait while you stumble and waiver about!"*

Then I seem to have been in a mixture of spirit and dreamland until I woke up! Libby definitely told me about my shortcomings concerning my prayer and then I must have dozed off. The books that I had ordered came this morning and I had been reading Here and Hereafter, the third book recorded by Anthony Borgia. It was so fascinating that I had clearly read too much and fallen asleep almost as soon as Libby had arrived! I had made myself a ham and tomato sandwich, which I was eating sitting on the side of the bed and reading my new book at the same time. A bit of tomato dropped onto my shirt and I heard Libby say, *"You are a mucky individual!"* So I knew she was there waiting for me.

After I had settled down she told me something that I can't remember now.

"Are you listening Bear?"

"Oh yes," I said. "I'm listening."

"If you don't say anything I rather assume that we've gone to sleep!"

"I was trying to be good," I said. "Naturally I didn't want to interrupt you and I tend to take the line that I don't want to be holding you back in anyway." I still feel a bit sensitive about letting her go and not holding her back so I leave her to take the lead.

We were discussing my ability to remember our conversations afterwards and Libby said that she was often helping me at the computer when I was writing it in my journal in case I forgot anything or got something wrong. After all it was nearly always late at night that I was writing it up.

"That doesn't seem to agree with your leaving me at the end of our little chats and then turning up again a couple of minutes later to see what I'm writing."

"There are two ways of doing it. Do you remember some weeks ago I came with you from the bedroom to the front room and stayed with you while you were typing?" (See page 34, Friday, 22nd October 1999)

"Yes, I remember," I said, "I asked if you were coming with me and you said you were."

"That's right, I did. Well the other way is to leave you, as I mostly do now and return when you are typing. In the meantime I can transfer myself from where I am while we are talking by thought transference to actually standing behind you while you're typing."

"What happened last night? You appeared to be shouting as though you couldn't make yourself heard either because I wasn't hearing you or you were trying to overcome some sort of interference."

"Well sometimes when thought transference is taking place it may be more difficult to get the amount of thought, the volume if you like, right. Sometimes I have had to read just my thoughts for you to be able to pick them up, so to speak."

I lost her a while because I had a picture of someone wearing a white shirt behind a counter, possibly a policeman and two people in front of the counter. One of them was saying,

"I brought him in because he wants a desk job!"

"Do you understand now?" I heard Libby say.

"Just now I lost you completely," I said and I told her what I had seen and heard.

"Yes," she said, *"that can happen. Somebody else's thoughts can get caught up with somebody else's. It's a sort of crossed line! It happens very rarely I understand. Either that or you went to sleep again and dreamt it!"*

Then I was asleep again! Perhaps I had dreamt it.

Sunday, 12ᵗʰ December 1999

I slept in until eleven o'clock this morning and that may help me stay awake longer, enough to talk to Libby without being rude enough to crash out on her.

I had another long chat with Marie tonight about some books that she thought I would find interesting. She and Adrian are coming up to spend some time with us over the Christmas/Boxing Day period. She was concerned about how I would be able to take it if Libby didn't come through for a period of time, say a week! I felt that as long as Libby told me in advance that she wouldn't be coming I would manage, but I didn't believe that she would deliberately leave me for long.

Monday, 13ᵗʰ December 1999

Again I was late to bed having watched some very interesting programmes about the ancient Egyptians. I said my prayer and then I heard Libby say, *"That was good, my Bear."*

"Thank you." I said. "And how are you today?"

"Oh I'm good thank you, very good."

"I suppose that it's rather silly to ask how you are when you are obviously well and happy, but sometimes you are merrier than at other times."

"Yes," she said, *"That's true. After all we are always happy here but there are times when we are happier than others!"*

"Marie said tonight that she wondered how I would react if you were unable to come to me for a while – say for a week. Is that likely to ever happen in the foreseeable future?"

"Not in the foreseeable future that I can see. We are both in need of each other. I want to see you too you know."

"I am constantly reminded of what your clairvoyant said when he told you that we would have "a very, very strong, very, very strong spiritual involvement".

"Surely that's what we are having now? We shall have this spiritual relationship continuing all the time that I am on Earth, because surely it can't end until I am with you in the Spirit Land?"

"Yes," she said, *"that's how I understand it. I have told you that you have a lot longer to live and that a lot of water has to flow under the bridge before you come here.* (See page 52, Thursday, 25th November 1999). *When you do come here we will be together again and can remain that way forever. However that doesn't mean that there won't come a time that you won't want me to come so often."*

"I can't envisage that."

"You must remember that there's a lot of water to flow under the bridge yet. I am always here if you want me. I know that you are still concerned about holding me back but we have dealt with that and you're not. You have let me go in love. If you want me to be with you less that is easier for you to do. Say your prayer like a good Bear and turn over and think about something else. Then I wouldn't dream of bothering you. If you want me then all you have to do is what you're doing at present. Just relax say your prayers and wait for me! You must remember that we are very fortunate to have such a strong relationship. As the man said, "Many

*people would envy us that". I'm talking about people up here
as well as on Earth. Those who love and are parted as we
have been aren't given the strength that we enjoyed on Earth.
We had complete trust and harmony on Earth and that is what
has given us the strength that can't be parted by death.*

*"You can always turn me away as many people on
Earth do to their loved ones, usually not meaning too, by
either surrounding themselves with grief or by seeking help
from the wrong quarters. If the spirit is shunned it will turn
away and not try to communicate for a while. It will then get
immersed in the many things of interest up here and
gradually it will not bother to keep a constant eye on that
person. It happens so often but our lives together on Earth
were so much bound up with each other that our spirits
couldn't be so easily parted. We lived for each other, so just
because I have moved on it doesn't mean that we will not be
able to stay together – unless you, being the one still on Earth,
want to change things?*

*"Remember Bear, we had and are still having
something very special that is not often achieved by many
other people. We have been given a great gift. Well that's
enough. I'm going to go now."*

"What are you going off to do now?" I asked.

*"I'm going to give the children some pony rides. Good
night my Bear."*

I am quite sure that as she turned to go she waved
back at me! "Good night my darling," I said, "Good night."

I slept for a while and then on waking I made myself
a cup of coffee and a couple of cheese rolls and carried on
with my reading of Here and Hereafter by Anthony Borgia. I
read the passage I had most wanted to read about. It was
about husbands and wives who have a deep attraction for
each other and want to continue living together in the Spirit
Lands. Should one of them have progressed further into

another higher realm, it is perfectly possible for him or her to choose to live in a lower realm to be with their loved one. They can then help their loved one with their progression. This was exactly as I had hoped, but it was very comforting to read that this is indeed so.

After reading this section I settled down to sleep when I heard Libby say, *"Well Bear, are you satisfied now?"*

"Oh yes my love," I said, "I am much more satisfied now. If that should happen to us I know that you will stay with me and as you are such a good teacher I will in time progress upward to be on the same plane as you may be entitled to be on. You always were a very good teacher and I have learned a lot from you."

"You are progressing well my Bear," she said, *"you are learning patience and to apply yourself to making other people happy. That's a very good start. You've always had the right values but you didn't always apply them for various reasons. Well, sleep well my love."*

"I shall. Thank you. Good night."

"Good night my Bear."

This morning I received the name of another good medium or clairvoyant who lived near Reading. At this moment in time I am interested to visit her for two reasons. Firstly I would like a tape, similar to Libby's, telling me more about myself and perhaps some future things to think about. Secondly I don't want to believe that all clairvoyants are like the alleged medium, who I had previously visited and who had been incapable of giving me any form of a message and admitted she was losing her spiritual abilities. My sole experience to date is that she got nothing of consequence right and that she was incapable, in my case, of seeing things that I would have thought the average person would be able to gather. Perhaps I shall go and see this second medium, but only time will tell.

I took Cracker to see Heike, the Vet, this morning. There is nothing wrong with her eyes that she could determine. We will try a different ointment. However it may be caused by my mother-in-law's cigarette smoke. Cracker's ears are not bad but a weekly clean would be helpful.

I spoke to Marie again tonight. Each one of us has a doorkeeper who protects us from spirits that we don't want to meet or from spirits that would be bad for us. Twice Marie was going to tell me something about doorkeepers and twice her mind was wiped blank so she couldn't tell me. Was I being protected from something that I am not ready to know about?

Marie wanted me to ask Libby if she knows anything about the Keeper of the Akashic Records. Marie was particularly interested because she couldn't find anything to read about it. The Keeper will take you through the records of one's life and you will have to face up to your wrong doings. How does one address one's wrong doings in order to progress?

Marie and I also discussed the difference between a clairaudient, a clairsentient and a clairvoyant. Apparently a clairaudient is able to make contact by hearing, a clairsentient by sensing and a clairvoyant by seeing the presence of a spirit.

My copy of Chambers English Dictionary gave the following definitions,

Clairaudience – the alleged power of hearing things not present to the senses

Clairsentience – was defined under sentient as conscious, capable of sensation, aware, responsive to stimulus – to feel

Clairvoyance – the alleged power of seeing things not present to the senses

I noted that *Clair* comes from the Latin for clear. I for one learn a little something every day!

I confess that I was a little nervous about things tonight. There were the thoughts I have about whether I should go and visit a second clairvoyant after my first encounter. Then Marie was blocked from telling me about the doorkeepers and finally Marie wants me to ask about the Keeper of the Akashic Records.

Up to now I had felt that this was all really between Libby and me and that it was nothing but good. It made me very happy to be able to talk to her and because we were so close and happy together and I was not grieving as I would have done without her presence and support.

Was this all suddenly becoming too deep for me? Was I progressing in my understanding too fast and was I about to enter deep water? Where the revelations that I was experiencing all part of my training to progress in Libby's realm and catch up, or was I going to slip back instead of climbing the ladder?

Whatever the case, what I was determined to remember and believe was that Libby wouldn't allow anything bad to happen to me if she could help it. However I have free will so let's pray that I make the right choice.

Libby came to me after my prayer.

"Bear!" she called.

"Hello my darling," I said. "I'm glad you're here."

"Well that's good to hear."

"You seem so light and bright. By contrast I feel heavy like a stone and you're like a brilliant light feather. I want to ask you about some things."

"Okay."

"Well firstly, I have been told about a clairvoyant who lives near Reading. Should I go and see her?"

"That again is up to you. I know that you'd like to have a tape like mine. It can be very comforting. It won't do any harm to go."

"Will you come with me again?"

"Oh, I don't know. I'd need to think about that. I'll tell you nearer the time, but I promise you one thing – you won't get a show like you did last time!"

"Alright, I'll try not to be too disappointed! Secondly then, as you know Marie has asked me to ask you what you know about the Keeper of the Akashic Records?"

"Right, I have not met such a person. I don't really think it matters if someone has written down an account of your life or not. The important thing is that you are able to address your mistakes or wrong doings in such a way that you are able to progress. If you take the attitude that what I did was right, bearing in mind the circumstances and I'd do it that way again – you're clearly not learning from the experience or likely to put it right. However if you realise what you did wrong and are sorry for it, you are likely to progress. It's no good being half-hearted or just kidding yourself. You must really mean it! If you can honestly look into your heart and say to yourself, "I was wrong!" and mean it, you are almost there. Okay, that's enough. I'm off now. Good night Bear."

"Good night my darling."

She was gone and I felt much relief from her answers. I do get worried easily about things that I don't fully understand and I confess that I still have a great deal to understand about all this.

Tuesday, 14th December 1999

I have just remembered something that happened yesterday morning. Marie had asked me previously if I had noticed anything that has been unaccountably moved. "No," I had replied. "I can't think of anything."

"Keep an eye open," she had replied, "sometimes they deliberately move things."

Mandy, who comes in and does a bit of ironing and cleaning once a week was in Libby's Mum's sitting room and I was talking to her. My mother-in-law asked Mandy to put a cup back on a shelf that was too high for her to reach.

"How did that fall down?" Mandy asked.

"Oh, it just fell down," said Mum.

Mandy and I looked at each other with that 'was it a spirit that knocked it down on purpose' look?

Undaunted my mother-in-law, Joan, continued, "It's the vibrations. It often falls down!"

What a let down, Mandy and I just laughed – nervously perhaps!

I said my prayer tonight and I could very faintly hear Libby say, *"That was good Bear."*

I found it almost impossible to hear her. She seemed so far away. It was so hard to hear her.

"I can hardly hear you," I said. "Can you speak up or send a stronger thought or something?"

We tried several conversations but only bits could be heard. It was so frustrating. I tried another tack hoping she could hear me.

"I've been hearing some stories about you today. The more I hear about you the more I fall in love with you."

"Don't be silly Bear!"

"No it's true. I love you more than ever!"

"You're collecting a lot of stuff," she said. This reference was to data I was collecting about her life before we met – photographs, anecdotes, memories from friends, etc. *"What are you going to do with it all?"*

"I don't know." I said. "But it makes me happy."

"Well that's alright then!"

Then there was a spell when I couldn't make out what she was saying but I felt sure she was talking to me. I tried again.

"I love you," I said, but I got no response.

"I'm going to type up my notes," I said. "If you can hear me I'll come back in a few minutes and we'll try again."

I finished the typing and I could feel Libby close to me. I decided to go to bed and hope she would be there to talk to me. As I left the room a thought struck me. If I could feel her presence when I was sitting at the computer perhaps I should try to talk to her there. I sat down, turned the light off, put my elbows on the table and covered my eyes.

"Are you there, Libby?" I asked.

She was there because I heard her say, *"Go to bed!"*

I hurried back to bed and settled down. There was nothing and I could feel that she wasn't there. I was disappointed of course, but we have had such good conversations that I can't complain if I have missed out tonight. Perhaps tomorrow or perhaps we'll talk later on.

I wrote up these few notes. On the way back to bed I called in to the bathroom. I concentrated and heard Libby say quite clearly and deliberately, *"I can't get through tonight. I'll talk to you again soon."* It was said in a way that was definitely her. I recognised her manner of speech distinctly.

"Alright my love," I said.

Wednesday, 15th December 1999

Marie and I discussed soul mates. Marie believes that Libby and I come from the same soul group. Some people believe that everybody comes from a group of souls and they can choose when and where they can come down to Earth. They can even choose their parents. When they die they go back to their soul group and they exchange information about what they have learned. They may have to come back to learn a lesson again. It seems as though you may have to learn to be on the receiving end of what you may have dished out!

Libby in thoughtful appreciation

Libby in reflective mood on a visit to Cambridge

The prize winning combination of Forest King and Libby at the Hurst Horse Show

Libby presenting the Forest King Trophy at the Hurst Horse Show

Pan Martyr
21.11.00

Angela, my guide who prepared me for the coming of my new beloved

Barn Owls had always fascinated me so that flying a Barn Owl in
Gloucestershire was a dream come true

The Rollright Stone Circle in Oxfordshire that played a large part in my spiritual life

The road junction near Orpington in Kent that was to change my life - and for the better

The vision becomes a reality as Jenny and Michael are married at the Sanctuary, Arthur Findley College, Stansted Hall in Essex on Saturday, 30th March 2002

Jenny and Michael on Honeymoon in Egypt

RED CLOUD

Jenny's portrait of my guide Red Cloud. He was a war leader of the Oglala Lakota (Sioux). One of the most capable Native American opponents the U. S. military ever faced, he led a successful conflict in 1866–1868 known as Red Cloud's War over control of the Powder River Country in northwestern Wyoming and southern Montana. Later, he led his people in reservation life.

Chapter 5

THE BIRTHDAY PRESENT

Thursday, 16ᵗʰ December 1999

It was now exactly ten weeks since Libby died. The inevitable business that we all had to face was the Christmas card situation. They were coming in a few each day and there were of course those addressed to Mr and Mrs Ayers, "To Libby and Michael. Love and best wishes to you both." There are always some people who hadn't heard, been told and so on. It was nobody's fault but naturally it hurt.

I bought and watched a fascinating video this afternoon. It was called Field of Dreams. I won't attempt to describe it or comment on it here except to say that I recommend it. It was certainly made by someone who understood the workings of the Spirit World.

After I had said my prayer, I heard Libby say, *"Well my Bear."*

"Well my darling," I replied.

"You've had a busy day. You've made a lot of progress."

"Yes I have. Can I ask you a question?"

"Of course you may."

"Well what's all this about soul mates?"

"Okay, well they certainly exist! Marie is quite right – you and I are soul mates. As to the way they work and so on I'm not completely clear yet. In any case it's too deep for you at the moment. You've got enough going on with your journal."

"Alright, thank you."

"And now I think that that's enough for tonight because you're very tired and you've been working very hard. Thank you for taking Mum to the opticians. That was good of you. You're a good Bear."

"Thank you my darling, I do what I can!"

"Yes, you're doing well. Good night my Bear."

"Good night my darling and thank you for all your help."

"That's my pleasure Bear. Good night."

"Good night my love."

It's now very late again and I have a great headache but I can look back on a highly successful day. I am suddenly finding myself very, very busy. I hope I can stand the pace but I have got a really good incentive. I feel that it is very important that whatever else I slow down on I must keep up my work on this journal.

As Samuel Pepys once wrote, "And so to bed!"

When I awoke this morning I made myself a coffee and did three-quarters of the Telegraph crossword and then decided to have a little more sleep before getting up. I settled down and wondered if Libby might be there.

"Good morning Bear," I heard her say.

"Good morning my love," I said.

"This is rather nice!" Libby said referring to having a chat in the morning, which we hadn't done before.

"Yes it is"

"Are you going to go through your journal to remove as many typos as possible?"

"That was the plan. Can you make sure I don't get disturbed by outside things today?"

"I'll certainly do my best," she said, *"but I think you ought to help Mum with the ditch."* The leaves were blocking

up her ditch and it needed a clear out before the rains came!
"She'd like that!"
"Yes, I'd better do that. How are things going with
you?"
"Oh alright. Everything seems to be in order."
"Good and how's the Greek going?"
"Oh very well, thank you. I'm enjoying it."
"I expect you are. Are you learning Ancient Greek or
Modern Greek?"
"Oh Ancient Greek."
"Yes, I thought you would be."
"Well Bear, I think you should get up and get on!"
"Yes I suppose I'd better."
"Bye bye Bear," she said.
"Will we talk again tonight?"
"Yes, I expect we will unless you need me before then!"
"I expect I will. Goodbye my darling."

    I decided to change my bottom sheet and pillowcases.
As I was doing this on her side of the bed I deliberately
touched her spectacles that I had left on her bedside table. I
had left the bedroom as much as possible as it was before
Libby died because I hated the thought of seeing it without
her things there. As I touched her glasses I could distinctly
feel her. It was as though her being came into mine. It
surprised me, but it felt wonderful.

    I spent the rest of the day in the bottom of the ditch
forking out leaves.

Friday, 17ᵗʰ December 1999
    I said my prayer and I heard Libby say, *"That was
very good Bear."*
"Thank you my darling," I said.
"It's very late!"
"Yes I know."

"Well my Bear, I'm not going to stay any longer because it's very late and you need some sleep."

"I do miss you especially at times like this. I know how much you did for me."

"Stop worrying about it. Everything will be alright. You've got a lot of people working for you up here."

"That very reassuring," I said.

"Yes it is. Now I love you very much and I'm going to leave you to get some sleep. Good night my Bear."

"I love you very much my darling. Good night."

I slept in until midday!

"There you are then Bear!" I heard Libby say after I had finished my prayer that evening.

"Hello my darling," I said, "what have you been up to today?"

"Nothing special. Just routine really. You've been very active though"

"Yes, I think I've made progress today."

Whenever I think about what has happened in my world since Libby died I find that I am amazed and delighted. So much has happened that I find it rather like a helter-skelter on an accelerating course. I have learned so much in the last ten weeks. Now things appear to be going so fast that the option of slowing down doesn't exist.

Saturday, 18ᵗʰ December 1999

I did a bit of the crossword before settling down to sleep. It was rather a tiresome one and it felt as if I was getting quite a bit of help from someone.

"Well Bear, what do you think about it all?" Libby asked.

"I think that things are going rather well," I replied.

"Yes," said Libby, *"I rather think they are."*

"I think that you've done splendidly. I'm very proud of you."

"Thank you Bear," she said. *"I think you've done very well too. Now do you understand what I meant by a lot of water has got to flow under the bridge?"* (See page 52, Thursday, 25th November 1999.)

"It seems to be more of a torrent at the moment," I said.

"Yes, it is rather, but it will slow down soon. I can't have my Bear swept away can I? That would never do!"

"No, it wouldn't." I said with feeling.

"Well, I must be going. Did I do well with your crossword puzzle?"

"Yes," I said, "you did very well."

"Good night Bear," she said chuckling.

"Good night my darling," I replied.

I am getting past the stage when I think that I must be dreaming although I'm wide-awake! I went back to bed and sat down. I said aloud to myself, "I'm going to read a little bit of my book, my love and then I'm going to sleep!"

Immediately I heard, *"I'm in the field with the horses."* It seems that we have a direct line! Nothing is incredible anymore and it was just as well that I realised that because the night wasn't over, but it had been a busy night. I knew Libby wouldn't be talking to me again tonight so I turned over to the other side of the bed.

I went to the Post Office at about one o'clock today. I had decided, at least I thought that I had decided for myself, not to go to the local Post Office but to drive to Barkham Post Office to see Pam and to post my parcels there. When I walked in the Post Office counter was closed! A lady behind the counter said, "Didn't you know that all Post Offices close at twelve-thirty on Saturdays?"

"No," I replied, "I would have thought that just before Christmas they would be open! Never mind, is Pam about?"

I asked Pam how she was and she said she was alright. She told me she had read half the book I had lent her and she was finding it very interesting. I commented about the closure of the Post Office and they weighed my parcels, sold me the stamps from behind the shop's counter and I posted them in the box outside to catch the afternoon post. If I had gone to the other Post Office I would have seen it was closed and I would not have been able to post my parcels! Surely I am being guided in just about everything!

We've had a couple of inches of snow this evening. Libby hated snow because it made life so much more difficult to feed and look after the horses. I must go down to the farm tomorrow and check that everything is in good order before Libby tells me to!

After my prayer I heard Libby say, *"Oh Bear!"*

"Hello my darling," I said.

"I do love you," she sighed.

"I know. What's been happening in the Land of Light?"

"Oh nothing much today, I've been with the horses. You gave me a surprise when you spoke to me last night!"

"I love you very much you know."

"Of course you do!" she said. *"You're a good Bear. I'm going now. Good night."*

"Good night my love."

Sunday, 19ᵗʰ December 1999

I spoke to Joan and Harry Johnson (Libby used to work with Harry) this afternoon and asked them to let me have any anecdotes and memories about Libby. They were off for three months on a round the world trip! I was so glad that Harry was well enough to go after his heart operations. They lost their only grandson, Graham, recently so they know only too well what grief is.

I have written the Christmas cards today. It has been difficult responding to those people who had already sent cards to Libby and me. Some people had of course sent them to the two of us as they hadn't heard of her death. I miss Libby very much today. My mother-in-law gave me some reminiscences over lunch but it hasn't helped me. I think I shall go to bed early and hope I can talk to Libby. I turned the light out straight away and lay down.

"Bear?" I heard.

"Yes my darling. I'm here."

"I'm sorry you're so down. It's not surprising. You've been very good and the Christmas card duty is rather depressing."

"Some people hadn't heard you had died," I said, "that makes it more difficult."

"Of course it does! I'm here if you want comforting. I miss you a lot too you know."

"Yes I know."

"You are going to find Christmas through to the New Year quite difficult – so of course am I, but I shall be with you and we will make the best of it together."

"Will you be with me tonight? I need you tonight!"

"I shall be with you every time you lie down," she said.

"Good!" I replied.

"Now go and write your notes and remember that I shall be here whenever you want me. Go on!"

"Bear?" I heard later as I settled down. I had been reading when I felt Libby wanted to speak to me.

"Do you feel better?" she asked.

"Yes, I feel a bit better," I replied.

"I thought you'd feel better after watching the film."

There was a long pause.

"Have you got anything interesting to tell me?" I asked.

"No, not really. Everything is fairly normal here. I've been with the horses all day. Do make sure your horses are alright. The weather with you is foul at the moment."

We had had two inches of snow yesterday evening and it had been freezing all day!

"I know how you hated the snow," I said. "Of course I'll see that they're alright."

"Over Christmas you'll be okay but later you may find it a bit difficult. Soon it will all be over and you can get used to the new century."

"Will that make any difference?" I asked.

"No, not really, as you always used to say it's only a change of a date on a calendar. It won't make much difference really. Are you alright Bear?" she asked.

"I'm alright my darling, thank you."

I had been reading and got up to go to the bathroom. She really was giving up time tonight to make sure that I wasn't getting too low. The sooner I went to sleep and give her a break from watching over her old Bear the better I thought. Libby clearly knew what I had written because after I had settled I heard her say, *"So you're trying to get rid of me, eh?"*

"No my darling, definitely not that – I am feeling better now. Earlier this evening it seemed such a long time to go and I felt so lonely and depressed. I'm fine now. You go off and do something useful. I'll be okay."

"Are you sure my Bear?"

"Yes, I'm sure."

"Are you telling me that you've had enough of me for tonight?"

"No my darling, if you were with me every second of every day I'd never be bored by you'"

"Okay then. I'll go. Good night my Bear."

"Good night my darling and thank you."

Monday, 20ᵗʰ December 1999

Twice I woke up and twice I had been wrestling with the words of the journal in my dreams. I decided to get up and make myself a mug of coffee and marmalade sandwich. It was three o'clock. While I was in the kitchen I found that I understood what I had to do. I went back to bed feeling more relaxed and happier than I had felt for a while.

Four books arrived today. I have enough reading matter to take me into the next century! I did three quarters of the crossword and settled down. After my prayer Libby said, *"Well Bear?"*

"Yes thank you my darling."

"You have had a tremendous up. It's not that surprising that you're having a little down."

"No I suppose not. You sound rather sad yourself."

"It's only because you're rather down. I don't like that. Come on Bear, cheer up!"

"I'm fine," I said, but I wasn't really.

"This is a sad time of the year for you. You'll have a few downs but overall you'll be fine."

"Of course, I know that we can't put the clock back but I do miss you. I'd give a lot to have you sitting on the other side of the table doing your parish work with me on the other. I miss not being able to do some of the ordinary things together."

"Like shopping," she shuddered!

"Yes, like shopping. It's a chore but we had some fun doing it together."

"Yes of course we did, but not towards the end when I used to get tired so easily." Libby was remembering how tired she used to get at times during her illness. *"Well,"* she said, *"that's enough for the time being. Cheer up Bear. We'll talk again soon."*

"Alright my love, goodbye." I said.

Tuesday, 21st December 1999

My enthusiasm has forsaken me. I feel that I should be asking Libby more about her life in the Spirit World, but I don't seem to have the drive at present. It's Christmas Day on Saturday! It has suddenly become very close. Naturally I'm not looking forward to it, but I must put on a brave face for the sake of others. My book is not riveting. I've read half of it and it could have been summed up in the first chapter! Back to the crossword or perhaps I'll try another book.

"That was a nice succinct prayer," I heard Libby say. *"Is this book better than the other one you were reading?"* I was now reading The Celestine Prophesy by James Redfield.

"Oh yes," I said, "this is much more interesting. Tell me, is there truth in what they are saying about light energy and beauty?"

"Yes," she replied, *"the basis is quite true!"*

"Then the Spirit World exists on that basis?"

"If you think about it you'll see that our world exists because of light, which is energy. The things around us give us energy. The flowers, fruits, the air and water for example give us additional energy. The whole of the realm is based on beauty. Everything is beautiful here."

I then found my head buzzing with things concerning light, energy and beauty. Then I woke up! I had dropped off to sleep again in the middle of Libby's explanation. I was cross with myself. She was explaining something important and fascinating and I went to sleep.

After my prayer tonight I heard Libby say, *"Okay Bear?"*

"Yes, I'm okay my darling."

"I know it's upsetting you dealing with the Christmas cards but just hold on and let Christmas and the New Year go quietly on.

"It is particularly upsetting when they are addressed to both of us," I said. "Does the start of the New Millennium really mean anything?"

"No, not as far as you're concerned so don't worry about it."

I saw a view over unspoilt countryside. Libby told me that it wasn't really unspoilt because nothing could be spoilt there.

"You'll love it here, my Bear," she said. *"It's much more beautiful than you can see. You must be patient though. Remember that I told you that something good was going to happen over Christmas? Well, you must look out for it because then you'll enjoy it all the more."*

"Alright I will."

"And remember to be patient, especially in January. Be patient and let things happen. You're pushing too hard. There's still a lot of water to go under the bridge but it's slowing down now. Be patient especially in January. Be particularly nice to the people from Greece coming into the cottage for Christmas. They need a nice quiet restful time."

"Okay," I said, "will you be with me on the journey up there tomorrow?"

"I'll be with you, but drive carefully and don't speed!"

"Right."

"Good night my Bear."

"Good night my darling."

Wednesday, 22nd December 1999

As I drove passed Twyford station at seven forty-five this morning on route for the cottage, I heard Libby say, *"This is a new experience for you seeing the rest of the world going to work!"*

"It certainly is" I replied. I had to leave early this morning as I had the booking for Christmas coming from

Greece arriving at noon! Normally I didn't venture out until much later than this!

We had a chat on the way up about domestic things. I was a little concerned that we had had a cold snap and I wondered if the cottage was alright! She assured me that it was and she was right! On the way back from the cottage Libby and I discussed Christmas and its effects on those who had lost a loved one. There are the Christmas cards, which most couples write together. It is therefore a shock when one is left alone to write them. My policy is to wait until I receive a card before I send one back. There is a reason for this. Firstly, it stops me from perpetuating the chain of cards sent to people who really would rather not increase their own list anymore and secondly, it gives me a chance to find out who didn't know my wife had died. I can then put the appropriate words in their card and this saves me from having to telephone or write a letter later. Surely the first Christmas must be the worst. This is my first Christmas without Libby. We spent fifteen Christmases together. I can't believe that it's not going to hurt.

One of the things that I have been thinking about is what advice I can give to those people who aren't as fortunate as Libby and I. We have had conversations virtually every night and often in the car as well. If the traffic situation requires my concentration then Libby disappears. Perhaps she doesn't trust my driving! When the road is clear again she returns to me.

Libby has told me that we were especially fortunate because we have earned enough Brownie points to be able to talk to each other. I asked her what she meant by this and she explained that we had progressed sufficiently on Earth to be allowed this gift. It certainly is a gift. We have earned the right to talk to each other apparently because we were so close together and lived for each other – truly close to each other. *"We come as a pair,"* Libby always said, *"and we do everything together"*.

We never had any secrets from each other. We always helped others together. We never deliberately made anybody unhappy together. Libby was always better at it than I was, but some of it must have rubbed off on me. When she said that we had earned enough Brownie points together I would say that she almost certainly earned more than I did, but that putting the sum of the two together we had enough to receive this wonderful gift.

There is another way of putting this. I accept that Libby and I are very fortunate to talk together so much. It's just like having a telephone conversation except that there is no worry about the size of the January bill! I am sure that there are many people that are grieving for a loved one who would feel a lot happier if he, or she, could speak to them. I am also sure that there are many occasions when they do just this. My mother-in-law, Joan, would love to hear from her daughter, but Libby has told me several times that she has tried, but just can't get through because her mother has put a protective barrier around herself. Many that mourn have a barrier around themselves to help them get through the day, the hour and sometimes the very next minute.

Sometimes I hear people say, "I suddenly had a thought and it was exactly what my husband would have said!" How do they know that it was not their husband who had put that thought into their head? I promise you that there are times when I don't know if I have had a good idea or Libby has put one into my head! I prefer now to say, "Thank you" for the idea rather than risk being conceited enough to accept it as my own. I often find that I am at the traffic lights or pausing in my typing and I hear a comment from Libby. *"Well done Bear!"* or perhaps *"That's good Bear!"*

I think that over Christmas, or any important day like an anniversary or birthday, it is especially important to be receptive. Listen to the thoughts that come into your mind. Be prepared to be surprised and delighted if you hear the words of your loved one. He, or she, will speak their thoughts in your voice in your mind, but it will be recognisable as coming from them by their enunciation, timing and feeling. With thought transference you can only receive other people's thoughts into your mind and translate them into your own wavelength or thinking voice. I was very concerned at first that I was answering my own questions when I spoke to Libby. I have since spoken to others who, without prompting, describe exactly the same process when Libby and I speak to each other.

Also on these special days particularly, go to a quite place. Curl up in an armchair or lie down on the bed. Take several deep breaths and relax completely. Keep your eyes closed. Perhaps a relaxation tape or gentle music may help. Personally I say a prayer to God, the Creator of the Universe. I pray for all those in the Spirit World. Then I pray for those of us that are still on Earth. I pray that we will be able to receive the help and advice of those who are trying to contact us. I pray that we may be receptive. Then I pray for personal things. I pray for Libby and my mother especially. Then, relaxed and ready, I wait looking into the darkness produced by my closed eyes.

I don't call Libby. I don't speak first. I wait, relaxed and await her coming to me. Hope rather than demand I think is the watchword. I find the best time is just before going to sleep. Sometimes I am so relaxed that I actually go to sleep while my darling wife is talking to me! She's remarkably good about it.

The day after Boxing Day will be a good test for me. It is my birthday. It is Libby's birthday. It is our

Wedding Anniversary. Undoubtedly it is a day that I must face head on and take whatever comes. At least it is one day and not three different days. I hope that I shall not be awake at ten minutes past six in the morning when I was born but I will be awake at ten minutes past six in the evening when Libby was born. We shall see and hear what we shall see and hear!

"That was a good prayer, my Bear," I heard Libby say.

"Thank you my darling. Was what I wrote about Christmas alright?"

"Yes, it was alright but it needs tiding up a bit but that can be done later. Now I want to talk to you about Christmas. I want you to be relaxed about it all. You must remember Christmas 1999 and not previous Christmases. I want you to only think about this Christmas and be yourself. When people come and visit I want you to stay with them and not rush off and play with your computer or anything else. Don't think about me not being there. I shall be with you."

"Alright."

"I want you to be kind to everybody. Be especially nice to Mum. She will feel things too. Don't tease her much or better still don't tease her at all! Remember that we shall all be watching our loved ones. Be patient, kind and friendly to everybody and don't drink too much. That's enough for you to take in for the present. Good night Bear."

"Good night my love."

Thursday, 23rd December 1999

I am collecting reminiscences and memories about Libby. My feelings are that if I keep them together in a folder they will always be there to read and enjoy should I need to cheer myself up. It will be rather like a photograph album but much more personal. I have asked some of the people that worked with her and also friends as well as the girls who kept horses with her. It will have two main objectives. Firstly, it will keep me busy. Secondly, these anecdotes will never be lost.

I telephoned Pam this afternoon to see how she was and invite her to feel free to call on us over the Christmas holiday if she wanted a friendly shoulder. She told me about a couple aged forty who had sold their house and were moving in January. They had gone Christmas shopping in Reading when her husband suddenly fell to the ground. He was dead before he hit the pavement. Tragedy is all around us. We must remember in our own grief that there are others whose loss is as great or greater than ours is.

"*Bear?*" I heard distantly after I had said my prayer. I had had to wait a little longer than usual and it had crossed my mind that Libby might not be coming.

"Hello my darling. Are you there?"

"*Yes Bear, I'm here.*"

"That's better," I said. "You're much closer now."

"*Well actually I was a little less punctual tonight.*"

"You mean you were late! Can you tell me what you were doing?" I asked.

"*Oh yes,*" she said brightly, "*I was with the horses.*"

"How are they doing?"

"*Oh they're doing well, thank you. They're a lovely bunch you know. I know you'd love them.*"

"I'm sure I would. I expect they all love you?"

"*Well yes they do, but you must remember that everything is based on love here. It's not just me you know!*"

"I expect you've got a lot to do with it."

"*Now let me talk to you for a moment. This Christmas I want you to be tolerant, patient and kind. I want you to remember that not everybody has your beliefs. You always used to say that there are as many religions as there are people and you were right. So don't overdo your views and your newly found knowledge. Don't push it down everybody's throat."*

"No my love, I'll try not to."

"What about this young woman who has lost her husband recently in Barkham? Are you going to try and do anything to help her?"

"I'm not sure yet."

"Well it's up to you. You've made the offer through Pam and I think that is enough. Your real job is the journal. That's how you are going to help most people. That must always come first, if you can help other people as well then that's fine.

"I like the idea of collecting reminiscences and memories. I think that it's a good therapeutic exercise. Hopefully it will help those who remember them as well as those who collect them. I think people will then keep the best and most natural memories to remember rather than those of the last few years or months. I'm not so sure about collecting photographs."

"Well I may need some to put in the book," I said.

"Perhaps. Well that's enough for tonight. I hope you sleep well."

"Thank you my darling. Good night my love."

"Good night my Bear."

I tossed about in the bed for a while but I couldn't get off to sleep. There was a gale blowing outside. I made myself a mug of coffee and read my book. I settled down again and I was considering my love for Libby and my lack of grieving.

"What's going on Bear?" I heard. *"It seems as though you're arguing with yourself."*

"I was considering my love for you and my lack of physical and mental grief at your death," I told her.

"Well if you want to have grief that can easily be arranged," Libby said, *"all I have to do is to go away. Then you'll grieve."*

"No, I don't want that!"

"Let me explain it to you. You haven't experienced physical or mental grief because I am with you. If I go away, as I did on a couple of occasions, you felt hollow and empty. I am able to stay with you and keep an eye on you, even when I'm with the horses or learning Greek. You feel full and complete, don't you?"

"Yes I do," I said. "That's right."

"Well, if you remain open and receptive I can fill you with my love. You are complete and whole. If I am not able to be with you it's because I need my full energies – such as when we had the visitation from a Higher Realm, you were on you own. You were cross with me later on because I hadn't been around to fill you with my love and you had experienced grief. You still love me as much as you did before. It's not necessary to love somebody to feel grief. If you love somebody that you've lost and you surround yourself with a barrier in order to cope with everyday life without that person, that person can't get through with their love to protect and help their loved one."

She continued with, *"You have got it completely the wrong way round. Because of our deep and personal love for each other and your prayer that God answered in the gardens at Nettlebed, I was able to tell you not to worry. You didn't worry. You didn't surround yourself with a barrier in order to cope. You knew that I was in God's hands. You were happy that I wasn't in pain and that I was what people on Earth call 'at rest'. Therefore you remained open-minded and receptive. I was able to talk to you. Little by little we were able to develop our communications. I can assure you that many clairvoyants can't contact the spirits here as easily as we can talk to each other. If both are willing and need to talk, it can easily be accomplished. We both missed each other. We needed to talk to each other. We needed to feel that we both still loved each other. Surely you can see that it was this love that filled you and stopped you grieving. The only thing that you have lost is the physical body of your wife and that body hadn't been much good lately. We still have our spiritual love."*

"Now I understand, my darling."

"Right, then be a good Bear and go to sleep."

"Thank you my love. I will."

"Good night then Bear."

"Good night my darling."

As I went back to bed after typing these notes in my journal, the gale blew very strongly around the house. I hoped that the farm buildings had all their roofs in tact, but I felt much happier now that Libby had explained the reason why I didn't feel the intense grief that I had expected to feel on her death. I have had much support from friends. I had been able to cry that relieved the tension. I also felt that I was much more sensitive in myself, which made it easier for me to cry if I needed to.

Friday, 24th December 1999

I had slept well for what remained of the night. Unfortunately we had visitors so I had to get up early!

Tonight I went into the bathroom on my way to bed and I heard Libby say, *"You were very good with Hans."* An old friend who had visited my mother-in-law this evening.

"Thank you my darling," I had said.

Then I went and lay down on the bed and put out the light. I always used to get undressed and settle down ready to sleep, but I now lie down on the bed fully dressed so that I don't have to dress again before typing up the journal. I said my prayer and I heard Libby say, *"That was nice Bear."*

"Thank you my darling." I replied.

"As I said to you in the bathroom, you were very good with Hans. He needs to understand more about death, especially as he lives in the past after the death of his father. You were able to tell him that death is nothing to fear. He was right to say that he can feel his father around him. His father would like to talk to him if Hans would only be more receptive. You and Mum were right to try and persuade him that he must live in the present. As he told you all his happy memories are in the past, but he must make way for new ones. Do you notice anything different tonight?"

"Yes, I do. Where you are everything is lighter, brighter and happier. I can see a ring of white clad figures dancing around in a circle."

"You can see all that, can you?" Libby said.

"Oh yes, quite clearly."

"That's very good Bear. You are coming on well."

"What is making everything lighter, brighter and happier?" I asked.

"Well, it's of course Christmas time. This is the time when we thank God, the Creator of the Universe, for creating us. It is lighter because energy flows down from the Higher Realms to us and this makes everything less heavy. Energy creates lightness. It is brighter because extra light also flows down from the realms above. It is happier because we are celebrating God's gift to us – that of life. I'm very impressed that you could see all that," she continued. *"You're doing really well."*

"Perhaps it is because you are able to send stronger or more meaningful thoughts down to me?"

"Well, perhaps there is a bit in that, but you are seeing the difference in the Spirit World from other times and that is

very good. Well happy Christmas Bear." It had now passed midnight so it was Christmas Day.

"Thank you my darling and a very happy Christmas to you too."

"You will remember that you are to celebrate Christmas 1999 and not previous Christmases that we have shared together. I shall be with you over Christmas – you must remember that."

"I will my love," I said.

"Well, I must say good night now," Libby said. *"I'll talk to you again very soon."*

"Good night then my darling." I said, "Good night."

"Good night my Bear."

As I finished typing up these notes I could hear the winds howling round the house. I thought of the people who had been evacuated along the south coast where they were expecting seas of over fifteen metres higher than usual. That's nearly fifty feet to the likes of me. They will not have a very happy start to Christmas.

Saturday, 25th December 1999

It was Christmas morning and about eleven-thirty we had a very heavy snowstorm! I wondered what the betting odds were! It didn't settle because of all the rain that we have had in the last few days. I have tried to tidy the front room where I work and we have also cleaned the deep fat fryer. I watched an old Morecambe and Wise Show and I haven't laughed so much since Libby died. It was the well known one that included the Angela Rippon dancing routine. It was such a pity that I hadn't put a tape in to record it.

We had a simple Christmas lunch of Chicken Kiev and we await the arrival of Marie and Adrian this evening. On Boxing Day we will have our traditional Christmas meal of sirloin of beef from our excellent butcher, Eagles in

Bloxham, Oxfordshire. I drank some red wine at lunchtime but otherwise I shall leave drinking alone. It will not make a substitute for Libby.

I had a little nap this afternoon. Mum and I have managed to keep ourselves busy and occupied. The day has been quiet but that is how we prefer it. Having our Christmas meal on Boxing Day is, I think, a good idea, because Christmas Day seems very much like any other December day. There are the Christmas cards about and presents, but by not making a big issue of today it is passing without too much pain. Of course as I write this I am missing Libby very much but I know that we shall be talking tonight.

Libby and I would have spent this morning at Betty Grove with the horses so I have avoided going down there today. People will be excited and I'll not risk putting a damper on their festiveness. I'll see them tomorrow. I think the secret of spending my first Christmas without Libby is to let Christmas slide quietly by. Be friendly and so on to other people, wishing them well, but keeping a tight rein on one's emotions and trying to get though it as just another day. This is a long holiday, until well into January with the Millennium celebrations, so there is a long way to go yet. This is only day one. I prefer generally to listen to music or watch a video rather than let the world in. It is of little concern to me to watch the rest of the world celebrating. If the world comes to my door I shall greet it, but otherwise I shall keep myself in quiet isolation!

Marie and Adrian arrived at eight o'clock and we had supper and an enjoyable evening. Marie read my journal and enjoyed it. She seems to think that it has the makings of a good book. Marie of course understands Spiritualism. She calls herself a spiritual person. "It's a good project – a very good project." She told Adrian that he must read it too. "I couldn't put it down," she said. That bodes well!

Sunday, 26th December 1999

It was half past two this morning before I went to bed hoping to talk to Libby. I said my prayer as usual.

"Hello Bear," she said, *"It's very late."*

"Yes, I'm afraid it is. Marie's been reading the journal"

"Good."

"Do you mind other people reading about our life together?"

"No. Why should I? We've nothing to be ashamed of. We've a good life together."

"Yes we have, haven't we?"

"Now I want to talk to you about Boxing Day. You're going down to the farm in the morning?"

"Yes, that's right."

"It's very wet down there after all this rain."

"It is, but there's not much I can do about that. I shall be getting the tractor soon and I am hoping to get a roller too, so when the ground is dry enough I can roll it down a bit and make it more level."

"That will help. I'm glad that Adrian's having AGM." (My mother-in-law's car registration was AGM and the Ford Granada was always known by its registration letters.)

"It'll have a good home," I said. "Adrian will look after her."

"Of course, now you've got the people from the farm coming in for a drink in the afternoon?"

"That's right."

"Well, it's a good idea but you'll probably have had enough red wine at lunchtime so don't drink too much."

"Of course not, my darling!"

"Well just see to it that you don't!"

"Right!"

"In the evening Marie is going to try something. Just be relaxed and patient, alright?"

"Yes, of course my darling."

"Okay then."

"How have things been up there today?"

"Oh, everything has been very nice – no, that's a silly word. Everything's been glorious! People have been very happy. Most of them have been keeping an eye on their own families on Earth. I've been watching over you and Mum. Did you feel me about?"

"Oh yes, I did," I said, "except for about six o'clock, Earth time. I felt a bit hollow around then."

"I went down to see the horses and I needed my concentration there, so you would have felt that I wasn't so close about then."

"I felt very full and complete most of the day," I said. "Oh Libby, I do love you!"

"I know you do Bear," she replied. *"I miss you very much. I want to be with you."*

I could see her then, head and shoulders looking to my left and she was about to cry. "You're not going to cry?" I asked.

"Of course not!" she replied. *"But I do love you. I wish you could be here with me."*

She was clearly crying.

"So do I my love, but you've told me that I can't come yet."

"Not for a least another twenty years!"

"I suppose that's a long time on Earth to wait, but we'll have eternity together."

"Of course we will," Libby said. *"Well my darling, I love you very much."*

She had stopped crying now and the picture of her faded.

"I know you do, my darling. Just now when you had a little cry I could see you in my mind's eye. Tell me does emotion make the presence stronger?"

"Possibly," she said.

"I can feel you very strongly now. You're very close to me."

"I know," she said very quietly.

We were very, very close. It was difficult to speak. We were just enjoying the closeness of each other. Eventually I heard Libby say very quietly, *"I must be going now Bear. I love you so much."*

"And I love you very much. Good night my darling."

"Good night my love," she said. I waited. The presence of my wife was still very close. After a while I saw an image of her white robe flitting away in the distance getting smaller.

I have given Marie some tapestries that Libby was working on and Marie is going to finish them. After our main evening meal I went and lay down in the bedroom. I had been thinking about Libby and so I went to the bedroom believing that she may want to talk to me.

"Hello Bear," I heard. *"I'm glad you've come and lain down."*

"Hello my darling," I said. "How are you?"

"Oh I'm fine. I'm sorry about my snivelling last night. I just missed you rather a lot."

"I've had my share of snivelling that you've had to put up with."

"Yes, but you've got more right to snivel than I have," she said.

"Oh I don't know about that," I said. "What are things like up there?"

"Things are back to normal."

"That's good," I replied.

"Well, I'll talk to you later," Libby said. *"Goodbye Bear."*

"Goodbye for now my darling," I said.

Marie went down to my bedroom about eleven o'clock to try and contact Libby. Marie was told to pick up Libby's glasses, but she didn't want to risk smearing the lens so she picked up Libby's watch. As Marie got through she came to a double gate. Marie asked the doorkeeper to let Libby come out. The doors opened towards her and Libby came out. She was wearing a lovely gossamer robe. In front of the gates there was a flight of stairs, which Libby descended. She was radiating light, which was too strong for Marie to look into. Marie found that she couldn't get anywhere although she had asked Libby to call me down from the front room, but she wouldn't. Libby wouldn't talk to her. Marie came back to the front room to say she wasn't getting anywhere.

Marie continued talking to me between eleven thirty and midnight on this Boxing Day evening. This is what she said.

"Libby didn't want to talk to Michael but wanted to talk to her mother. She was more concerned about her mother. She wanted to speak to her mother. Libby came down. She was quite tearful. She wants to get through to her mother but she can't. She has made her peace with Charles (Libby's father) who was not in the same dimension. He had come though but now he had gone.

"She is worried that if she doesn't tell Mum she's sorry they won't be in the same dimension. She wants to say she's sorry. She got something wrong. She feels that because she never said sorry that she wouldn't be close to her. She misses her. If she doesn't say sorry she won't be with her.

"There was a lot she needed to say to her father that was never said, but it's gone now. Her mother has a little problem that needs sorting – a niggly little problem. Libby would rather she got it sorted.

"Libby is aware of what Joan is telling her especially at night, but she's not opening herself enough and Libby can't come in. She hears her Mum sending her love but Mum is too frightened to step off and go that one step further. Libby does get her thoughts and wants to be closer.

"Libby thinks she didn't get things quite right. She wishes with time and hindsight that she had seen to them. Libby regrets certain things especially that she didn't spend the time that she could have spent with her. At the time it was more important to work with people from outside the family unit that needed her more. On reflection she regrets she didn't do more! She's welling up with so much love she didn't show her Mum. She wants to give her a big hug – that everything's okay. She wants her to know that she is okay. Mum worries about her.

"Libby is crying. Libby can't go back and do it all again but she wishes so much that she could. Libby says the vision of love is different than on the earth plane. She wishes she had stepped back and actually looked at the situation better, but at the time it was the right thing.

"Libby feels that a mother's love is so precious. Libby feels closer to Mum than she has ever felt, but doesn't know that Mum knows this. She's sad that it wasn't two-way. Libby said that her mother is a stubborn old fool but Libby needs her. For once in her life she should open up and let someone in! For some reason Libby needs forgiveness – Mother's forgiveness.

"Libby explained that Michael was not to worry about this. It is a different kind of love than ours. He's not to be jealous. It's the love between a mother and her daughter. Her mother has to stop pretending.

"Libby is pacing up and down. She's quite adamant that it wouldn't have worked. Libby is very tired. That's what she's been working on today. She's not wasting any more words. She just wants her Mum to know that she's alright. She wants to make peace.

"As she's going away Libby said, "Love to Holly." Marie didn't understand but it was clearly a reference to Libby's thirty-three year old mare, Folly, at present still alive and well at Betty Grove.

"Libby will try again later. She was very emotional and crying."

Marie came back out of trance with her face drenched with tears. The information that Marie gave me I found to be incredibly accurate. Marie had written something down in an envelope and sealed it afterwards and given it to my mother-in-law. I had no idea what it said.

Monday, 27th December 1999

Later Marie and I were discussing the thing that Libby didn't want to talk about and I explained to her what it was. Libby had had an abortion. Marie then wrote the following down on a piece of paper, "As Libby walked away she was cradling a baby wrapped in a shawl. She could now understand the words "Mother's love."

I was shattered!

As I write these words my emotions are very mixed. I am thrilled that I am a father – really thrilled. I am saddened that we didn't share the child on Earth. I wrote above that I thought the comments Libby had made about her mother were incredibly accurate. Now I am utterly amazed that I fully understand what she was saying. I have tears in my eyes as I write this. It's the biggest bombshell I have ever experienced in my life.

Clearly the baby in Libby's arms was symbolic because the child would be nine years old by now. Libby was telling Marie that she had found the child and that she understood what a mother's love should be. Libby had told me on Thursday, 2nd December (see page 74), *"Something good is going to happen at Christmas"* and a reminder on Tuesday, 21st December (see page 133), *"Remember that I told you that something good was going to happen over Christmas?"*

Another incredible thing happened. On Thursday, 9th December (see page 102) Libby told me that she'd be home for Christmas. She was! Marie brought her home with these revelations!Looking back, the build up to these things came about through some organisation behind the scenes. It had started with Marie saying on the phone one night that she'd love to spend Christmas at Melton Cottage because it's so peaceful. I told her that she and Adrian should come. Marie said that she always spent Christmas Day with her mother so they couldn't come.

I told her that she should talk to her mother about it because these things had a way of working themselves out. I even said that perhaps she was meant to come! How right I was. It was certainly meant to happen. I was not told immediately about the baby, because Libby told Marie not to tell me just yet. Now it had all happened on our Birthdays and Wedding Anniversary!

Now at about one o'clock we were going to bed and Marie suddenly remarked that as it was now my birthday I should open my cards and presents. I did so. Shortly afterwards Marie gave me Libby's bombshell! Libby has given me the best possible present that she could give me!

I am going to bed now to talk to Libby. I shall not get much sleep again tonight. I'm much too excited. I said a quick prayer to God thanking Him for this wonderful news.

I hope He understood my haste. Of course He did! I heard Libby say, *"Well Bear!"*

I was really so excited that I didn't answer her immediately.

Are you there?" she said.

"Yes my darling, I'm here! I'm so excited. I was shattered when I heard the news about her. I was absolutely shattered!"

"It's a him actually."

"Gosh!" I said. "Is that him I can see with a blue shirt and white shorts with you there?" I had a picture of a little boy with golden hair dressed in a sky blue shirt and white shorts running around in a grass field a few yards from Libby.

"Yes," Libby said, *"That's him!"*

"It's absolutely fantastic!" I said. I could hardly contain my excitement. "How did you come to find him?"

"Well one of the things you do here is to review your life. When I was reviewing mine I realised that he must be here. So I went and looked for him."

"You needn't have done," I said.

"Oh but I did!" Libby replied.

"No, I didn't mean it that way. I meant that not all parents would have sought out the child that had grown up so much."

"Oh but I just had to find him! You remember that I organised horsy rides for the children?"

"Yes."

"Well you see, it wasn't quite as you may have thought. I wanted him to learn to ride and look after and love horses – naturally enough. I couldn't just take him out without the others. That wouldn't have been fair so I organised the riding for all of them and he helps me."

"What's his name?" I asked.

"Well," Libby said hesitantly. *"I wanted to talk to you about that. What would you like to call him?"* She paused. I thought but I didn't say anything. *"Well, they called him John."*

"I think it's not a good thing to change his name at nine years old. I think John's fine. John Ayers," I said. "I like that."

"That's good," Libby said and I think she was a little relieved.

"I think he's a grand lad," I said. "I'm very proud of you. I think you've done wonderfully."

"I did have a little bit of help from you!"

"I suppose you did," I said remembering the occasion well. After Libby had become pregnant we had discussed when and where it had happened. "What a birthday present," I exclaimed!"

"I hoped you'd like it. I said something good would happen!"

"Yes, but you didn't tell me just how good. It's wonderful! It's fantastic!"

"I think you should go and write up your journal now," Libby said. *"We can talk again later."*

"Yes alright," I said. "Thank you my darling."

"Thank you my Bear."

Afterwards I went back to the bedroom and lay down on the bed again fully clothed. *"You're still up then Bear,"* I heard Libby say.

"Yes," I said, "I'm still up. This news is so exciting. It's absolutely wonderful!"

"You really must stop saying that it's absolutely wonderful!"

"I'm sorry but it is. When is his birthday?" I asked.

"Don't you know? It's the 8ᵗʰ of September!" (See page 38, Sunday, 7ᵗʰ November 1999)

"I thought it might be!" I replied. "I'm so pleased that you won't be alone anymore."

"I certainly won't be, but I shall still be talking to you regularly. You mustn't think that this changes anything between us."

"Of course it doesn't!" I said.

"Do you understand why I was crying last night? Why I miss you so much? I want more than anything for you to be here. I want you to be able to share in his life – his growing up."

"Well you must tell me all about it. He will be grown up by the time I come to you."

"That is true," she said. *"But you have a lot to do on Earth. We will be together when you've done your allotted tasks."*

"I shall be an old man by then!"

"When you come here you will soon be in perfect health and in the prime of life! Oh Bear, I do miss you so!"

"I miss you so very much, especially now, but you are still such an important part of my life and you make me so happy. I shall now console myself that if you hadn't died I wouldn't know I had a son and you wouldn't be able to bring him up. I suppose that I can put two and two together and link your early death with the bringing up of John?"

"Yes, you can do that. You see you are able to cope much better than I thought without me on Earth. If I hadn't come here you wouldn't have learned about the Spirit World and written the journal. It was all meant to happen this way. And now I really must go so you can get some sleep. It's terribly late again. Good night Bear, I do love you."

"And I really do love you," I said. "Good night my darling."

"Good night my Bear."

When I eventually went to bed I read for a while from The Tenth Insight – Holding the Vision by James Redfield. Marie had told me about soul groups. (See page 116, Wednesday, 15th December 1999) I asked Marie this morning when she first heard about soul groups and she told me that it was five or six years ago. Marie hasn't read the Tenth Insight and the book hadn't been written when she first heard about them. It struck me as quite remarkable that tonight, with all it's revelations that I should read about soul groups.

Soul groups are a group of souls who are on the same resonance and who work together to help each other in the Afterlife. The book describes how parents are chosen and how the spirit enters the body at conception. John would have known that he was only coming to Earth for a short time because it was all done through the soul group who have knowledge of the future. It was clearly important that Libby wasn't a mother on the Earth plane but she was in the Spirit World. It could be said that I wasn't to be a father with Libby on Earth but I am one now and I feel that this journal may well reveal how a man can be a father although his wife and son are in the Spirit World. Libby and I will talk a lot I'm quite sure about John and how he is going to grow up with Libby. One day I am sure I shall be able to speak with him as I now speak to Libby. There is certainly a lot of water to flow under the bridge yet!

I had a visit from one of the girls from the farm. She was asking me questions about spiritual matters that twenty-four hours before I wouldn't have been able to begin to answer. My knowledge and experience is growing at a fantastic rate.

Marie and Adrian left after lunch. Frankly I was glad that they were going home because I wanted some time to myself to get back to normal after all the revelations of the last few days. They are coming back to see us again in

January so I will be looking forward to that. I also need to catch up on some sleep.

It's been one of the happiest Christmas/Birthdays that I can remember. I miss Libby but she has always been around. She gave me the most wonderful birthday present – a son!

I was in the bathroom during the evening when I clearly heard Libby say, *"Happy birthday Bear!"*

"Happy birthday my darling," I replied.

"Happy anniversary Bear."

"Happy anniversary my darling," I replied. We were both laughing happily together.

I spent the evening reading. I had a nap. I spoke to friends and relatives who were kind enough to telephone me to wish me a happy birthday and see how Libby's Mum and I had fared over Christmas. Then I felt that Libby was waiting to talk to me so I said my prayer and asked God to look after Libby, John and my mother. Then I heard Libby say, *"Happy birthday Bear!"*

"Happy birthday my darling."

"Have you enjoyed your day?"

"Oh yes, it's been a wonderful day. Have you got John with you?" I asked.

"No, he's not actually with me at the moment, but he has been with me all day."

"What have you been doing?"

"Well, John and I have been wandering about this land looking at the flowers and the rivers and enjoying everything."

"What's he doing now?"

"Oh, he's with the horses."

"Is he alright on his own?"

"Yes of course. There's no danger here. Accidents just can't happen."

I was struck by a change in Libby. She was much softer, more relaxed. Much more loving, more rounded somehow. Up until now I had the feeling that she had been busy working, getting things organised. She had to wait for me to learn and be able to accept things. Perhaps she could relax a little more. She was certainly able to share the joy and happiness of us having a son. I have felt different too. Since I have known about John I have felt more complete, more relaxed and life certainly felt more enjoyable and worthwhile. I can understand that Libby was relaxed now that I had sufficiently progressed to be able to receive this wonderful news. I couldn't have had a more wonderful present. I do not think in terms of Libby being anywhere other than where she is. I can now fully accept what has happened. A mother's place is with her child and Libby has to be both mother and father to John. Both our mothers had to do this before her. The big difference is that both our fathers went off with other women and left our mothers alone with their children. In our case John went to the Spirit World first and Libby has since gone to join him. I am the absent father. However I shall not lose sight of him or his growing up because Libby and I will talk about him a lot. In time Libby will surely prepare him to talk to me!

Tuesday, 28th December 1999

Before going to bed I made myself a mug of coffee and a Stilton cheese roll. As I was cutting the Stilton cheese I heard, *"I'm glad I'm not sleeping with you tonight!"* Libby was almost the perfect woman, but she didn't like the smell of Stilton!

I have been spending most of the afternoon sorting out my favourite photographic memories of Libby. Her mother also gave me some of her drawings and some photographs of Libby as a young girl. I was collecting these together as a sort of photographic record of her life. As I was looking at a photograph of her aged ten on a cruise with her mother, Gran Ethel and Poppa Tom (the name she used for her grandfather) I thought, "You were a good looking child." Immediately I heard Libby say, *"Oh sucks!"* I have enjoyed looking at the photographs very much. I have found it very therapeutic writing up the journal, collecting people's memories and now making a photographic collection of her life.

I had a quick word with Libby before I went out. I lay down on the bed and waited.

"Well Bear," she said, *"what do you want to talk about?"*

"I wanted to know how John was."

"Oh he's fine! He's a super little chap and he's quite advanced for his age."

"And how are you my love?" I asked.

"I'm fine," she said. *"We've been down with the horses today. He loves the horses."*

"That doesn't surprise me considering who is mother is!"

"Well, no. I suppose not!" Libby chuckled. *"I'm rather worried about my mother. Can you ask her to try to take that extra step so I can talk to her?"*

"Yes of course I will," I said. "But I don't know if it will do any good! What about this medium I'm expecting to meet tonight?"

"She's okay. Just be your usual charming self and listen. Don't tell her too much about us. She can wait until the book comes out!"

"Alright my darling. Thank you. Bye."

"Goodbye my Bear," Libby said.

So later I went out for drinks with one of the families that kept a horse at Betty Grove. Joan, my mother-in-law, was feeling tired and frankly couldn't be bothered to make the effort. She is eighty-one and she gets more tired as the day goes on and the last few days have been rather hectic.

At the drinks party I met a lady called Carolyn. I listened but didn't learn very much that I didn't know already. She was mainly into healing. However she gave me the name of a clairvoyant who lived fairly near whom I shall add to my list!

I went to bed and said my prayers for those in the Spirit World and on Earth.

I heard Libby say, *"Hello Bear."*

I said, "Hello my darling."

As I looked I saw in the distance a figure with white light shining from it very brightly. "Is that you?" I asked.

"Yes," said Libby. *"I thought that you were wondering about me in my spirit attire as I had appeared to Marie? I felt that you were wondering why you hadn't seen me adorned so."*

"Can you come any nearer?" I asked.

"No." Libby said. *"You're not ready for that yet."*

"I do love you!" I said.

"And I love you too. You do know that don't you?"

"Yes, I know that."

The radiant figure faded away.

"Are you there?" I asked

"Yes, I'm still here," Libby said.

"Thank you for showing me. You looked wonderful, but it's cosier talking together like this," I said. Libby had forgone her spirit attire. She was as usual nearby in my mind although I couldn't see her.

"What about visiting a clairvoyant?" I asked. "Carolyn gave me the name of a lady tonight. Is it a nuisance to you if I see them?"

"No, it isn't a nuisance at all." Libby replied. *"You can go and see them if you want to. I shall tell you all I can if you ask me questions and I shall show you things when I think it is right for you to see them, but it will do no harm for*

you to go. If you want to explore and find out more, then you should go."
"Thank you my darling. Is John alright?"
"Oh yes, he's fine."
"Will you teach him to talk to me when the time is right?"
"Yes of course."
"He'll be at least twenty-nine when I come to meet him!"
"Don't you worry, you'll talk to him."
"Thank you my darling."
"That's alright my Bear. You must go to sleep now."
"Yes, I must. Good night my darling."
"Good night my Bear."

Wednesday, 29th December 1999

On the way up to Shenington I had heard Libby say, *"Good morning Bear."*
"Good morning my darling," I had replied.
We had had a little chat about nothing in particular. We lapsed into silence for a while and I started thinking about Libby and the photograph that I had taken when we were on the way to Scotland a few years before. We had been following a car with the registration letters BAT, which eventually pulled into a lay-by. Libby had stood in front of the rear number plate blocking out the numbers so that only the letters showed and I had taken a photograph!
This happy memory had made me feel very sad. I began to feel hollow and empty inside although I could feel that Libby was still with me. Libby told me to breathe deeply and concentrate on the picture I had last night of her in her spirit robes. I concentrated on that vision. I breathed love into myself. It was difficult because I couldn't give it my full concentration because of the traffic on the M40. Slowly however I did manage to feel love coming into me and I certainly felt better because of it.

On the way back, after welcoming in the family who had booked the cottage for the week of the New Year celebrations, Libby was there with me as I drove south on the M40. Suddenly I felt a change in her presence.

"Are you with somebody?" I asked. "Have you got John with you?"

"Yes," Libby said.

I felt him very strongly with Libby. Then I clearly heard, *"Hello Daddy!"*

I was supremely happy. "Hello John," was all I could manage to say. Libby was completely quiet during the next few minutes. After a pause I managed to say, "How are you, John?"

"Oh I'm very well thank you Daddy." He was a very well mannered little chap. I was delighted and there was a great grin on my face for the next half an hour or so – even after he had gone.

"Were you pleased to find Mummy?" I asked.

"Oh yes I was. She makes me very happy. Are you coming to see me soon?"

"No," I said, "I'm afraid that I can't do that John. It is apparently going to be a long time before I can come and be with you, but we are going to be able to talk to each other a lot and Mummy is going to look after you until I can come and see you. Do you like the horses?"

"Oh yes Daddy, especially King. I do love King and he loves me too."

"He always was an exceptional pony." I said. "Do you go for rides on King?"

"Oh yes!" John said. "Mummy and I go out together. I ride King and Mummy walks with us."

"Are you happy with Mummy? Are you pleased Mummy found you?"

"Oh yes! I'm very fortunate because not everybody is found by their Mummy."

"I wish I could come and see you," I said, "but we will have to be patient and I will come and see you as soon as I can!"

"Thank you Daddy," John said.

The traffic on the M40 required my attention. When it quietened down a bit I could only sense Libby with me.

"Where is John?" I asked.

"He's gone off to play nearby. What did you think of him?"

"He is absolutely wonderful! Of course he would be being our boy."

"He's a lovely chap," said Libby. *"There's a lot of his Dad in him!"*

"And there's a lot of his mother too!" I said. "He's absolutely wonderful. It's fantastic!"

I was still grinning from ear to ear as I now drove down the Marlow by-pass.

"Darling, I do love you so." There were little tears of happiness in my eyes.

"Thank you Bear. I love you too and I think we are both very proud of what we've been given."

"Yes indeed! Is that why you had to leave me so soon, because John needed you?"

"Partially, John needed his mother, that is true, but that wasn't the only reason. I had finished my work on the earth plane and I was needed here to look after the horses. I had further work to do. I hated leaving you but you have much more work to do on Earth. It is terribly important that you publish the journal. It is more important that you tell those who need help on Earth than for you to be here to be John's father. I shall bring him up as well as I can and you will be in touch with him to help and guide him."

"It's a fairly unusual situation," I said, "for a child to have his mother with him in the Spirit World and his father on Earth!"

"Better that than to be abandoned by both parents!" Libby said.

"Yes of course!" I said.

The traffic on the M4 was heavy and needed my attention and although I could feel Libby's presence and guidance, I had to concentrate on my driving. Then I turned off the M4 and had to concentrate on the roundabouts and junctions until I arrived back. Libby stayed with me until I returned home, but then, having seen me safely into the garage, slipped quietly away.

Marie spoke to me later this evening. She was keen to know all that had happened since she had left. Eventually I had to hang up. I was shattered, too tired to talk anymore. I went to bed very early after the late night party last night, the early start, the change over work at the cottage and the excitement of the journey home. I read a little as I drank my coffee and then settled down.

I heard Libby say, *"Hello Bear."*

"Hello my darling."

"You're very tired. Go to sleep. We'll talk later."

"Alright my darling," I said sleepily. "Good night."

"Good night my Bear."

Thursday, 30ᵗʰ December1999

I went to bed and prayed to give Him my thanks for all that I had received and for the insight to the work that I had been allotted. I then prayed for those in the Spirit World and on Earth. After a pause I heard Libby say, *"That was a serious prayer!"*

"Yes it was and I meant it."

"Yes of course you did. You have been thinking about things and you want to ask me some questions?"

"That's right! Did you do a deal when you came to the Spirit World that if you could keep in contact with me we would publish the journal?"

"Oh no!" Libby said. *"It was nothing like that! It became clear that we could accomplish both things quite happily."*

"Really! What should the book be called?"

"You will know when the time comes! You haven't got there yet. Leave it as it is. Continue to call it your personal journal, but you will know what to call the book when the time comes."

"Where is John? How is he?"

"Oh he's fine! I usually leave him with the horses because it's so much easier to talk to you without him being here. Yesterday it was quite difficult getting us both through to you!"

"Oh but it was wonderful! I've never been so happy!"

"Wonderful is becoming one of your favourite words!" Libby said.

"Yes, I suppose it is!" I chuckled. "But it is all so wonderful!"

"Silly old Bear!" said Libby smiling. *"What other questions did you want to ask me?"*

"I can't remember now!"

"They couldn't have been very important then."

"Oh I expect they were," I replied.

"There's always next time! Well I'm going to get on."

"Alright my darling," I said. "Goodbye for now."

"Goodbye until then," Libby said.

I went back to bed after typing the above and saw my notes on the bedside table concerning the questions that I wanted to ask Libby. I settled down but I didn't say anything.

"Did you want me?" I heard Libby call.

"Well, if you're not too busy, I do have the other two questions that I wanted to ask you."

"Okay," she said.

"What can you tell me about the dakini?"

"My word, you are getting on, aren't you? Do you realise it's only twelve weeks since I died and you're coming up with questions like that! Well, the dakini are spirits found in the Buddhism of Tibet. They are spirits that act as guides. In the Western World they would be known as angels. They are really messengers or guides from the Spirit World to those on Earth. Does that answer your question?"

"Yes! That's very helpful indeed. Now I've learned that soul mates are spirits of the same kind like you and me in a soul group. I've also heard recently that this is not strictly so because there can be other souls that can come into a soul group from elsewhere?"

"That is so. I think you've already worked this one out. When a soul group is contemplating somebody's path to be taken in life, it is quite possible for a member or members of other soul groups who are more expertly experienced in a given subject to be invited to advise."

"That is very helpful my darling." I said. "Thank you."

"That's alright Bear. Any time, any place, any where!"

"I'll let you get back to your work. Good night my darling."

"Good night my Bear."

Friday, 31st December 1999

The last day of the twentieth century, I wonder if it really does make any difference or is just an excuse for a party. It only happens to most people once in a lifetime – if that. Neither my mother nor my father experienced it and my wife, Libby, never did – on Earth anyway! I have no plans!

I shall either be asleep or I shall spend it with Libby if she's not busy doing something else. We were never a couple that needed this sort of celebration. Our Birthdays – yes! Our Wedding Anniversary – yes! But to celebrate a split second when the calendar changes – no! Not really. If Libby had lived I suspect we'd have been with the horses to make sure that they were alright when people let off those wretched fireworks. Perhaps I've answered my own question! I ought to be on the farm to make sure the horses are safe.

I spent the morning at the farm renewing the goats' bedding and trimming their feet. After lunch I had a nap to make up for the late night tonight. I settled down with the intention of saying a prayer to God about the millennium, but I heard a voice say in a very excited way,

"It's absolutely incredible!"

"Is that you Libby?" I asked.

"Yes it's me," she said. *"I had to talk to you. It's absolutely incredible!"*

"Are you going to tell me what's so incredible?" I asked.

"Well there is so much more energy, light and love here. It's flowing down from the Higher Realms."

"Like it did at Christmas?"

"Yes just like that – only more so."

"Has it been like that all day or has it only just started?"

"Well it started this morning, or a least what you'd call morning. It was very little at first but then it increased and got more and more until now it's far greater than I've known it since I've been here. The feeling of love is tremendous! We all feel much nearer to God, who is the Divine Source of all light. It's as though we've all been lifted up closer to him."

"Does it affect John too?" I asked.

"Oh yes and the animals too, the horses are trotting around with their ears pricked and their eyes alert. It's wonderful!"

"There's that word again!" I couldn't help saying!

"Well it's a jolly good word of yours!" Libby retorted. *"What are you going to do tonight?"*

"I was going to go to bed early, but then I thought I ought to go down to the farm and keep an eye on the horses. I can't do an awful lot because it's so wet down there. At least I can be on hand if they get spooked into any sort of trouble."

"Our horses shouldn't be any trouble but it may depend on the ones that you have as guests."

"That's right, but there are bound to be fireworks at midnight, so I thought that I wouldn't take any chances."

"You're a good Bear!"

"I do my best!"

"Take care of yourself tonight. Goodbye for now, I'll talk to you again soon."

"Goodbye my darling."

Just after nine o'clock I felt a strong feeling that I should check the farm and leave the stable lights on when I left. There had been minor firework parties during the evening, but the present ones were noisier. I put on two sweaters and a coat to be on the safe side as I didn't know how long I should be at the farm.

I took the Range Rover down the track. The ruts were full of water and mud after the heavy rain we had had during the last week. I drove down passed the farm gate and checked the goats and Raffles, the ram, at the end of the Bottom Field. They seemed to be alright. Parking the Rover outside the farm gate, I unlocked it and put the car park and stable lights on. Min, the black and white cat, had made herself a nest in the shavings in the first stable and was curled up fast asleep. The greys, Folly and Jane came towards the gate of the Bottom Field. They were alright but I didn't want them standing around in the mud by the gate so I walked up the

Middle Field where Cindy and Thomas were. Cindy was slightly jumpy and came over to me. I let her nibble the fingers of my left hand until she gave my little finger a sharp nip. She thought that I should have brought her some pony nuts!

I walked further up the field and looked out over the River Lodden towards Reading and Lower Earley. There was a fairly continuous rattle of firework noise with the occasional rocket and the odd flash of light. As I watched I heard, *"Thanks for coming Bear."* Libby was watching out too!

I walked up to the Top Fields until I could see Slipper and Savannah in Top Field Right and then Amber and Crystal in Top Field Left. They were quietly grazing. *"You can go now if you like,"* I heard Libby say, but I waited for another half an hour and looked out at the crackle of fireworks exploding across the river. I thought that this is what it must have sounded like when there was "sporadic fighting" that we were shown in news bulletins from countries abroad. Suddenly there were several very loud explosions like canon with the echoing rumbles afterwards. They were very loud and I couldn't help reflecting that they must have cost a bomb!

The air was at the dew point or slightly more, because although it wasn't actually raining, everything was wet – especially my hair. There were still flashes and bangs from the south over the river, but every now and again there were flashes and bangs from the east and west as well. Thomas came over and was friendly. He was not agitated and probably only wanted to see if I had any food. After about half an hour I walked back down to the buildings. Everything was quiet on the farm

I examined my little finger where it had been nipped and was reassured that it was still there but there was some blood coming out by the nail! I went into the first stable and stroked Min. She put her head up in welcome and she was clearly pleased to see me. Leaving the farm lights on, I locked the gate and returned.

As I wrote these notes in my journal, I could still hear the fireworks from Lower Early across the M4. It was now half past ten and I thought that I ought to go down again. Suddenly I noticed something. It had gone quiet! I went to the front door and went out. I listened. The barrage had stopped. There was only a crackle of the occasional firework. Ten minutes later the noise started up again. This time most of it was coming from the town of Winnersh! I reflected on the benefits of living in the industrial south!

I decided that I would have a mug of coffee before going down again. We had clearly had the worst of the fireworks for the time being. My next concern was what would happen at midnight! I pondered on the thought about these people with so much money to explode. Do they ever think about animals, some of whom are petrified by thunder and fireworks? I was glad that Portia, my Golden Retriever, was safely with Libby in the Spirit World. If Libby was still with the horses at Betty Grove Farm, then on this occasion I imagine Portia was with John, but Cracker, Libby's Golden Retriever who still lives with me, was fortunately bang proof!

I had seen Min safely tucked up in the stable and I wondered where the other two cats were holed up. Tiger, the large tabby, would be fine but Monte, the black longhaired cat, would be a bit nervous. The chances were that they were curled up together somewhere.

The fireworks still exploded on the other side of the M4, but they weren't as frequent now at eleven-twenty. I was having my coffee and then decided I should go down to the farm again. I somehow felt that Libby would be there with me and if I did have to drag myself into the new century that's where I wanted to be with her. I wondered if she would bring John with her.

Chapter 6

THE NEW CENTURY

Saturday, 1ˢᵗ January 2000

By a quarter to twelve, before the New Year arrived, I was standing in the Middle Field Left and it was drizzling. Libby had greeted me halfway up the field as I trudged through the mud with, *"Hello Bear! I'm glad you've come back."* She was alone because I couldn't feel John's presence at all. Then, as I stopped and faced the River Lodden the Arborfield church bells were ringing over to my left. There were a few fireworks going off still. At five to twelve they started up in earnest. By midnight the noise was continuous along the Lodden valley. The drizzle had become heavier and it was now light rain.

I heard, "Hello Daddy!"

"Hello John," I said delightedly. "What a wonderful surprise! What do you think of all these fireworks?"

"Oh I think that they are rather jolly! Some of them are very pretty. I had to come because I wanted to be with both my Mummy and Daddy."

"That's just as it should be."

"Do you like the fireworks too?"

"Yes. They are rather spectacular," I said rather grudgingly.

The sniping had turned into a full-scale battle. The whole valley now was a continuous noise as if everybody was trying to outdo everybody else. The main fireworks for about fifteen minutes after midnight were pretty ones. Four horses now surrounded me, but as the rain got heavier they just stood with their heads down.

"Weeeee!" I heard John say as a particularly colourful rocket exploded over the trees.

The incredibly barrage of sound and colour continued. There was absolutely no let up.

I heard Libby say, *"Thank you for coming."*

"Where else should I have been?" I said. "I wanted to be at Betty Grove with you and John!"

"Don't get wet," was all Libby said.

The continual noise of fireworks still echoed along the valley. I had to admit I was fairly impressed. A huge colourful rocket exploded in front of me above some trees.

"Look at that one," I called out to John.

"That was terrific Daddy."

"Don't get wet Bear!" Libby said.

"I'm alright." I replied with my head pushed down into the top of my coat.

It was a full half an hour before there was any let up in the continuous rattle along the Lodden valley. I walked down to the stables. The rain was getting pretty heavy. I put my head in the first stable to wish Min a happy New Century. She wasn't there! I went in search of the tomcats, Tiger and Monte, but I couldn't find them. Perhaps they were wishing Libby and John a good New Century! I left all the stable lights on, mainly for security but also as a hollow gesture towards the New Century. I drove up the lane and stopped at the style to check the horses in the Top Field Left. As I did so one of our neighbours between the farm and Libby's Mother's cottage let off a banger. I nearly jumped out of all my clothes and skin as well. I said something very rude and then apologised in case anyone was listening!

The rattle down the valley was back to sporadic gunfire now. The main battle, which had lasted about half an hour, was over. I wondered who had won. Clearly those who manufactured and those who sold fireworks had made a killing. As I arrived back at Melton Cottage I wondered how the fire service and the Accident and Emergency Departments were coping. I also wondered what the poor and needy were thinking. Perhaps I'm too much of a Jonah sometimes. I had been impressed by the firework display after midnight. I didn't think that there were that many fireworks in the world – let alone in the Lodden valley! Most of the time I had been completely surrounded by exploding money! Well come on! It only happens once a century!

It was now a quarter past one and there were still sporadic firework parties going on! Cracker, who as I said earlier is pretty bang proof, was shaking indoors during the main battle and had only just condescended to go out for her last night ablutions. Perhaps we could all go to bed at last!

It is now the new century. Libby died eighty six days ago. I have learned so much during that time that I find it difficult to appreciate that it is only three months. I have lost my wife on Earth, but I have gained a wife and son in the Spirit World who spend time with me. I'm really a very fortunate fellow.

At last four great stumbling blocks have been negotiated – my first Christmas, our first Birthdays and Wedding Anniversary and now my first New Year without being able to hug and kiss my wife, but Libby hasn't deserted me. She had been with me and helped me through. God bless her.

I went to bed at half past one. The Lodden valley was quiet again. I have to admit that tonight has been quite an experience.

I said a very sincere and practical prayer to God and then I heard Libby say, *"That was good Bear."*

"Thank you my darling," I said. "That was a wonderful experience at the farm tonight."

"Yes, it was pretty good."

"We are surely most fortunate to spend so much time together and to be able to talk so freely?"

"Yes, that's true, but if only people won't put up such grief barriers they would be able to have much more contact with their love ones."

"I am especially fortunate that I had my prayer answered and that you spoke to me at Nettlebed so I was prepared. You are a particularly spiritual person and some of that has rubbed off on me."

"Yes, but you must remember that usually by the time the funeral is over, people have got their grief barrier around them. These particularly occur about the time of the funeral. They have to get through the experience. All their loved ones can do is to do something physical – like moving something in the house to try and tell them that they are there and that they are alright. Remember that when I first tried to talk to you, it wasn't that easy until I had learned the best way to do it. Then you had to be receptive enough to understand when I was talking to you. It isn't easy for people on Earth to understand that when a thought comes into their heads and they say, "Oh, so-and-so would have said that!" that it probably was so-and-so who did say that!

"Unless people understand how thought transference works, they imagine that they are thinking these thoughts themselves. The whole point is that you receive my thoughts in your mind and so they come to you as if you had thought them yourself. It's only the mannerisms that are different. If you can get this through clearly in your book you'll get masses of letters from people saying, "Thank you. If only I had understood. I now know that so-and-so was speaking to me!"

Now it's very late and you're very tired. I shall talk to you very soon. I'm going off to see my horses. Good night my Bear."

"Good night my darling."

I woke up on this morning of the new century to a beautiful sunny day and I reflected on last night. It was the perfect way for me to spend my time as we went into the new millennium. It needn't have rained – that is true! Everything else was perfect. The fireworks were, by any standard, spectacular. I had watched them with Libby and John! I couldn't have foreseen this even a few days ago. I am extremely fortunate. I wonder how many people were as fortunate. I like to think that there are many more than I could imagine, except perhaps that they may not have the courage to talk about it.

I went to lie down on the bed early this evening hoping that Libby would be there to talk to me. She didn't come. It came into my head that I should play a relaxation tape. I relaxed and lay out on the bed. I allowed the tape to take over and I concentrated on the words. Afterwards I felt relaxed and I turned on my side in a sleeping position. There was no sign from Libby. I felt that she naturally had work to do after the last week from Christmas to the New Year.

My thoughts wondered if I had lost my ability to be receptive or whether and I hoped more likely, that she was busy. Perhaps on the first day of the new millennium they had special visitations from the Higher Realms. I had not said a prayer to God because I had felt that it was too early in the evening. I had prayed just before I was ready to sleep in the past and that seemed to have worked well. Libby was always there afterwards and had clearly heard my prayer too.

I am mentioning this in my journal because I want it to be remembered that Libby didn't always come whenever I lay down and waited. I also want to remember this in case it is the beginning of something different in my life. Heaven please forbid that Libby won't come as often or perhaps ever again. I can't honestly believe that after all that has happened between us, she would have gone away knowing that we were not to talk again, perhaps for sometime.

I feel sure that there is something that has delayed or prevented her from coming. She has her work with the horses, her life as a mother with John, her rides for the children and her Greek studies. She could have been visiting friends. She could have been taking instruction. She may well have been organising something. There are umpteen reasons why she wasn't there. I continued to tell myself not to worry. I clearly felt that I was told to play a relaxation tape. Surely that was to tell me that she was busy and that she would come to me later. I hope and pray so.

However I can't avoid thinking that I must remember that my experiences with Libby are unusual. They are not the norm. Perhaps I need reminding of this occasionally. I must be positive. I feel relaxed but rather cold and hollow. I must be patient and wait.

After my prayer Libby called, *"Bear? Bear?"* She was clearly very excited.

"Yes, I'm here."

"It's incredible here. There's so much more Light, Love and Energy after yesterday. We all feel so much more Love towards each other. We are raised up, closer to God, the Divine Source of Love, as though we have all progressed and been rewarded for our work."

"And John too?"

"Oh yes! Everybody in the realm – don't you understand? The whole realm has moved closer to the Great Light source."

"That's wonderful! The only problem that I can see is that I've been left behind. I'll have to work even harder to catch you up if I want to be with you when my time comes."

"Oh Bear! You silly old Bear! That's not the case at all. You have been working very hard during the last three months, very hard. You've already made great progress. You've progressed a lot, you know."

"Thank you my darling, that's encouraging."

"You didn't think that I'd progress so far that I'd leave you behind, did you?"

"Well that's not an easy question to answer," I hedged.

"I think you're just a very silly old Bear!" Libby said laughing.

We spoke about other things I know, but when I woke up about an hour later they had gone. I woke up, as if from a dream, willing myself to remember, but I couldn't. I cursed my human frailty. I have read this passage through several times hoping to remember, but I can't. The only comment that I can make is that I believe that Love, Light and Energy in the Spirit World are the same. The increase in our vibration causes them to be present in ever-greater quantities – the better our lives become the greater are our vibrations. If we lead a poor life on Earth our vibrations are low. We have little love. Our Light source, that we absorb from, is low. We can only acquire low levels of energy. The poorer our lives are, the lower our vibrations are and the further from God we are! God is the Supreme Source of Love, Light and Energy. The more we progress, the greater our vibrations and the closer to God we are, hence my concern that Libby could progress faster than me and leave me far behind.

"Bear!" I heard as soon as my head touched the pillow. *"I'm glad you're back. There's more I want to tell you."*

"Thank you my darling."

"The reason why I wanted you to listen to the relaxation tape tonight was because when you relax your vibrations increase. You go onto a higher plane yourself. You are in fact closer to God at such times. It is easier for me to contact you if you are on a similar vibration to me. If you like it makes it easier if you are on the same wavelength! If I am on a higher wavelength and you're on a lower wavelength then I can still contact you, but I feel much more uncomfortable. In fact if you ever did anything really naughty I would immediately be able to tell by your decreased vibrations!"

"Good Heavens!" I said. "That's another good reason for me to behave myself!"

"And don't you forget it!" Libby laughed. *"You see,"* she continued growing serious again, *"God is the giver of all Love, Light and Energy. He can give these gifts as far away as the Laws of Nature allow. The closer you are to Him the greater the amount of Light you receive."*

"It seems to me that if you have a degree in physics you can get on better where you are!"

"No, not really. It's very simple or so it seems from here. God can control the Light that He sends out so that it goes where He wants it to go. You remember when God answered your prayer in the garden at Nettlebed? (See page 27, Monday, 4th October 1999) Well, He did so by sending down a beam of golden light. He could control that beam so that it came at exactly the right second and you saw it clearly in front of you. It was meant only for you to see at that precise moment! You never saw it come or go, did you? You only saw it there! How did you feel when you saw it?"

"Well, I felt awed, elated, relaxed and completely at peace," I replied.

"Don't you realise that at that precise moment you were very close to God. He had raised your vibrations so

that you were near him. He doesn't lower His so that He can be close to you! He simply raises your vibrations and then aims his Light so that it comes only to you. What did you feel later when He spoke to you in the garden?"

"Very much at peace," I said remembering the experience in as much detail as I felt at the time.

"You see," Libby continued growing serious again. *"You were relaxed to such an extent that you felt completely at peace and so your vibrations were quickened as you were very close to God."*

"What was the warm breeze that I felt just before He spoke to me?" I asked. (See page 30, Friday, 8th October 1999)

"Oh I thought you knew that. That was the Breath of God. I thought that was why you chose the hymn at my Thanksgiving Service, 'Breathe on me Breath of God'."

"Well yes, that's right, but it was the Minister's suggestion and it seemed very appropriate to me."

"Yes, it certainly was," said Libby thoughtfully.

"That reminds me of something," I said. "At the Thanksgiving Service, Marie told me later that I got the distance just right when I walked behind the coffin. She told me that there was just the right amount of room for you to follow it when you were riding King. I thought that you would just be there outside watching?"

"Oh no, I wasn't going to miss anything! Besides it's the proper place to be. If you hadn't been concentrating so much on the coffin and keeping your head straight, you'd have seen us. I willed you to relax so you could see us but I couldn't get through to you. I was very limited in my ability to talk to you in those days. At one point I thought you might get too close and get stepped on!" Libby laughed at the thought but I didn't think it was that funny!

"It must have been a wonderful sight." I mused.

"It was pretty terrific I must say!"

"Well, what else do you have to tell me? Is John with you?"

"No, he's with King."

"I hope he's getting some schooling?"

"Oh yes! Don't worry about that. He's getting plenty. Schooling here is not all about learning your two times table. There are plenty of personages that you would approve of who are happy to give their time to a little boy! You must remember that a lot of the good things on Earth have come down from the work of what I shall call 'august personages' here in the Spirit World. A great deal of music has been written here and Paul McCartney said on television that one of the songs he is credited with was not written by him – he only wrote it down!

"You'll find that a lot of composers as well as artists, poets and others have had inspiration from here. The world where you are is a very materialistic one. We are constantly getting," Libby paused clearly trying to find the right word, *"resonance coming up here that show how materialistic the Earth people are. There are exceptions,"* Libby went on. *"There are definite moves in the fields of medicine where some people are finding help by the laying on of hands, the use of plants and herbs, what some call alternative medicine, but generally there is this materialistic feeling that they must have more and they don't need it! There are some good references in the Bible about it. Not everything, because it was written down hundreds of years after Christ died, is without worthiness. Much of the good thoughts have come through. One quotation that comes to mind now is,*

"Consider the lilies of the field, how they grow; they toil not, neither do they spin."
[St. Matthew Ch.6 V.28]

"I think that's how it goes! Because of this materialism it is so difficult, almost impossible, to put things in the minds of people on Earth who could 'discover' new things. Hundreds of years ago it was much easier. Man had an open mind. The Renaissance was a wonderful time of progress and discovery."

"That's fascinating stuff!" I said.

"You are a good example, my Bear! You have an open mind. Although before I died you had had a conventional religious upbringing, you were sufficiently open-minded to accept that, as you often said, there were as many religions as there were people. You also used to say that basically the people around the world where worshipping the same God, but in a different form. You were rather sceptical about the work of mediums and the possibility of talking to the dead. I rather think that you felt like so many others that we, as human mortals, were not meant to delve into these matters. What do you think now?"

"Well, that is a big question!" I said, playing for time to think. "If we are given gifts by God, such as you and I have been given the ability to communicate, we should use them to the best of our ability."

"Good answer! You see that the reason why some folks say that we are not meant to delve into such matters is because they are unable to accept that spirits exist. They either have had no experience themselves or else they are frightened. It is extremely important however that they don't meddle! You know that because you tried to make contact with your Spirit Guide, your dakini, one night and you had a definite warning not to do this."

Libby was referring to one night in bed when I was feeling particularly confident in my new experiences with the Spirit World. I had heard Libby's tape when she was with the clairvoyant. I thought that it would be a good thing if I could meet my Spirit Guide. I lay back and relaxed in bed. I asked if my Spirit Guide was there. I remember saying that I didn't mind what he or she looked like because I was prepared! What I wasn't prepared for was a rising feeling of dread and horror that I experienced. I shouldn't have done this. It was clearly wrong for me to delve at that moment in time.

"And now my Bear, that's quite enough for one evening. Write up your journal and then when you come back to bed, read your book and then go to sleep! Good night my Bear."

"Good night my darling."

Sunday, 2nd January 2000

I am now reading Post-Mortem Journal by Jane Sherwood. It gives a totally different aspect of the Spirit World. It is about the arrival of T.E. Lawrence in one of the lower realms and his "cleansing" from his wrong doings on Earth. Although I knew of the darker realms from previous books, I am now learning about the facts about how one is confronted with ones "sins" and how one can then progress on from there to be in the lighter realms.

I said a serious prayer to God asking for his help for those in the Spirit World and on Earth to progress. After a while, not straight away as usual, I heard Libby talking to me. She told me that I must be careful because reading about the lower realms was beginning to depress me.

"It's quite alright to read about it, but you mustn't get drawn in. You can be interested in what happens there, but I am trying to keep you in the Light and Love of the realm that I'm in. You mustn't allow yourself to get depressed about what happens down there in that dimension. Whatever you do you must guard against dark spirits, because they do exist. You must never try and contact them – never for any reason. There are many people up here that are looking after you as well as me, but you must be careful. You are very tired and

that lowers your energy levels. Always try and keep yourself full of Love. I warned you that there would be ups and downs in January – well, they've started. Have a nap now and you'll feel better."

When I woke up Libby was still there and wanted to tell me more.

"Up here, when you are ready to do your work," she said, *"it isn't allotted to you. You find the work that you feel you are best suited to. I had been walking with friends when I found the horses. I asked who looked after them and I found that there was an elderly gentleman who was extremely kind and loved them all very much. He told me that he stayed with the horses because he felt that somebody should. It was really time that he moved on to a Higher Realm where his wife had already gone. Sometimes he visited her and sometimes she came and visited him.*

"I told him that I had several horses of my own here and that I would be only too happy to look after his charges when he is away visiting his wife. Now I find that he goes to see her more often and stays longer, so that I am really the one in charge now! When he comes back he seems to visit me as much as the horses. Recently I was at the cottage and he visited me there. He met John and was extremely interested to know all about you."

"Tell me more about the cottage?" I asked.

"Well, it's very much like your mother's cottage in Shenington. I decided that I needed somewhere because John needed a home. He needs somewhere to play and learn – somewhere where people can visit him as well as me. He has friends from before I found him of course and sometimes some of them visit him."

"Tell me more about the cottage," I said again.

"It's quite small really. I don't need much space except for visitors. There are two rooms downstairs which

are used mainly for loafing and entertaining. There is no kitchen or bathroom of course. The two rooms upstairs are mainly for enjoying the views over the countryside. You can see for miles. There isn't much of a garden, but there is a stream that runs nearby with the most beautiful flowers growing on its banks and there are some spectacular shrubs and trees. The dogs enjoy it. There are no fences or hedges so that they can come or go at will. TC (our tabby cat) *is in charge so that everything is perfect, or will be when it's time for you to come. You'd like it very much, but I will have to get it extended by the time your arrival is due!"*

I looked at Libby's photograph in front of me. I loved her very much. As I looked I was breathing in deeply as I remembered her ten years ago. I heard Libby say, *"Don't do that Bear, it's not good for you."*

"I was breathing in Love," I replied. "Isn't that what you've been telling me to do?"

"Well yes Bear, that is true enough, but you were also thinking sentiment. That was what I was saying wasn't good for you. You will learn that there is a great deal of difference between sentiment and love. Love with a capital is the same as Light and Energy. It comes from the Divine Source. You can't breathe in that kind of love from a photograph of me taken ten years ago."

Libby was talking quietly with a great deal of affection.

"What I am trying to tell you is that it doesn't do you any good sighing and mooning over an old photograph. Your life on Earth must go on. There is no way at all that we can ever have what we had before I died. I know that sounds hard, but we simply can't go back! We have a new relationship now, one that most people can't find. If only they were more open and patient, other couples could talk to each other as we do. We only talk as often as we do because we have a job to do! If you analyse how much of our conversation is about

the Spirit World in relation to the earth plane, you'd see that we don't actually talk about ourselves very much now. I'm always here if you need me, of course – you know that.

"I am teaching you so much for two reasons. I want you to progress and be a good Bear, so that you and I will be together in the same realm one day when you've finished your work on Earth. That work just happens to be helping others who are crying out for help and can't find it. The Church won't admit that it's good for the bereaved to talk to spirits. They are frightened because it upsets their control over their congregations. That's what I've heard you refer to as the members of their club. You are right, of course. There are religious groups here who have their own churches and hold their own services and carry on much as before. They can't accept that there is a whole, greater, wider issue here. God is Love. Love is Light. Light is Energy. God's Love is made of Light and Energy. To all intents and purposes they are the same."

I let her go on. I found that it was fascinating stuff and the more I learned the more I wanted to know.

"There are churchmen who have had experiences with mediums and talked to spirits, but they have to keep quiet about it! Those who live totally by the Church's rules find it very difficult to come here and expand themselves into the great scheme of things. Their Church protects them and they are all frightened of making their way in the outside realms without that protection. Some people do learn to leave the club, as you call it. Anyone who wishes to try, will have as much help and advice as they need. There are many spirits here who understand. They have been through it all themselves. There are many people too, up in the Higher Realms, who will give advice. Sometimes they will even come down or in rare circumstances they have been known to invite

that person to come with their Spirit Guide to the Higher Realm."

"Are you saying that the Church is leading its congregations astray?"

"No, I'm not saying that. The Church throughout history hasn't a very praiseworthy record of Love. The Church is lead by a board of directors like any other company! They see their job as protecting their religion rather than helping those in need. They tend to look after their own jobs like anybody else does. The members of their "flock" are of less importance as long as they remain as members. Religion should be looking out all the time for new evidence of God's Light on Earth. All religions need to be a living entity, growing in strength as it learns more of God's purpose. Most religions are steeped in history and are loath to change anything in case they rock the boat. What they don't realise is that it is the directors that are rocking the boat."

"You always spoke of Him up there", I remembered. "You and I didn't go to church much because we didn't need a man made building to communicate with God."

"That's right," she agreed. *"He is in the fields, on the beach, along the roads and in our homes. You always prayed to God as I did – when it was important. It isn't necessary to speak to God only when in a church. I noticed you always said a prayer when we visited a church because you had a conventional upbringing, but you also said a prayer to God whenever you needed to pray. You always asked or thanked God wherever you were and whenever it was necessary. Remember your prayer at Nettlebed? (See page 27, Monday, 4th October 1999) You didn't go to the chapel or the church in the village. You prayed as you walked down the path in the garden. You felt that God wasn't listening. You felt nothing. You cried out in anger to Him. You weren't afraid because you stood up and were counted. God sent you a clear answer. He raised you up from your*

anger and brought you closer to Him. You said that afterwards you felt at peace, remember?"

"That's right," I said.

"Now then suppose you had been in a church. Would you have shouted out to God? What would you have been told by Church ministers? Do you think you would have said that you had become angry with God? The most likely explanation that the Church would fall back on is the usual story of a God that you must humour. If you make him angry He is likely to punish you and you will burn in Hell! I love you very much, my Bear, I think you are very special, but why should God treat you any differently?

"When He sent you the golden shaft of his Love to tell you that He was listening and that all would be well, some Churchman would perhaps have suggested that it should have been a thunderbolt to burn you up for angering God Himself. Instead He did what you asked of Him. Later in the same gardens He told you that He had heard you. (See page 30, Friday, 8th October 1999) Now is that the kind of God that the Church is telling the world about? My darling Bear, the Divine Creator of Everything is the God of Love. He is not able to be angry or unkind to his children. Prayers here are always answered if only those on Earth can work out how! Do you remember me telling you about how I had to be very careful in trying to look after you, because I mustn't do anything that would upset the lives of others?" (See page 87, Monday 6th December 1999)

"Yes, I can understand that," I replied. "I suspect that many prayers are directed in such a way that if they were granted other lives would be upset."

"That's right. Now I must leave you, but before I go I want to explain something else. During the last couple of days I have given you a great deal of information. You have done well to record it all. It is important that this message is clearly put down in your journal. I have been trying to help you to remember it all as you were typing it up. Soon you will

have need of what I have told you. I'm not going to say more than that. You must have patience and as usual you will know when the time comes."

"Thank you my darling."

Monday, 3ʳᵈ January 2000

As if Libby hadn't given me enough to think about, she was waiting for me when I settled down to sleep. She was trying to convince me that what we had on Earth together was finished. I can still remember her body and our love. She told me that these things were gone forever.

"You must look out for your own needs on Earth," she said. *"You mustn't look back for your love. You must look forward."*

"I find it very difficult to look forward," I said. "You have the ability to do that."

"I only have this ability to see a certain amount in the future. It's not nearly as much as you may think. You must also remember that you have a free choice in what you do. That makes a big difference to the future. If you choose differently from what I expect, then things change. All I am trying to tell you is to look forward and not backwards. What we have now is a different relationship to what we had before. I am spirit and you are mortal. Our love can be as strong as before, but our relationship is different. You can always choose another path."

"You sound as though you are trying to get rid of me," I said.

"That's nonsense, Bear. I love you very much and whatever you choose to do that won't change. When your time comes we will be together here. If you choose to move on, you are entitled to do so. You have that choice."

"It's really a bit unsettling," I said.

"No it isn't!" Libby insisted. *"You go and think about it. Nothing's changed except you are learning more about the facts of life. Nobody ever dies! They change their physical bodies for better ones that suit their environment and requirements. It's no use having a heavy body if you want to transfer yourself somewhere else just by thinking about it."*

"That I understand!"

"Bear, all I'm saying to you tonight is don't think about our past love. Think about your earthly requirements. Look into the future and not into the past. We still have the present. I still love my Bear, but I don't love you for what you were, I love you for what you are! You must love me for what I am. Got it?"

"Yes my darling, I've got it."

"Well then, go to sleep like a good Bear!"

About mid-evening, I had been paying some bills and writing letters, I distinctly felt that Libby was ready to talk to me.

"Hello Bear. Do I make you nervous?"

"You know my typing goes to pieces when there's someone looking over my shoulder! I'll go and lie down on the bed and we can talk."

I put the light out and lay down. I could hear Libby calling, *"Bear? Bear? Bear?"*

I called back, "Hello my darling, I'm here. Can you hear me? I can hear you."

All I got was, *"Bear? Bear?"* I got up and went back to the front room. *"Where have you been?"* was all I got for my troubles.

"I want to talk to you about things. There are beautiful flowers here. The trees are perfect in shape because they never have any disease or insects or wind to contend with. The streams are of pure crystal clean water that is sparkling,

as you've never seen water sparkle! The grass is so soft that it's like walking on a very expensive thick-piled wool carpet only more so. The temperature is just right – not too hot nor too cold. The light comes from everywhere. It's not like the sunshine on Earth. There are no shadows. It is constant and is just there! There is no breeze or wind – unless you want some and then it's just there, rippling through your hair. The air is alive with perfume from the blossoms. If you can image a perfect English summer's day with all flowers in full bloom..."

At that point my mother-in-law came into the room with some things for me to take down to Pershore in the morning. I was due to transport her Granada Estate for Adrian and bring back a Massey-Ferguson 35 tractor to use on the farm.

"Can you feel any thing?" I asked her.

"No," she said looking puzzled.

"Your daughter's here in the room. I can feel her very strongly."

She tried very hard, but could only say, "No, I can't feel anything."

"Tell Mum to get that niggle sorted out," Libby said. Mum's hand immediately went up to her heart.

"Libby's saying that you must open up," I said very quietly. "She says that you must take that extra step and try." I told her Libby was getting a little cross. "She says that she keeps trying to get through to you."

I could feel Libby's presence very strongly. She felt as strong as when we first talked together. A few minutes later Joan, my mother-in-law came in again. She had found that there was a programme on the Discovery Channel called, Life after Death. It had been on for half an hour! I watched the second half of the programme. It was certainly very interesting because it was about Near Death Experiences.

Fortunately I have Sky Digital, where they have a second Discovery Channel called "Discovery + 1 hour." This gives the opportunity of watching a programme and then taping it later if required! Libby had not been able to speak to her mother but she had prompted her to find this programme in the What's On section. Surely I was brought into the front room to be available. Had Libby and I spoken in bed as usual, the light would have been out and Joan wouldn't have disturbed me.

Another thing has been demonstrated tonight. I have been fairly certain that when I am typing some of the longer passages early this month, Libby had been guiding me to get it down correctly. As she was an excellent touch typist I wonder if she will soon be able to type it direct for me. As I go to bed tonight and prepare for the journey to Pershore in Worcestershire and back, I am reflecting on what has happened since Libby died. This potential tragedy had been turned into a wonderful experience for me. I have had a steep learning curve during the past three months. There is one thought that is uppermost in my mind. Life has not been at all dull! Libby never ceases to surprise me.

Tuesday, 4th January 2000

I said my prayer to God as usual, but Libby wasn't there. I slept until ten to eight and left Betty Grove Farm at eight-thirty with the trailer. It was very soon apparent that Libby was with me and she stayed with me in the Range Rover until we came to the top of Fish Hill, just outside Broadway in Worcestershire. Libby hated steep hills and Fish Hill especially!

By about one o'clock the trailer on the back with the Ford Granada was off loaded and the Massey-Ferguson 35 was loaded on. I left at three o'clock after lunch and coffee. I drove alone through the Cotswolds and round the Oxford

Ring Road. As I came up to the traffic lights to continue round the ring road towards Henley-on-Thames I clearly heard, quite loudly, *"Hello my Bear!"* She sounded very excited and pleased with herself, but I had no idea why.

"Hello my darling! Where have you been?"

"Oh I've been round and about!"

"I've missed you." I said. After a few moments I decided to have a little bit of fun. "Is that case on the passenger seat in your way?" I asked.

"No it's fine," Libby said. *"I don't need a seat, thank you. Oh Bear, are you winding me up?"*

"Yes I'm afraid so!"

"I really never know when you're winding me up!"

"You don't happen to have a sandwich with you?" I asked grinning.

"No of course I don't. I... Bear, are you winding me up again?" Libby asked.

"Yes I'm afraid so!"

"You really are hopeless!" Libby said.

Silence for a few miles and then I asked, "Can you arrange for a toilet and a sandwich bar to appear soon?"

"No, I certainly can't! I'm not here to look after your every want and need!" she said crossly. *"What did your last servant die of?"*

"Breast cancer," I couldn't help replying.

There was a pause and then I heard Libby say, *"I suppose I asked for that!"*

After driving through Henley-on-Thames and turning off towards Twyford, we came to Wargrave. This little village on the side of the Thames had a very narrow high street and a set of traffic lights. Cars were, as usual, parked on the left-hand side of the road and it was not too easy to manipulate the Range Rover and the even wider trailer with a tractor on board!

"Can you keep the lights on green so I can get through," I asked. The lights stayed on green. I got through! "Can you really do that?" I asked.

All I got was a little chuckle and a *"What do you think?"*

I wasn't all that sure, but I didn't say anything further about it and we enjoyed each others company through to Winnersh. As we arrived at the traffic lights, there was a lot of traffic and I said,

"Can you get me through on green?"

We sailed through!

"You are a clever little girl!" I said.

I drove on and decided that I was too tired to deliver the tractor to the farm in the dark.

"I'm not going to the farm," I said. "I'm going straight to Melton Cottage. I'm too tired to fiddle around in the dark and then walk back along that muddy footpath."

"Okay!" Libby said. *"You have a free choice."*

I turned up the lane and parked outside Melton Cottage.

"Thanks for your company," I said.

"Entirely my pleasure," was her reply.

I went to bed early. I was very tired. I said my prayer to God and thanked Him for giving me a safe journey to Pershore and back. I thanked Him for letting Libby come part of the way there and back. I asked Him to let me continue to love Libby and for her to continue to love me. I asked for our love to continue so that, when my time came, Libby and I would continue our love together. As I prayed for our love I could feel my heart getting fuller and fuller. By the end of my prayer I was very conscious that my heart was completely filled with love and strength.

I finished my prayer but Libby did not come. I felt alone, but I was certain that God had answered my prayer and that our love would continue and eventually Libby and I would live our lives together after I left this Earth. I had developed a headache by the time I went back to bed. I had intended to take a pill and amuse myself with the crossword, but as soon as I entered the bedroom I knew Libby was there.

I thanked her for spending so much time with me on the journey.

"It was particularly good to have your company from Oxford. I was beginning to get tired and lonely. You made good company," I said.

"That's good, but really you mustn't tease me. I never know whether you're serious or not!"

"I'm sorry my darling, but it's difficult for a Bear to change his proverbial spots."

"Well at least you've got your tractor to play with! Just be careful with it and don't frighten the horses."

"Of course not!"

That's all I remember until I woke up a little later!

Wednesday, 5th January 2000

"So you went to sleep on me!"

"I'm so sorry but as you can tell, I'm very tired."

"That's alright," Libby said. *"I was going to tell you about John."*

"Oh do tell me," I said excitedly.

"If you are not too tired!" Libby teased. *"Well he's been with some Old Masters today. When I say old, I'm not referring to their age, but the time that they have been up here."*

"I understand. What sort of Old Masters are they?"

"Well they've been teaching John about art and music mainly."

"Does that mean that he's going to paint pictures and compose music?" I asked.

"Not necessarily. They aren't teaching him to actually do these things – more how to appreciate them."

"That's wonderful!" I said. "I wish I could have had coaching like that."

"Me too," said Libby.

I yawned involuntarily.

"Oh I'm so sorry I'm keeping you up!" teased Libby, getting her own back on me for teasing her earlier. *"Anyway you'd better get some sleep before you leave me stranded again! You've got to get that trailer back to the garage first thing. Good night my Bear."*

"Good night my darling." I said sleepily.

As I came back from the garage I saw the post van and I knew that the post had been delivered. I felt that there was a difficulty that had been delivered. So much so that I prayed to God that whatever it was would be alright! I'm very tired after yesterday's journey, but it seems to me that everything will work out. I must help Joan with the pump in the well that's not working.

Thursday, 6ᵗʰ January 2000

This evening I made an appointment to see a clairvoyant near Wokingham. I was watching a film and I felt that I needed to make a couple of phone calls. Afterwards it came to me that it was a good time to ring this lady. She sounded very pleasant and I was looking forward to meeting her. She asked if the name Joan meant anything to me! Of course I said that it was the name of my mother-in-law. She said that she was testing to see if she had a link. She also said that there was a great change coming in my life. She said twice that she was very much looking forward to seeing me as though she really meant it. She asked what car I would arrive in so she could look out for me. She charged £20.00 for half an hour to an hour depending how things went. She doesn't use a tape recorder as she finds them distracting but I can take notes.

Of course she could easily have got this information from Carolyn, who was recommended through a lady who keeps a horse on the farm. I would go with a completely open mind and I wanted to see if she can tell me things that she couldn't have got from other sources. The main object was for me to find out things in my life. I felt at a crossroads. This was not just because of Libby's death. I had, I think, come to terms with that. I couldn't see where I was going. I didn't fancy sitting around for the next twenty years or so waiting to join Libby. I knew that the journal had to be published and I wanted to help other people.

I felt strongly that it was right for me to make the appointment to see another clairvoyant. I couldn't explain why except to suppose that Libby and/or her friends wanted me to do this. Libby wasn't there tonight although I tried three times. On the third occasion I was thinking about John.

Suddenly I heard, "Hello Daddy."

"Hello John," I said. "What have you been doing?"

"Mummy and I went for a walk and we looked at the flowers."

"I expect they're all the colours of the rainbow?"

"Oh yes they are. Mummy isn't here now. She's had to go away and do something important."

At this moment I think that I drifted off to sleep because the next thing I remember was something about the journal and then John wasn't there. Every time I slept tonight I dreamt about the journal.

Saturday, 8ᵗʰ January 2000

It had been a depressing day although the weather was bright and sunny. I didn't feel in the best of health and I slept the afternoon away again. In the evening I typed up Harry and Joan Johnson's recollections of Libby. At work she was always known as Liz. Their memories made me cry but I considered that a good thing. It always helps to relieve the tension. I was also administering whisky and soda. I shall go to bed early and hope to sleep the flu like symptoms away. I remembered that when Libby was a bit down, as I am now, she'd say to me, *"Bring me something nice!"* I wished she was here. That would be nice.

Sunday, 9ᵗʰ January 2000

After sawing up some logs and having lunch I intended watching the video Truly Madly Deeply that I had just bought. I was tired and depressed but the weather was as beautiful as it was yesterday. If the weather was bad then (See page 27, Monday, 4th October 1999) I would have felt more depressed. It was a condition called Seasonal Adjustment Disorder. It meant that you felt more depressed when there was less daylight.

I went to sleep in the middle! However I rewound it, watched the rest of it and found it moving and thought provoking. It's about grief after the death of a loved one and how to pick up the pieces and get on with your life. However I don't feel that the ending applied to me! I was not ready for another relationship. Not now anyway. I found that time was hanging heavily at present. I was going to bed in the hope that Libby will be able to talk to me. I missed her very much and needed her comfort and advice.

After doing some of the crossword, I plucked up courage and asked God to give me strength. I have lost my confidence and need help badly. Libby came to me. She told me that she had been getting cross because she had wanted to talk to me and I hadn't responded lately.

"You know what the matter is?" she asked. *"It's three months since I died. You'd missed that hadn't you? I told you that January was going to be a bad time for you. Well, this is all part of it. You must pull yourself together – nobody else can do it for you, you know!"* She paused. *"Bear,"* she

said very softly, *"I know it's not easy, but I am here to help you. I've managed to keep you afloat up until now. I'm not going to give up and neither are you. You've done very well in the last few months and you're not giving up!"*

"No of course not."

"You are going out tomorrow night. Enjoy yourself, but be ready for Monday morning. There's nothing this medium can tell you that I can't, but you'll feel better if somebody else tells you. You must bolster your confidence again. You believed what Marie told you? Well, you need somebody nearer, someone to be on hand should you need outside help. Remember that you are going to see her about yourself and not about me. That is important."

"Alright, are you still there?"

"Of course I'm still here! I'm always here if you want me. That's when it's hard, when you won't let me in. It's been hard on me too, you know. You've had this depression for five days so you'll soon come out of it. "

"Yes, it started on Wednesday," I said.

"I never fully understood what you meant when you told me, while I was on Earth, that whatever good things you put on the scales to balance the depression the scales never moved. I understand now, but you have to stick in there. I remember you telling me that all you could do was to tell the depression that it couldn't stay there forever and when it went away you'd be okay again."

"Yes, that's right," I said sadly.

"So you'll soon be alright again! You believe it!"

"Oh I do. It's been one of the worst I can remember, but it will have to go."

"That's good and remember what I've told you about patience!"

"I remember but it's easy for you to talk about it when you've got forever to look forward to!" I replied.

"What you seem to have forgotten," Libby said, *"is that you have eternity to look forward to as well. It's just that I have started a little ahead of you."*

"I see what you mean. I'll try and remember that!"

"You'd better," she replied. *"Have you had enough for tonight?"* Libby asked.

"No," I replied.

"Do you feel any better," she asked.

"When I'm with you yes, but when I go off into the front room I feel very lonely. I know you're there, guiding what I type, but I still feel depressed, alone and empty."

"That's because you revert back to your doubts about the journal and whether you really believe in it. You see you've had your confidence shaken and that's one of the reasons why I want you to visit the clairvoyant. It'll help to restore your belief in yourself. At the moment you doubt whether what has happened to you is real. She'll be able to tell you things that you'll believe because at the moment you doubt everything. She has no reason to make things up. You'll know if she does as you knew about the woman in Bracknell. If this lady tells you things about yourself you'll literally get the message."

"How long ago did you foresee this happening to me?" I asked.

"Well," said Libby, *"to be truthful, it's always been on the cards."*

I always hated that expression "to be truthful" because it implied that without saying it one would not be telling the truth, but I knew what Libby meant.

"You see Bear, you've stood up very well, but the time was bound to come when, after your tremendous high, you were bound to have a crash. Now it's happened. We've got to get you through it and we will."

"What do you mean by "we"," I asked.

"You and I and those in the Spirit World that think that you're worth spending time and patience on. Time is no problem because we have plenty of that! Patience is something we all have to learn. There is plenty of that here too, so consider yourself very fortunate and just you remember that!" she said laughing. *"Don't drink too much of that whisky. You'll sleep well enough tonight without it, I promise. Good night my Bear."*

"Good night my darling."

I was very grateful for all the help that I was getting. It was hard to come to terms with losing one's wife at any time, but I found it especially difficult as I was still suffering from Chronic Fatigue Syndrome. Libby was only fifty-two when she died and I was still trying awfully hard not to be bitter or angry about the years we had lost together on Earth. It wouldn't help her or me if I got cross. It was no good feeling sorry for myself. I must be grateful for at least I have Libby to talk to and that's a real consolation.

I was now feeling extremely fatigued and I took Libby's advice and got to bed for a good nights sleep. I could certainly do with it because I was going out tomorrow night and I'd several visits to cope with during the week. There were also new visitors to see into the cottage on Saturday.

Monday, 10th January 2000

I received a copy of *Living Images* by Coral Polge. It was the autobiography of a medium who, as a professional artist, could sketch her contacts in the Spirit World. As I was going out this evening I thought that I would see if Libby wanted to talk to me. I waited but she wasn't there.

Suddenly I heard, "Hello Daddy."

I was surprised and delighted.

"Hello John, is that you?"

"Yes Daddy, it is."

"How super to talk to you, what have you been doing?"

"Oh I've been riding King. He is the best horse there is Daddy!"

I had clear images of King in his prime and a small boy riding him. As one picture faded another appeared. There were four or five different ones, but all of King, some of his head in close up and others of a little boy with blond hair riding him.

"Is Mummy there John?" I asked.

"No Daddy. She's gone to see a man. I don't know who but I could find out?"

"Well, don't worry old chap. Tell Mummy that we talked and that I shall be about later tonight if she wants me."

"Okay Daddy. Bye."

"Bye John."

Pam gave us a lovely supper. Afterwards I went into the storeroom below the country Post Office to smoke a small cigar. In the first room I felt Martin's presence. I walked into the second storeroom but he wasn't in there. I walked back into the first room. His presence was very strong. I didn't know what to say. However I plucked up courage and said, "Please go and talk to Libby. Tell her I love her." After that he was gone.

I finished my cigar and went into the kitchen to tell Pam what had happened. I was rather amazed. Pam held my hand and said, "Thank you so much." It clearly meant a lot to her that Martin and I had made contact. Pam is very sweet and she will find an evening to come round for supper and read my journal. After my doubts about letting anybody see it, I felt confident that Pam will be a good person to read it.

I went to bed thinking about my visit to the clairvoyant tomorrow morning. I felt strongly that Libby wanted to talk to me. I said my prayer to God and waited but she didn't come. I thought of John and I heard, "Hello Daddy."

"Hello my boy," I said. "Is Mummy there?"

"No Daddy, she's busy."

"Alright old chap, I'll talk to her later. Good night."

"Good night Daddy."

Libby came to me for a few moments. I couldn't understand anything she said to me. Then I was in a huge aeroplane hanger looking down a row of propeller driven planes. They were facing to my left and there were very many of them. They were metallic in colour, silvery. Did I drop off to sleep and imagine it all?

Tuesday, 11ᵗʰ January 2000

As I prepared to go out this morning, I was reflecting that I was uncertain. I was with the medium from ten-thirty until two o'clock. I was feeling better for my visit. I had bought in some flowers and I had been playing music while I typed my notes. I had a lot to think about

I was looking forward to our talk to night. I said a very detailed prayer to God tonight, but Libby wasn't there afterwards. I finished the crossword and very tired, I settled down to sleep.

"What did you think of it all Bear?" Libby asked.

"Well, I thought it was terrific. It helped me a lot."

"And what are you going to be?"

"A very good Bear!" I said.

"Yes, you certainly are," Libby said laughing.

"She was very good. I have learned a lot."

"She should be good if she had the same birthday as us."

"Yes, that was good and she's so near too."

"You can learn a great deal from her. There's a lot I could tell you just as well, but she's in a position to help you in some ways that I can't manage so easily. For example she

can open doors for you. You can meet a lot of people through her and she can teach you about practical things. "

"Where have you been these last few days?"

"Not everything that I do is to do with you! There are other things. Well I'm glad you're feeling so much better. Study it all," she said, *"there's much that you must learn and you must live your life along better lines. "*

"Right," I said. "Thank you for getting me out of that depression."

"Well you weren't much fun! It's good that we're back to normal again!"

"Yes, it feels good. I know I've been very down. I'm sorry."

"Well, you must get to sleep now. Good night Bear. "

"Good night my darling."

Wednesday, 12th January 2000

I tried something new tonight. I lay out on the bed and tried to relax and breathe in love and light expelling the darkness. I said to myself when I started that I would try this for an hour. I breathed in light, which I saw in my mind's eye and the more I breathed in light, the lighter my mind's eye was. To begin with it was very dark with only small particles of light but, very slowly and gradually, it became brighter. Several times I asked God for more of His love, more of His light. He always gave me more, but it was a gradual and slow process.

I felt that my mind, behind closed eyes, was my soul. It was very dark with only a little light. As I breathed in more, the darkness was gradually banished until it was, perhaps sixty per cent light when I finally opened my eyes. I had been doing this for exactly sixty minutes according to the clock. I felt much more relaxed and pleasantly tired.

Thursday, 13ᵗʰ January 2000

Libby was waiting when I was ready for sleep. I asked her how I had done with my relaxation and breathing in love and light. She told me I had done quite well for a first effort. I must persevere with it.

I asked her about the violet flame. She told me it was the light of those in the Higher Realms. Those in the Lower Realms emit horrible colours because they are impure due to their misdeeds. In the Middle Realm, where she is, they emit white light. In the Higher Realms they emit violet light and God's light is gold as I saw in the garden at Nettlebed. (See page 27, Monday, 4th October 1999) I asked her where I would find the violet flame, but she told me not to be impatient and wait. I would know when the time was right!

I amused Libby when I describe my attempts of breathing in love as a kind of lovemaking. I do miss her very much. When I told her that I wished I could give her a hug, she told me that I'd have to be very careful because her present body wasn't as strong as an earthly body. I told her that I'd still like to try and she said that she wished she could cuddle up to me in bed.

Thank goodness the depression has lifted. We are able to get back to enjoying our conversations again and having some amusement together. I now wonder how far I must progress in order to be able to invoke the Violet Flame. Tonight I asked Libby about the clairvoyant I had visited. I told her that Marie had said that she doubted that Libby was there. I asked her if she had been there and she said that she had been.

"This is important," I said, "did you send those things through to me or not?"

"I was aware of what was going on, but I didn't send you the messages that you received."

"Then the whole thing was a set up and I'm not to believe any of it."

"That's right."

"Then I can't believe anything anymore!" I said.

"Remember what I told you at the beginning when you asked if you should go and see a medium. I said that if you wanted to see them it wouldn't do any harm. If you want to find out more about them – you should go."

"What about visiting the clairvoyant?" I asked. "Is it a nuisance to you if I see them?"

"No, it isn't a nuisance at all." Libby replied. *"You can go and see them if you want to. I shall tell you all I can if you ask me questions and I shall show you things when I think it is right for you to see them, but it will do no harm for you to go. If you want to explore and find out more, then you should go."*

Well, I suppose that I asked for this! I had a sleep and later, after looking at what Libby had said to me, I lay down on the bed and waited for her to come to me. She didn't come immediately and I thought gently to myself that I wanted to talk to her. I tried not to call her, but I suppose I had made it known that I did need to talk to her.

"Well Bear?" I heard. It was friendly, a little formal, questioning.

"I need to be sure about all this!" I said.

"About what?" Libby said innocently. She always could act the innocent if she wanted to.

"You know perfectly well," I replied, "about this clairvoyant visit. I'm getting confused about everything."

At that moment an extraordinary thing happened. I had put my finger and thumb up to my eyes either side of my nose as I was talking. There was a light that shone into my eyes as if somebody had switched on a powerful searchlight. It was a white light, but not pure white, slightly tinged with gold. It was very strong, but not strong enough to hurt my closed eyes. It remained for some seconds and then it went. I pressed my finger and thumb together over my nose, but I couldn't recreate the light.

"You saw that light?" I heard Libby say. *"Well I created that to show you that this is true. Go on squeeze your finger and thumb together and try to recreate it."*

I tried several times. I couldn't make a light of any kind come into my closed eyes.

"You see, you can't do it! That was my love. My light, if you like, coming to you to prove to you that what we have is real. You can't always believe what other people tell you, but you can believe what I tell you! Sometimes you must learn to listen more carefully to what I say. Exactly, what I say!"

"When you talk to me," I asked, "why don't I feel your presence anymore? I hear you in my head. I don't feel you about as I did when you first started to come to me?"

As I was saying this I began to feel her presence slowly but surely building up beside me. It felt stronger and stronger. Neither of us spoke. I could feel her positively there.

"Why can't I smell you?" I asked thinking about a comment made by the clairvoyant?"

"Because you know that I didn't wear scent or cosmetics on Earth except on very rare occasions. How would you feel if I came to you smelling like a perfume shop?"

She's right of course because I wouldn't have believed it was her. Then, as I enjoyed her presence about me, I found that I could smell her. It wasn't a perfume or a scent – it was, what I can only call, the essence of Libby. It was wonderful.

"Well there you are!" she said. It had a ring of 'your time is up now!' *"Listen to what Marie has to tell you and you will learn much more about mediums. Bye Bear."*

"Goodbye my darling and thank you."

Tonight, by telephone, Marie told me her reasons for doubting the clairvoyant. I wrote everything down for later study. It made very interesting reading. I had now had three very different lessons about clairvoyants. I am certainly learning a great deal about them!

Marie gave me the following information about the Violet Flame. "It is the Crown Chakra. It is the seventh Chakra situated at the top of the head, often depicted in Hindu or Buddhism as the thousand petals of the Lotus flower, reflecting colour. It is the spiritual centre of art, religion and beauty. It means wholeness or holiness. Crown Chakra is a purple stone, such as amethyst. It stands for creativity, inspiration and developing spiritual awareness. It is the most holy colour of all.

Libby and I had a word or two tonight, but I found it difficult to get it clearly. To start with she appeared to be calling me. She was very faint. I asked if she was there.

"Yes, I'm here."

"Do you want to tell me anything?" I asked.

"Do you want to ask me anything?"

I felt she was going and then I saw her in the distance half-floating and half-running away across a field. I had seen her go like this before.

"Good night my darling," I said and she waved back to me.

Chapter 7

THE VISION

Saturday, 15th January 2000

I woke during the night and made myself a mug of coffee and some ham rolls. I was told that if I drank it on Libby's side of the bed and used her bedside table something extraordinary would happen. I did just this and I was told to lie down and turn the light out. I held her spectacles for a while and then her shoes. I felt her presence very strongly, especially from her shoes. She told me that other people had held her spectacles and watch. This was why I experienced a much stronger presence from her shoes.

Thoughts about the clairvoyant kept coming into my mind – she had had help from others. That's what had happened. There were things like, "She doesn't like me smoking!" This was to prove to me that Libby was there when she wasn't! Things like the journal, which I couldn't remember if I had mentioned. I hadn't! She'd been told. There were other things Libby told me that had been prepared and put into the session. It was a set up, which was to show me how some mediums worked.

I was told that I should add Marie to the dedication of the journal. Do it now! While I did this and some other adjustments, I have no doubt that Libby was guiding me. There were phrases, out of the blue, like "you may like to do this" or "you may like to check that" that were typically used by her.

The visit to the clairvoyant had confused me. I had had some strange doubts about one or two things but I had dismissed them. I now realise that Libby was trying to tell me things, which I had just put down to my own thoughts. I should have known better! Perhaps it was all part of my learning curve. I had put these thoughts away and make my assessment on my own. I wanted to believe that I had had a good session and not been taken for a ride! I now know, because Libby had reminded me that I hadn't given anything away during the first half of the session.

I had opened up between the two sessions. Anyway I now know the truth and have another clear experience of mediums at work! I must thank Marie and Libby for showing me what I should learn from it all. I am now going back to bed feeling that my confidence has been restored. It is difficult for me to understand that I should have so many doubts about what Libby and I achieve. I shouldn't have any at all.

However, there is somewhere deep inside, an ingrained logic that says that these things can't be happening. Until I can override this I shall not achieve the full benefit of my experiences.

Libby and I had a good talk in the car. She told me a great deal about the last visit I had made to the clairvoyant. She told me how the information had been gathered, through the daughters of one of the ladies who kept a horse at the farm. I supposed that the daughters would have thought it would be fun to help with information directly or indirectly. Libby also told me never to see a clairvoyant in the same area as the local paper. There had been a four-hundred word article about Libby in the Wokingham Times. It was made quite clear that my mother-in-law had told the writer a great deal about Jerry and Adrian. Marie told me how to set up an analytical table to assess the accuracy of the medium reading.

The incoming lady at my mother's Shenington cottage had lost her father in October and we had a great deal to talk about when I asked if she had any contact with him! I left the cottage two hours later than usual after a very interesting discussion.

Sunday, 16th January 2000

We exchanged our love and Libby gave me some advice tonight. She told me to relax and be patient. I must forget about the clairvoyant and her pronouncements. They were not important but were only meant as a lesson for me. I should take a rest from my studies and get on with earthly jobs that need doing until the book Soul Mates by Thomas Moore arrived.

She would be there if I wanted her, which of course I did. TC was asleep at the present moment but was waiting for me to come and stroke him and all our other animals in Spirit were well and happy. The SAD lamp, which I had been considering buying was a good thing and would help me. I must relax, relax and relax.

Tuesday, 18th January 2000

After I had prayed to God, I heard Libby call me. I said, "Hello darling."

"Hello Bear," she said. *"Don't worry about the Inland Revenue Tax or the Thames Water. They'll be alright. I told you January would be difficult. It will soon be February. Are you pleased with the cottage bookings?"*

"Yes, they're coming in well. January is the most important month for them and they're okay. How is John?"

"Hello Daddy."

"Hello John. How are you?"

"Oh I'm fine thank you Daddy. I've been riding King! He's terrrrrific."

"Yes he is, isn't he? Do you like the dogs too?"

"Yeees! But I think I like the horses better!"

"Do you love your Mummy?"

"Oh yes. She's a wonderful lady. I'm very lucky she came and found me."

"Yes I know."

"Well you will come and be with us one day?"

"Yes I will my boy," I said.

"Goodbye Daddy."

"Goodbye John."

"He's a good boy," said Libby.

"Yes he is. I wish I could be with you."

"Well, it was either you or me. One of us had to come and look after him."

"I think it was better that it was you," I said thoughtfully. "You know about Mother Love."

"I wish you could get it through to my mother. I'm sorry she's being a pain at the moment.

"That's alright. I'm doing my best."

"Yes, you are." Libby replied. *"I'm going now Bear. Good night."*

"Good night my darling."

Wednesday, 19ᵗʰ January 2000

The solicitor has told me that he is about to apply for a Grant of Probate. This will settle Libby's will and will remove one of the uncertainties from my plate. He says the amount concerned will be a positive one, so I shouldn't have to sell anything. I will then make a positive move, balance my accounts and pay off the credit cards. I have been marking time to see where I am being led financially! It seems very strange and uncomfortable to handle everything myself after Libby and I did everything together.

Arborfield and Newland Parish Council have set aside £500 for a memorial to Libby for her services to the parish. At the moment it stands as a bench or a tree but I shall try and think of something more useful. One of the councillors told me that the council was waking up to just how much work Libby did put in for them!

Tonight I feel very tired and wretched. I said my prayer and Libby came and spoke to me. She told me that I must be strong because January will soon be over. Things will get better after January. After Probate is granted, she said that help would come to me. Libby told me that she knows I believe in her and what I am told. It is me that I don't believe in. She and John love me. I must be patient and wait for the help that will come.

I need a new drive to get me going again. I was doing well to get past the doldrums. Soon I will get onto an even keel again. I told Libby that I loved her and that nobody could replace her. She said that she and John would be waiting for me. Until then she would always be with me. In the meantime I must make my own way with what help was available. Help was at hand and I should use it, but she will be with me and in the end we shall be together. Dear God, I hope so.

Friday, 21st January 2000

I had a telephone call from Barclays trying to sell me family insurance. I told them that my family had died in October. I then telephoned to my bank and complained about this thoughtless act of telephone sales – they are without any thought for the condition of their customers. They were apologetic and I trust that the message will be passed on.

Libby came and talked to me after I had said my prayers. She told me not to let things slide but to keep doing what had to be done. I must hang on. I was doing well she told me. She understood my depression but that I must keep going until the end of the month. February would be better. She and John were with me. I heard John say, "We are with you Daddy." They will support me. Libby had told me that January would be a bad month and she was right.

Saturday, 22nd January 2000

I said my prayers tonight but Libby wasn't there to talk to me. The experience wasn't wasted however as I was able to examine my mind's eye so to speak, without her presence. It was absolutely blank and empty. I tried speaking thoughts to myself, but there was nothing. This completely proved to me that Libby does come and talk to me. Of that there was no doubt! When I have a moment of doubt they were unworthy and I should ignore them. I should have enough faith and belief by now.

Sunday, 23rd January 2000

Libby came for a chat when I went back to bed again. She hadn't been there earlier on because the chap who used to look after the horses had come back to see her. He was very pleased with the horses. Libby still gave the children pony rides. John apparently won't let anybody else ride King!

Libby said, *"You'd think that they had always been together."*

"By the time I come up to join you he'll be a grown man!" I said.

"That's true."

"Anyway it means that when I do come I can have you all to myself!" I said hopefully.

"Only if you're very good!"

"Oh I'll be good if I get you as the prize! Can you tell me now if you'll be there when the time comes?" I asked. "You sounded rather doubtful when I asked you before."

"Well," Libby said, *"you've got to be very good Bear. There's a long time to go yet and things change. There are others who are better equipped to bring people here and they have their job to do. If you're not good then you'll have to go elsewhere and work your way up here. You'd better start being good on Earth and make sure you can come straight here. You'll have a bit of sorting out to do anyway – everybody does."*

"What you're really saying is that if I go down to the Darker Realms, I'll have to wait until I can come up to you?"

"Yes, that's true if you're a naughty Bear!"

"Well I shall do my best anyway."

"You're doing alright," Libby went on. *"You are much better after a day on the farm. January is nearly over and you're certainly over the worst. Keep going."*

"Yes I will," I replied. "Did you hear my outburst yesterday?" I had been outside and I had called out, "Libby, I love you and I miss you so much. Take care of everything!" I had felt a very strong desire for her and I wanted more than anything else to give her a hug.

"I should think the whole of Berkshire heard it," Libby said laughing. *"I don't suppose there were many in the Spirit World who could have missed it. I had to walk miles to get the frightened horses back!"*

"Now I know you're not truthing with me," I said. "The whole of Berkshire might have heard me, but unless the occupants of the Spirit World and the horses are tuned into my vibrations I don't think that many would have heard me."

"You are doing much better now," Libby responded. *"You were right to offer Adrian some work on the farm. They have done a lot for you and it's only right that you should do your bit to help out now. There are still plenty of jobs to do on the farm with or without the mud."*

There was a natural pause and I said, "Does that mean my time's up?"

"No of course it doesn't! You know I'm always here if you want me?"

"Yes I know that and I'm very grateful for it," I replied.

"Anyway it is about time I went. Don't forget to take your tools up to the cottage. You'd better go and write that down before you forget it. Night night."

"Good night my darling."

I do feel a lot less depressed tonight and I think I'll sleep well.

Monday, 24th January 2000

Libby didn't come and talk to me tonight but John did. He told me that Libby was away. She had told me to be good. She would come and talk to me soon. John had been with King today. He was in a field nearby and after he had said goodbye he ran off. Probably back to see King.

Wednesday, 26th January 2000

When Libby came to me tonight she seemed very far away. The signal was weak!

I asked, "Is Jesus Christ really the son of God?"

"Yes, we're all God's sons and daughters."

"But did he really come down to Earth?"

"Yes he did. He was a great spiritualist. He preached and died and he was resurrected."

"Was he really born from a 'virgin'?"

"Yes, but you needn't try and understand about that. Just have faith. Bear, I want to talk seriously to you..."

The signal completely broke down. I wasn't able to receive any thoughts and, although I waited for a while, she was gone. I wonder if I'm becoming less receptive or less good. Certainly the communication is becoming less and more difficult. I know that we still love each other but the fact remains that we are having less. It is totally unfair to complain about the lack of good talks with Libby. We have had so much together and I know that this is a short lull only. I am tired and Libby is busy. What could be more natural than a little lull? I wonder what she wanted to tell me tonight.

Saturday, 29ᵗʰ January 2000

Libby and I had a long discussion on my way back from Shenington to Sindlesham. Libby explained what she has been doing during the last few days when she has not been able to talk to me. She has been learning how to welcome people into the Spirit World.

I said, "That will be very good practice for you when my time comes!"

"That's what I thought!" she retorted.

She also told me that I was going to meet somebody during the next few months. She would need my help as much as I needed hers.

"You need looking after," Libby told me. *"She will also need looking after. If you want a relationship, you can love and appreciate each other on Earth and this will not affect the spiritual love between you and I."*

Libby said that she would always be there to look after me from a spiritual point of view. It would clearly make no difference to us if I formed another relationship because they would be of different kinds. The love affair that Libby and I had on Earth **was** over. Our spiritual affair had begun when she died and was such a strong bond that it would not be broken by any other earthly affair that I might have.

David Kennedy, author of A Venture in Immortality describes his close and happy life with his wife Ann and then after her death married again shortly after the publication of his book. It could only have been with his wife's consent and she knew that he needed looking after so he could concentrate on his work as a minister in Scotland.

Whatever happens I know that Libby and I will be together. What I must work out, with her help, is how to do my allotted tasks to the best of my ability.

Tuesday, 1st February 2000

At last January was over. My light box came and I tried it out. I liked it. Tonight Libby came to me. She told me that now I would get strong again. My work was about to begin. I would get strong.

Wednesday, 2nd February 2000

I said my prayer and Libby again told me I must get strong. I told her how much I missed her, especially physically. I asked after John and she told me that he was there.

"Hello John," I said.

"Hello Daddy."

"How are you?" I asked.

"I'm fine thank you Daddy."

"Are you happy with Mummy and King?"

"Yes thank you Daddy," he replied.

"Will you look after Mummy for me until I come?"

"Yes Daddy."

"You're a good boy and I love you. Bye bye John."

"Bye bye Daddy."

"Sleep well Bear," Libby said.

"Good night my darling."

Thursday, 3rd February 2000

For the last couple of weeks, but especially this week, I have felt much affected by my Chronic Fatigue Syndrome. I have been extremely tired, depressed, aching and unable to concentrate for long. I have had a great many headaches. I required a lot of sleep to catch up with my needs. I was sure that the light box was helping but it was as though the past weeks and months have taken a toll and rather like the start of a holiday, the symptoms just have to come out. Perhaps it was a case of things that had to get worse before they can get better.

I said my prayer to God and then Libby called, *"Bear?"*

"Yes," I said, "I'm here. You sound very happy."

"Oh yes I am."

"Can you tell me why?"

"Well, things are looking up!"

"Are you talking about up there or down here?"

"Down there with you. There's a lot of help coming."

"What sort of help?" I asked.

"Oh, you'll have to wait and see!"

"Oh come on," I said impatiently. "You'll have to do better than that! Tell me something. Give me something to look forward to."

But Libby said no more. Then I saw clearly a vision of an attractive young lady with shoulder length golden hair sitting on the left of the picture under an old beech tree and in front of her, kneeling on his left knee, was a younger, slimmer and better looking me. She was wearing a long white dress and white pointed high-heeled shoes and he was dressed in a white suit with white shoes and carrying a white hat.

He was clearly proposing and she was smiling so she was clearly accepting and the sun was shining over them. After I had taken all this in, Libby was gone.

Saturday, 5ᵗʰ February 2000

I woke up at twenty past nine, an hour after I should have left for the cottage! Fortunately the visitors renting it understood and would see themselves out.

Libby was waiting for me as I left for the cottage. We had a long chat on the way up. She told me that I would get stronger now. January was over and the evenings are drawing out. She said that I have been very ill for the last few weeks. We talked again as we used to do. It was a great relief to me to feel so much better than I have for so long. We agreed that the light box was a big help. However she told me that I mustn't have it on in the evening. This is why I initially could get to sleep and then overslept!

I asked her about the vision that I had seen. The white clothing was symbolic. It meant that we were both good people. I will meet her in about six month's time. That is around August. I shall know that it's her when the time comes but she may need a little persuading. However she will soon realise that we are meant to be together. Libby says it will be alright.

I asked Libby, "How am I expected to love two people?"

"The love we have for each other is spiritual love. The love you will have for her is physical love. The two are quite different. You and I will still be together spiritually and I shall still look after you as I have always done. You two will be together and share things that it is difficult for us to share. I am with you as often as I can be and that won't change. You need somebody to be with and to be able to share everyday things."

"You do realise that the greatest gift you can give me, apart from your continued love and help, is for me to be able to spend my time with someone until it is time for me to come back to you."

"That's nice Bear."

"How are you getting on with meeting people and preparing them for the Spirit World?"

"Very well, I have been down several times with someone much more experienced. It's going well."

"And what about the Greek? You must have mastered that by now?"

"Yes, pretty well."

"What have you been using it for?"

"I've been doing some translating."

"I suppose you have been brushing up on your other languages?"

"Something like that."

"I suppose that it's silly to ask after the horses? They must have a perfect life with nothing especially good or especially bad happening in their lives. All they have to do is to graze and enjoy themselves."

"Yes, that's right."

"How is the horse from Hampshire that was so badly frightened?"

"She's gaining confidence and doing well. She's a sweetie really."

"What about the horsy rides for the children? Is that going well?"

"Yes, they love that. John particularly enjoys it. I think he likes being with his friends and doing something exciting."

"Of course he does! He also enjoys showing off his wonderful mother!"

"Oh I don't know about that."

"I do!"

There was a long pause while I negotiated the traffic.

"The cottage bookings are going well," Libby said.

"Yes, I'm pleased up to a point. There are fifteen for next season starting with April but I still have five unbooked weeks at the end of this present letting year."

"You'll get four," she said.

"That will be good if they're full weeks and not weekends," I replied. She wasn't going to be drawn any further.

"The trouble with you Bear, is that you lack faith. You are right to question, but you must increase your faith and trust. You believe that I'm here and talking to you. You believe that we're going to be together. You believe what I say and then worry in case I've got it wrong.

"Sometimes you worry in case you've got it wrong and perhaps misinterpreted it. You must learn the difference between using your heart and your head. If you gave away all your money to charity and then had nothing to live on, you'd be letting your heart rule your head and you'd be stupid. If you fell in love with somebody but, because of your sense of duty, you stayed and looked after my mother, you'd be letting you head rule your heart and you'd again be stupid."

"Yes, I do understand that."

"If I tell you that something is going to happen, you worry in case it doesn't. It will!"

Libby came all the way up to Banbury and then was gone before I reached the cottage at Shenington. She was with me again when I left the cottage and she saw me home again. I felt better after the journey than I had for many weeks.

I said my prayers to God but Libby didn't speak to me. However I felt strongly that her presence was about me and that was enough.

Saturday, 12ᵗʰ February 2000

Tonight, as I typed up various parts of the Journal, there is no doubt that I was being helped. I did a rehash of its presentation. Several times there were thoughts put into my head such as *"Don't do it that way, there's a better way!"* and *"Don't zero the calculator, you'll need that number again!"* Every time the message was right. Clearly Libby, who was better at this sort of thing than I was, was helping me. Surely she was also telling me she was back!

I said my prayers to God tonight and I felt sure that Libby would talk to me. I waited patiently for her call of *"Hello Bear!"* but it never came. Instead I heard her, through my thoughts, telling me that I didn't need her to come and talk to me every night. I had moved on sufficiently to be able to cope now without a chat every evening

Libby said she was about and knew what was going on and I was doing well. I must continue to get strong and fit. A lot was going to happen. I was moving on. I was starting a new journey on a new path. It was very exciting. She asked me if there was anything that I wanted to ask her and I said that there were a million things but I always seemed to forget them when she was there with me!

"How is John?" I managed to ask.

"Oh he's fine," Libby replied.

"What should I be reading?"

"Well if you want to continue your studies you should read Soul Mates".

"What about these books that I've ordered from Stansted Hall?"

"You'll find them very interesting and helpful. Good night Bear. Keep on getting stronger and fitter in the spiritual sense as well as the physical. Remember that you can talk to me at any time and I will be there to look after you. You don't really need so much guidance now. You're doing well and you're going to learn a lot more. Good night Bear."

"Good night my darling."

The books that I had ordered from Stansted Hall in Essex are by Arthur Findlay. They were a trilogy made up of On the Edge of the Etheric, The Rock of Truth and The Unfolding Universe. I had also ordered The Torch of Knowledge, Psychic Stream and The Curse of Ignorance [Volume 1 and 2]. Stansted Hall is I suppose the focal point for those interested in the Spirit World. They hold day, weekend and weeklong courses and have a very good shop. I had asked for a programme of events and I was planning on making a visit.

I had also ordered three other books from The Inner Bookshop in Oxford. They are, one by Allegra Taylor entitled Healing Hands and two by Allen Kardec and are called The Mediums' Book and The Spirits' Book. These books were out of print in this country but were coming in from America.

Tuesday, 15th February 2000

Is it too much to ask that the person I am going to meet in August, according to Libby, will have a house big enough to take me and also my furniture? How can I ask Libby to make all the arrangements?

Libby my darling, I need a beautiful new partner to replace you. I need her to be blonde with a good figure and a pleasing face. She must want me physically to make love to her. I don't want one with other people's children. She must love me completely, especially my faults. She must understand that I have a Chronic Fatigue Syndrome and Seasonal Affected Disorder. She must have a country house that is animal proof, especially for cats and dogs and horses. There must be room to take all my furniture, vehicles and books etc. I shall need my own study and library. She must be an excellent cook, enjoy red wine and be well educated and intelligent. She must also be long suffering, tactful, loving and faithful. She will need a great sense of humour – especially if I make a joke.

When the time comes for me to die I shall forget her utterly and come and join you in the Spirit World my darling. What do you think about my needs my darling? Is it too much to ask for you to devote your precious time in the Spirit World advertising on Earth for a perfect creature, fully equipped with all the assets for a sixty year-old bearded man, with a huge pot-belly and unclean habits? When all the answers to your advertisement come in you will of course make a short list of one and prepare the introduction, won't you my darling? I imagine that you will book the table for two in a romantic, candle-lit restaurant, where the acoustics are soft enough to dull my poor jokes and the light pale enough to enhance my features. You must promise that she won't be blind, deaf and mute?

"Well, what do think of it so far?"

I'd give a lot for Libby to talk to me when I go back to bed. I don't believe she will be though. Am I a Bear of little faith or a realist? I'm sorry my darling – I ask too much.

Wednesday, 16ᵗʰ February 2000

Late to bed again, but oh joy of joys, as I turned over and settled down I felt Libby's presence very strongly indeed. We talked and she gave me the proof I needed about my future. She told me that it was very important that I got ready for what lay ahead. It wasn't long now until August.

"And in August I'm going to meet someone who will be able to help me and take the pressure of day to day things off you? Is that right?"

"Yes, that's right." Libby said.

"I shall know immediately I see her, will I?"

"You will know when you meet her," Libby answered.

"And will she know too?"

"Yes, she'll know too. She'll need a little persuasion though. After all she's a woman! But she'll know!"

"So next February, twelve months time, I shall be in my new home with her."

"Yes, that's right."

"It seems to be a long way off," I said. "Time seems to go very slowly. It's only five months since you died and it seems like fifty years."

"Well it does seem a long time," Libby said. *"But after all we've got all the time in the world! The doors are opening Bear. Go for it!"*

"I will my darling."

"Well I must go now and let you get some sleep or you won't be good for anything."

"If I go and type all this up in my journal, will you come with me and make sure I get it alright?"

"Yes if you like. Go on then!"

Libby was still there when I went back to bed. She stayed with me until I went to sleep! I slept wonderfully well.

Chapter 8

THE WAITING

After the vision, I spent much of my time waiting for August 2000 to come round. I did this whilst exploring spiritual matters through reading books, attending workshops and sitting in two circles. One was in Banbury, Oxfordshire and the other in Cheltenham, Gloucestershire.

Libby was, as always, there for me and often John came too and spoke to me. However if I quoted here all the conversations that we shared it would fill several volumes and would be more than this little book could take. So I am going to just record a few special ones and then get on with the business of how Libby brought this beautiful blonde lady of the vision into my life.

First, I would like to say that she didn't come in as predicted by Libby. It took an additional year. There was a very good reason for this and it must be recorded that the information that Libby had worked on was in fact solid. The spiritual plan was for Jenny to be brought into my life that August of 2000.

Her relationship with her partner was over. It was finished. So the way was clear, but it was not foreseen that by an accident of fate they met again at the International Spiritual Federation Congress in Austria and for some reason Jenny used her free will and gave the ten year old relationship one more try. It didn't work but I was left at the 'bus stop' with my thumb in the air, saying to each lovely lady that passed, "Is it you? Is it you?"

Second, I would like to say that when I met Jenny in the August of 2001, she had blonde hair. I had been shown her with golden blonde hair. What was interesting was that Libby showed her to me as she was in February 2000. I have a colour photograph of Jenny at this time and her hair matches exactly what I was shown in the vision and not how it was when we first met.

During the extra time that I had to wait, I met a wonderful medium named Linda Williamson, who gave me many excellent spiritual sittings with her guides. They confirmed what Libby had told me and gave me much, much more.

Once, much later, I mentioned Linda's name to Jenny and she said how impressed she was that I knew such an outstanding person. Whether she meant that she was impressed with the fact that I knew Linda Williamson or that she was impressed by her books and reputation, I wasn't quite sure, but I think it was a little of both. Anyway I was happy much later to give Jenny a sitting with Linda as a Christmas present!

It was the following year during 2001, that Spirit took me out of both circles in the same week when disharmony occurred in each one. I was quite bereaved because I enjoyed both weekly circles. The circle I had been in at Banbury had six people and that at Cheltenham was smaller with only two, but I missed both groups. I need not have worried because I was told to sit by myself at Betty Grove Farm where I had moved after Libby's mother had sold her home for building and moved away to Pershore in Worcestershire.

Linda had told me in a sitting that I would be there for about six months and I would then meet this lady and soon move in with her at her home. So I was content to 'camp' down at the farm for the summer knowing that in the autumn my predicted new love was coming into my life for good. So this was the waiting time and I record here some of the interesting moments before the vision was fulfilled in the next chapter.

Wednesday, 1st March 2000

On the way back from Newbury I asked Libby to tell me about her passing. She told me that she knew that I was in the gardens at Nettlebed. She also knew that it was time for her to pass on. She had waited because she didn't want to leave me. She found herself looking down on the bed and the room in the Palliative Care Home. She then saw me in the gardens with Sally. (See page 29, Monday, 4th October 1999) She became aware that there was somebody there to meet her. She cried and didn't want to leave me. She was worried that I wouldn't be able to cope on my own. She said that he assured her that I would be alright. She asked if she could help me and she was assured that she could. She saw me crying for her. She thanked me for crying for her. She knew that I prayed for her. She thanked me for praying for her.

She then went on a journey and eventually opened her eyes in a spirit friend's house. She looked out of the window and saw the beautiful flowers and trees. She asked again if she could help me. She was told she could and would.

She saw all that I did in making the arrangements. When I came back to Nettlebed to see her in the Chapel of Rest, she prepared herself to speak to me for the first time. After God had spoken to me, she watched me walk round the gardens and guided me to the top of the steps. There she showed her presence to me and spoke to me to reassure me. Afterwards she watched over me as I drove home. (See page 31, Friday, 8th October 1999)

I have been helped a lot because I was a good person and I had much work to do. The doors were opening. It was important that I got into <u>everything</u> with a completely open mind. The situation was very difficult for most people. There were many that were into Spiritualism for what they could get out of it. They were misusing their gifts and it wasn't right. I must investigate and know the difference between the good and the bad ones.

Libby told me that I was beginning to make my way on the right path. She said she knew that I would make the right decisions. I had already started to do so. She gave some examples of how I had helped other people. I must continue to do that good work. I would know when and how to do it. I must ask for nothing but the satisfaction that I was doing God's work. I was a good person. I didn't know that, which was why I was a good person.

There was much work for me to do. I had started doing it. Libby would always be with me and I should have a lot of help. Libby said that she was almost always there. She didn't always talk to me. Sometimes it wasn't necessary.

I must not get proud or pompous about the work I was doing. If I did, I won't be able to do it. This was the problem with some mediums and clairvoyants. They were given the gift and they misused it. When the gift was taken away they couldn't always admit that they had lost it. Then they would try to carry on without it and make money out of their reputation and their false work. I must discover the difference between the two. There were the real and genuine ones and then there are the fakes (or rubbish ones).

I was doing well and Libby was proud of me, but I mustn't let it go to my head or I won't be able to do it. Libby insisted that I should not be alone. I would have a lot of help from on Earth and from the Spirit World. Libby told me that she loved me. I told her that that meant a lot to me as she knew, I loved her. She said she knew that. Libby left me as I came off the Motorway. She told me to drive carefully and later she came back again.

"How's John?"
"He's here if you want to talk to him."
"Hello Daddy," said John brightly.
"Hello my boy." I said. "And how are you?"
"Actually Daddy I'm rather excited!"
"Why is that John?"
"Well, I've been jumping on King."
"That's good! You love him very much, don't you?"
"Yes I do!"
"And I expect he loves you too?"
"Well I think he does."
"I'm sure he does!" I replied.
"And who else do you love?"
"Well, I love God of course and I love my Mummy and Daddy."
"That's good because we love you too."
"I must say goodbye now Daddy. I'll talk to you again soon."
"Goodbye John. I'll look forward to that."
"Well Bear, we must go now. Keep up the good work."
"I'll do my best darling."
"I know you will. Goodbye Bear."
"Goodbye my darling. Goodbye John.
"Goodbye Daddy."

Tuesday, 14ᵗʰ March 2000
    I said my prayer tonight and was told that if I wanted a message I must turn over to the other side of the bed. I did so and heard Libby say, *"Bear?"*
    "Darling!" I said.
    "I love you Bear," Libby said.
    "I do love you too, but you know that, don't you?"
    "Yes Bear, I know that."
    "How is John?" I asked.

"Oh I'm very well thank you Daddy."

"What have you been doing today?"

"Oh I've been to school, but I rode King earlier."

"What have you been learning in school today?"

"I've been learning about music and painting." John replied.

"Those are good things to learn about," I said.

"Who is gooder, you or Mummy?" John asked.

"Oh Mummy I should think," I replied. "But we'll have to wait until I come up there to see!"

"That won't be for a long time Daddy, but I shall be there to greet you."

"Thank you my boy," I said. "I shall look forward to that, but I expect I'll see you before then."

Thursday, 13ᵗʰ April 2000

I learned a great lesson tonight. I was reading about Jesus suffering on the cross at Calvary. When he cried out, "My God, my God, why hast thou forsaken me?" It suddenly came to me. Jesus had reached his lowest point just as I had at in the gardens at Nettlebed. (See page 27, Monday, 4th October 1999) I had cried out, "Are you listening God?" I had been at my lowest ebb and God had answered me as He had answered Master Jesus on the cross.

Saturday, 17ᵗʰ June 2000

I was driving up to the cottage at Shenington when Libby came through to me and I said to her, "Tell me about Satan."

She said, *"That's not a very pleasant subject for a beautiful morning like this!"*

"That's true but I need to know more for the sake of my progress. *He exists in our minds and therefore he is,"* she said. *"Remember that everything has an opposite. Where there is love there is hate. Where there is light there is darkness. Where there is good there must be evil. Love vibrations are light and fast, whereas the opposite is heavy and slow. The high vibrations of love are where you must always keep yourself. Like attracts like so if you have low vibrations you will attract low spirits. The lower you are in your mind, the nearer you are to Satan and the farther away you are from God.*

"If you suffer a depression you are at your lowest ebb and if that depression leads you to attempt suicide, then you are doing Satan's work and doing great damage to your spirit. Always remember that. Suicide is not an option. You must not take yourself out of the world before your time. The only way that this could possibly happen is for you to pray to God to take you up. That would mean changing your path and your plan. God can do anything because He created us and we are His children. He will not let us suffer unnecessarily. You will remember that when I was in such pain due to the cancer before I passed, I told you that I was taken out of my body on a silver cord and I was released from much suffering?

"It is better for you not to even consider thinking about Satan, darkness and evil. Be aware of their existence but concentrate all your thoughts on love. That way he cannot tempt you into thoughts of lower vibrations. Once tempted, like attracts like and your thoughts become lower in vibration. He will then be able to put further low thoughts to you and bring you lower still and so on. Remember Bear that the same applies to love.

"The more love you have and the more love you give, the more love you feel, the further you are from evil and the more love you will be given. The law works in the reverse as well. Take love and give love and you will be given more love to give. That is what is important.

"If you keep your thoughts and actions in love then he can't get a grip on you. That is where you must always be – thinking love, doing love, giving love. Remember that Bear. For everything that happens in life there is a reason for love. Remember the not so good things that happen. They are simply tests of your love, so that love will help you come through these tests. Always give love. Think love. Help other people even people that you don't particularly get on with or people that have done harm to you – think love about them. Then these evil things can't get to you and you will have more love to come.

"Remember that although when bad things happen to you in life on this earth plane, they hurt and they seem to go on for a long time, but in the course of eternity these are but short moments. It is important that we bear our problems with love and come through them. The more love that we generate towards our problems, the more love we will have and the shorter the time of trial will be.

"It is really very simple Bear. Remember that Jesus said,

"Love thy neighbour as thyself".

If we lived our lives on just this one principle alone, we would be making great progress and we would be closer to God."

"There is the first police car of the morning," I said, "on the hard shoulder with somebody that they have pulled in!"

Libby said, *"Spare a thought for them. You should give your love to the police! You should give your love to the motorists that are with them. They have been pulled up because they were doing something wrong. They both deserve to receive love.*

"Remember that there is a part of God in all of us. So if you love your neighbour then you are also loving God and moving closer to Him. Love thy neighbour as thyself. In you there is a part of God. Spend your life loving and you are loving God.

"Think of all the good people you have known and ask yourself, "Why are they good?" Because they love! They give love. The truth is very simple Bear, live your life in love and you will be moving towards God. That is the principle purpose of life on Earth. We come to Earth to sit in the classroom and learn. The most important lesson to learn about is love, because love is God."

Later I was reflecting on the fact that soon after Libby passed, she used to talk to me before I went to sleep. Now, although she does pop in, she doesn't say very much, but we always have a lot to talk about as I cruise up the motorway.

I heard Libby say in response, *"Well Bear, you are too tired when you go to bed. You stay up too late and at least when you are on the motorway I've got a captive audience."*

She's got an answer for everything that wonderful lady.

Tuesday, 20th June 2000

In the Banbury circle Doreen, our wonderful medium, saw John with his picture of the dog with a bird in its mouth. As Doreen thought, "Oh poor bird," it fell out of the dog's mouth, walked around in a circle and flew away. The dog was a Golden Retriever such as I had always kept. The picture was a wonderful present for me, his father on the first Tuesday after Father's Day.

Very soon on the way back after the circle, I heard John saying, "Like my picture Daddy?"

"Yes John, I liked it very much."

"It was a funny one, wasn't it Daddy?"

I could sense that he was smiling and laughing.

I said, "Yes it was. I wish I had been able to actually see it."

"But it was in your mind's eye Daddy, wasn't it?"

"Yes it was. As Doreen was describing it I could see it in my mind."

I asked John how he had painted it and he said, "Well I didn't actually paint it. I applied pigment and that isn't quite the same thing."

The picture that I had seen in my mind's eye was Portia, my departed Golden Retriever, standing head to the left and tail to the right with a pheasant with long tail feathers in her mouth, looking beautiful and immaculate. I asked John how he had applied the pigments. In the back of my mind I thought it must have been a very fine brush. While I was thinking about that he said, "No Daddy, you apply pigments by thought."

He said that it was much easier and much more accurate because if you apply your pigments by thought and it isn't quite right, then you think about what it should be and it's right!

"Anybody can produce a picture Daddy, providing that they have the ability to think clearly in their mind exactly what it is that they are trying to produce. There are so many wonderful colours up here for us to use," he said.

There were wonderful soft blues that he was rather partial to. He also likes the different sorts of reds that are available to him. Doreen described the dog as being painted in a reddy-brown colour. John said that because he rather liked reds a lot that it might have been a bit redder than my memory of Portia, the Golden Retriever that Libby and I had loved, actually was.

Sunday, 16ᵗʰ July 2000

I prayed to God for guidance and protection. Pam had asked me if I knew anyone who could deal with a poltergeist. After making some enquiries I was put in touch with Linda Williamson and this was the first day that I met her. We had arranged to visit a family on the Nine Mile Ride near Finchampstead in Berkshire, where Henry VIII used to ride the nine miles to his hunting Lodge. This family was having trouble with a poltergeist. It was a complicated situation.

There was a family of four, mother, father and two teenage sons. In an annex on either side of and connected to the bungalow, lived her mother and his father – one on either side. The old man was suffering from senile dementia and various other physical problems. He was apparently a very selfish man, who expected everything done for him, but was away in hospital on the day we called. The mother's mother looked after herself as best she could but she had severe arthritis in her right hand.

There was clearly much tension in the family with the various relationships, which was not helping the situation. We listened to the catalogue of activities caused by poltergeist activity. The younger child was unable to feel at peace in his bedroom and so Linda and I went and sat there.

Firstly Linda clairvoyantly saw an Ouija Board and a glass. Someone had been playing with it and this we concluded was how the spirit had got in. We didn't mention this to the family. Then Linda became aware of a large strong and aggressive man who told us that "they" had been having a lot of fun with the family. He admitted that he had played around with television sets, made noises on the telephone and done various other things. "They" had been having fun.

I told him, through Linda who was now in a light trance, that it was not his home and that he must move on.

He said, "It had been my home. I got involved in a fight when several men set on me."

I told him, "It isn't your home anymore. It belongs to these people now. You must move towards the light."

"It's very far away," he said.

"All you have to do is to start to move towards it. There are your family and friends who love you waiting to welcome you."

"I have no friends. There is nobody who loves me."

"If you move towards the light you will find that there are people there who love you and want to help you."

"I can see people there!" he said. "There is an angel there. I've never seen an angel before."

"Move towards them," I said encouragingly.

"There are a lot of people there."

"Is the angel still there?" I asked.

"Yes," he said.

"Move towards them. They are there to help you. They love you and want to help you. Move towards them."

"They are telling me that what you are saying is true," he said and he must have moved forward because Linda told me that he had gone.

Then through Linda I was told, "Michael, this is your work. This is the beginning of your work for Spirit. You are here to give healing – not by laying on of hands, but by helping people to move on."

We felt that the room was now more peaceful and we went to the kitchen. We told the family what we had done. Linda then clairvoyantly told them about the father's mother. Linda was correct in every detail that she gave. Linda then asked them to leave us so we could sit alone in the kitchen.

She felt that there was somebody saying, "Help me."

Linda saw an old lady sitting in front of an open fire. She was cold and Linda started shivering. The lady said that she had waited a long time. She had died in her chair alone. They had come to take her body away but she had been unable to move on. Now she could and she went. The kitchen felt at peace as though a breeze has blown through it and had cleansed it.

Afterwards I felt relaxed and at peace. I know I have helped this family and that Linda was the one to help me. I have moved on. My work for Spirit is becoming plainer and clearer. I shall wait for them to give me more work but in the meantime I know I must wait and be patient. Things will happen in their time and not mine.

Tuesday, 18ᵗʰ July 2000

Immediately after circle tonight, after the other ladies had left to make the coffee, Doreen went back into trance. She said, "I'm covered in brambles."

I shut the door and sat directly in front of Doreen. She started pulling at the top button of her blouse, undoing the button and pulling at the top of her bra.

"Smells!" said Doreen. "Smells! (Pause) No! (Pause) Smells!"

I asked where she was.

"Under the brambles!"

"Do they scratch you?" I asked.

"My... no. (Pause) The box!"

"Is there a box?"

"Are you in a box?"

"No! I came (Pause.)"

"Can you see a light?"

I saw Doreen smile and I asked if she could see the light, because there were people in the light. I told her to look into the light and see the people there who loved her and wanted to help her. She must move towards the light. She need only move a little way but she must move towards the light.

Doreen smiled again as though she was looking into the light and saw friendly faces. She seemed comforted and put her thumb into her mouth and was more relaxed and comforted. I urged her again and again to move towards the light. She took her thumb out of her mouth. I kept urging her to move towards the light. I told her again to move towards the light – just a little. When Doreen relaxed I knew that the child had gone into the Spirit World.

I asked Doreen if she could hear me. I asked her to come back to me. I held her hands and coaxed her back out of the trance. She was very deep and it seemed to take some time. Perhaps it was only a minute but it seemed a long time to me.

Then Doreen said,

"Um. Michael?"

I said, "Yes, it's Michael. It's alright!"

"Would you like a glass of water?"

"Yes." She drank it down.

Doreen said, "I've been off again."

"It's alright."

"I can tell you where I've been."

"It's alright. I know about it. We've rescued a child."

I was very happy with this success of my first spirit rescue.

Before I had left even Banbury, I heard the excited voice of John,

"Daddy? Daddy?"

I said, "Hello John, is that you?"

"Yes, it's me and you've done very well."

"Thank you John. Can you hang on and talk to me on the motorway?"

John said, "Yes, yes I'll talk to you later Daddy."

Suddenly I felt very happy and alive. It was a wonderful experience to have helped that child into Spirit from where it was earthbound underneath the brambles. I was sure that John was there to help me. Certainly he knew all about it.

"Okay Daddy," I heard John say as I drove onto the motorway.

"Hello John. Talk to me my boy," I said.

"Daddy, it was very important what you did tonight. It was particularly important because I want you to be able to help young people, young children, who haven't been as lucky as I have been by being looked after. The little girl tonight was only seven. She had died when she got caught in some brambles and couldn't get out again."

"What was the box John?" I asked.

"It was a box that she had been playing in – sort of hide and seek situation. The other children couldn't find her and when she came to crawl out of the box she got caught in the brambles and couldn't escape. You were able to help her on the way to Spirit. We couldn't get to her because she was so young and she didn't understand about the light. When we tried to talk to her through the light, she saw us and just smiled at us. Perhaps she thought she was having a dream. She didn't know she had to move forward into the light. So there was nothing we could do. You were very good and helped. Now she is with us and she is happy."

"Thank you John," I said. "It is wonderful to be able to help somebody. I am pleased that it went off successfully. I was worried about not being able to release the little girl but I was also worried for Doreen. It was the first time that we had worked together in a spirit rescue and I didn't want anything to happen to her."

"Oh she was quite safe Daddy. We were looking after her. What we couldn't do was to look after the little girl and get her to move towards the light, but you did that!"

"Yes but I did ask for help!"

"Yes but you didn't need it Daddy. You were doing alright!"

"Thank you John, that's a great comfort."

"Did you know that you had seen her face before Daddy?"

"I'm not sure John. I was trying to remember."

"You saw her face in your dreams last night. She was a little dark-haired girl with long brown hair."

"It certainly seems very familiar John, but I can't promise that I remember."

"That's alright Daddy. You are doing a very good job."

The following Sunday, while I was in church in Oxford, I was aware of a small beautiful child in front of me. She was facing me and as she smiled I knew that she was the rescued child and she had come to say, "Thank you."

Tuesday, 17th October 2000

As I was driving in Oxfordshire I was told to go to my destination via the Rollright Stone Circle. I had been there before and so I was happy to drive there and park the car in the lay-by outside. I walked into the centre of the stone circle and waited.

"You haven't brought your recorder," I was told firmly.

This was true. I had left it in the car as I didn't know why I had been asked to come here. When I returned to the centre of the circle and switched it on I was immediately given the poem below without a break. I still retain the tape. It proves to me that it was given by Spirit. I could never have possibly written it, let alone have recited it straight off without a break.

THE ROLLRIGHT STONE CIRCLE

In the middle of this circle I do stand
Surrounded by these stones upon the land.
The visitors, who come here, may not know
That our spiritual ancestors made it so.
If you watch the stones with care
You can make out faces there.
Surely there are messages upon the wind
If we could only listen and tune in.
Here it was in olden time
That our forefathers came to find
Spiritual answers to their prayers
To understand the life upstairs.
These hardened stones were placéd here
To make magnetic fields appear
To increase those simple vibrations
That can move mountains and alter nations.
Surely we have not moved too far
To understand what these things are?
Have we become too blind to see
That they are here for teaching you and me?
A chill wind blows as I think of this.
How awful it would be for humanity to miss
The wonders that have been left behind
And remainéd here for us to mind.
This is not the warmest place to be
But I'll remember serendipity
And as I go I'll hope to find
My place on Earth and peace of mind.

Saturday, 21ˢᵗ October 2000

I understood that as God had created us all, Jesus was a spirit like us all, who came to Earth for understanding the feelings and experiences of this earth plane. He was a greater medium than any of us and was able to be a truly wonderful instrument for healing and he taught great philosophy. He was and is a great example to us of what we should be and yet we fail to live up to his teachings and examples. We should read what he said with all this in mind to help interpret all he said. What that was isn't new. It has been there for two thousand years but when we read the words with the knowledge that God was a part of him, as He is with us, we should understand so much more.

As I was about to go back to bed again I felt that I should sit back in meditation. I closed my eyes and I felt a spirit breeze come up my legs to my waist. I saw Libby's face quite clearly in my mind's eye and I felt her presence. I said, "Are you there my darling?"

She replied quite sharply, *"Be quiet Bear!"*

A little later as I felt her presence fading I said, "Is it over?" and she replied, *"Only if you want it to be!"*

A few minutes later I opened my eyes. I felt strongly that Libby was trying hard to come to me in a stronger form to comfort me. God bless her.

Tuesday, 24th October 2000

I had a frustrating start this morning because I found that I 'kept losing things'. I had been told by another well known clairvoyant on Saturday that things were being moved at home and I should ask for them to be put back! Anyway I 'lost' some batteries that I needed for my Dictaphone and they turned up next to my coffee cup!

Then I couldn't find the battery charger and then I couldn't find the mobile phone! I asked Saint Anthony, who always helped Libby and me during the many times we needed his help. I found the battery charger in the 'wrong' suitcase. Then, after a frustrating search I found the mobile.

It was in a shoe, where I had packed it after a trip. I had not used it since then and this pair of shoes was in the back of the car with all the paraphernalia that I carry. I didn't believe that the mobile could be there, so I hadn't searched very seriously. However my eyes were drawn to a pack of unused audio tapes that I had forgotten that I had.

In opening up the back of the car to retrieve them, I was told to look on the other side. When I did so, I saw the cord of the mobile trailing out of the shoe, which was covered by the spare duvet that I carried in case I needed to spend the night away. I was so very grateful to Saint Anthony for his help yet again. I would not have found that mobile 'phone in a month of Sundays!

Later I turned to my picture of the Master and prayed for him to see that it was fitting for him to help me now to find my path and serve our Creator. I felt very strongly that he said that he would and I was grateful and happy to know this. May he keep me on my path and may I learn to give love again. Then I asked Master Jesus for his love and understanding and I know that he said that he would give this to me. God bless him.

As I finished my prayer, I knew that Libby was there and wanted to talk to me. I expected this to be about a friendship that I had decided to end. I turned over to the side that she always came to when she spoke to me.

I said, "My darling, I feel that you are there and want to talk to me. If that is so then I am ready."

"Remember that nothing that I have told you has been untrue. Love and honour God. Remember that your friend is Jesus – for you are fortunate that he loves you. I will guide you and help you. Learn as much as you can. Spend the winter studying. You'll come out better in the spring ready for your work. Then you will know where it is and what you have to do. For the moment, put behind you all the roots that

*are withering away. You will find new roots and new work.
You don't always recognise it Bear, but it is there. We are
working for you and are ready to guide you. Now that you
have made this big decision you will be able to continue on
your path for you have much to do and we will help you
because we love you. You are good. You know you are good.
We know that you have failings but at heart my Bear, you are
so good.*

*"God bless you. Sleep well. I will stay with you tonight,
so rest in peace. Give to God what is due to Him. Give to
Jesus your respect and love and he will give you guidance in
truth. God bless you Bear. God bless."*

"God bless you my darling. Thank you for coming."

*"How could I not come? I love you so and you need
me so. I am here. Never forget that. You don't need the
props of my earthly life. You only need total belief and
knowledge that you have, to know that I am here to support
you, to guide you and to love you. Good night my Bear. God
bless you."*

"God bless you my darling. Give my love to John and
all those who help me. Take my love and blessings and may
I be worthy to serve my Creator."

Friday, 27th October 2000

I spent the day rushing around trying to get things
done. I had meetings with two people from the farm that had
fallen out, but I think that they can sort themselves out now.
There are, no doubt, things that I have forgotten to do but they
will have to wait a week now!

I left shortly after three o'clock, so I had a leisurely
drive up. As I set out I heard Libby say, *"You can relax now
Bear! Nuneham Courtney will be good for you. Take it
seriously, as I know you will. It will save you a lot of chasing
about and you need to look towards the light and understand*

the more spiritual side. Use meditation to become more aware. You are doing well. Don't get me wrong! The physical stuff you have explored and it's not really necessary for you to concern yourself with Jenny's Sanctuary or the Noah's Ark. So don't be hurt if you are ignored! You are not rejected. We took you out. You are too precious and too important for the work that you have to do to be damaged in anyway.

"So be good Bear! Be vigilant! Be loving! Set yourself apart a little."

I called in at the Global Retreat Centre at Nuneham Courtney and collected some leaflets about their activities. As I drove from there up to Deddington, the sky was beautiful. It was broken cloud, a mass of colours. There was a beautiful blue, showing through a mass of clouds as if painted by water colours. There were so many shades from white to grey and it reminded me somehow of the sea when the cloud is out and far away. It was very, very beautiful.

Monday, 6th November 2000

I postponed my dental appointment this morning due to the state of my health and a desire, confirmed by Chris at the surgery, not to spread my germs in their direction.

I went to bed early tonight because I felt strongly that I should watch a movie before going to sleep. I flicked through the titles because I wasn't really interested in anything but an early night and an end to my cough and cold!

There was one film that leapt out at me. It was called Message in a Bottle. It was a love story about a man who still loved his dead wife but met another woman.

Tuesday, 7ᵗʰ November 2000

Last night I dreamt about Forest King. I dreamt that he had died and yet I knew that he hadn't. Later he was found safe and well! Libby was also there in my dream.

My first job today was to order a copy of Message in a Bottle from the video shop. I bought a used copy for £5.00! After lunch I went to bed and slept for three hours and after some more paperwork I sat in meditation from seven-thirty for an hour in place of circle.

My circle presence was difficult for me. I felt disturbed and restless.

I felt very alone tonight. I must be alone and learn from the experience. I must work hard here and get everything up to date and sorted. I feel that in the New Year there will be new things to erupt into my life. I must be patient.

Wednesday, 8ᵗʰ November 2000

I woke at three o'clock and found it difficult to get back to sleep again. At one point I saw a white light in the garden through the undrawn curtains. I have not drawn them since the days of Libby's funeral, when I felt that she wanted them open. The light I believe was Libby. She has been in my thoughts a great deal lately. I am trying to let Libby go and yet I need Libby to support me, especially just now, when I am feeling very low with this virus.

As I tried to sleep I saw in my mind's eye a place that I had visited before. It is a wood of beech trees sloping down to a lake. Through the trees I saw Libby in etheric robes shining out the beautiful light of love. As I watched I felt my heart fill with love as I hadn't felt for a long while. It made me feel good. (The number seventy-one was given to me.) It was a truly wondrous feeling and I thank and bless her. She can feel my loneliness and empty soul. She will I know help and guide me. I know that she is in spirit, but I am in human form and I am often tempted not to listen because my earthly emotions want something else. Perhaps, as she tries to draw away so that I can stand on my own two feet, I am left exposed and I am unable to cope with the trials and tribulations that I must master in my life. Have I lost some of the spiritualness that I had? My spiritual batteries feel battered! I need the love and togetherness of a circle to refresh me and lead me on. I somehow feel that my way is blocked and I need help in forging my way through.

"Where do you think you're really going," someone from Spirit said to me, "do you really think you've found your path through Serendipity?"

Libby knows this. Bless her. I need something that, as I write, is missing. The need for meditation is a possible solution. Later today I hope to find an answer to this question at Nuneham Courtney.

I am being pushed back into the grief that I thought I had managed to overcome. I feel tears running down my face as I type this. I miss Libby so much now that I am alone. How I overcome this is my problem. It is not anybody else's. I feel distraught and I can't sleep. I don't feel like working. I have lost my balance and I must be careful not to fall. I can't think of anybody that I can call on to help me out of this pit. I must find my lonely way through it somehow. I have lost the ability to give love to others. I want love and understanding for me, right now. Self-pity? Yes, that's what it is. How do I get rid of self-pity? There is only one way – to have patience and trust.

Thursday, 9ᵗʰ November 2000

I did sleep! I stayed in bed until eleven-thirty. In the post there was my confirmation of the One-Day Retreat at Nuneham Courtney for Sunday.

I went to the Farnham development class. On the way I had been given an inspired poem. After typing these notes I wrote it down. It was called Through the Grey Mists.

Saturday, 11ᵗʰ November 2000

At ten minutes to nine, as I was doing some numerology, I clearly heard a male voice say, "Michael". It made me jump! I sat in meditation and asked three times if there was anybody who wished to talk to me in love but I got no reply. I could still hear the word in my head very clearly.

I heard no more and went to bed at ten-thirty, hoping for a good night's sleep.

Sunday, 12ᵗʰ November 2000

I drove up to Nuneham Courtney for the One-Day Retreat. It was a good day and I have taped it all for further reference. In my prayer during the day I was seeking strength, love and healing in order to progress on the path chosen for me to pursue.

Whilst I was typing my prayer, I turned to the picture of the Master behind me and prayed to Him to see that it was fitting for Him to help me now to find my path and serve our Creator. I felt very strongly that He said that He would and I am grateful and happy to know this. May He keep me on my path and may I learn to give love again. Bless Him.

Later in the prayer, I felt that my forty days would end on Thursday, 16ᵗʰ November 2000. Then I asked Master Jesus for his love and understanding and I know that He said that He would give this to me.

Monday, 13ᵗʰ November 2000

I prayed to my Father and Creator as soon as I went to bed. I was anxious to re-find my spiritual path that I felt I had lost and was prepared to study and go down whatever paths were necessary.

As I finished my prayer, I knew that Libby was there and wanted to talk to me about the friendship I had released. I turned over to the side that she always came to speak to me. I said, "My darling, I feel that you are there and want to talk to me. If that is so then I am ready".

"Bear, you have done the right thing," she told me. *"You have at last realised and the pain will not be as great as you fear, because you know that you have done the right thing. You have received many, many, many warnings, but my Bear, you had earthly desires and hopes, but they were not to be. My poor Bear. Come back stronger in your love for us here in Spirit. Be cleansed and the doors will open for you, for you have much work to do. The time will come soon when you will be purified and you can take up your cross again.*

"You are fortunate that Master Jesus lights your feet. He will help you to look within yourself. You must do this. You will sleep well tonight. You will receive love and blessings and help. Can you feel me Bear? I am with you."

"Yes my darling, I can feel your presence."

"Be strong. Your love is great."

"Yes, it is filling my heart again."

"I will always be with you Bear. I will always be there to hold your hand and to guide you. Our love was so great on Earth. It is even greater in Spirit. As I once told you before, our love will remain and that spiritual love will be there to greet you when you pass. I know that you think that it is a long time but it will pass and we will be together again here in Spirit. You will meet John and you will love him as he loves you. You will be part of our soul group."

After my nap I was working on the computer when I received a telephone call from Pat McQueen of the Yateley Branch of the Institute of Spiritual Mediums. She asked me if I would read an inspired poem, or two shorter ones, at the December meeting. I am delighted to do this as it is important for me to share the work that I have received from Spirit.

I am very tired tonight and I shall go to bed early. I need all the strength I can get at the moment. I have organised a sitting with Linda Williamson. I have done some more paper work. I have reorganised my day out to the Barn Owl Conservation Trust with Linda from Barkham. Libby has told me that it will be a good day. I am playing some of the tapes that I bought at the Global Retreat Centre. I like them. Not a bad day, the only cloud is the fact that I must find somewhere to live by the beginning of March! I wonder what it will be like to have my own bachelor pad again? I think I may be looking forward to it! At least Libby and I can be alone together and I can concentrate on spiritual matters.

Tuesday, 14ᵗʰ November 2000

I feel very depressed this morning. I sat at the computer and I said, "I'm feeling very down this morning my darling".

I heard her say, *"You have made the right decision. Be strong".*

"Thank you" I replied.

"Try meditation", I heard.

I set up the tape player in the bedroom. I shall try the tape called, Knowing Yourself.

I meditated the first three lessons. I felt the coldness of spirit come up my feet and calves. I felt much calmer mentally afterwards and I stopped there.

On my journey up to Banbury for circle, I felt that I should ask Him for enlightenment tonight for Doreen and I are both going through difficult times on Earth. We shall be grateful for any guidance and truths that our Creator thinks fit to give us. On the journey up I prayed to our Master for His enlightenment to help cope with the difficulties we were both having to deal with as we wished to be able to serve our Creator and to play our part in His Universal Plan.

I was thinking of Libby and John and hoping that they would continue to guide me, when I heard John say, "Hello Daddy. You are doing the right thing. We are pleased and happy that you have made the decision you have made. You need to be free of earthly cares. If you had remained in this relationship you would have been too unhappy to do the work that is still ahead of you, that work that our Creator has put along your path. He has much work for you to do. So rest awhile and put everything in order because by the spring you will be very, very busy Daddy".

It was very interesting that John spoke to me at the beginning and at the end as the nine-year old son that I know and love. However, in the middle he spoke to me as a mature man. I felt that this was because the words were so important that I needed to know just how important they were.

"God bless you my boy" I said, "and thank you. Thank you for coming and for your reassurance".

"Mummy is here," I heard him say. I was so delighted.

Then I heard Libby's voice in my head. It was so good. She said, *"Drive carefully my Bear. You are very precious. I do love you so. You are doing what has to be done. You are clearing out the baggage that you don't need. Enjoy your work and travel light. You will have a home but it may surprise you where it will be. I can't tell you more, but you will know when the time comes. So be reassured."*

"Thank you my darling," I said.

"Take care. You still have free will and you can be headstrong. Take care of Alan. His time is not yet. The circle is not your responsibility at the moment. So don't

worry about it. You will know how to sit and where to sit when the time comes.

"Remember you have roots in Berkshire. You still have some work to do there. The inspired poems that you receive will be a success. They will bring comfort to many people. When you read your two poems at Yateley in front of the ISM members, read the first one that you ever received and also The Ages of Man. *They are the most important for you to read."*

The inspired poems that Libby was to advise me to read were When and The Ages of Man.

WHEN

When the sky's a mixture of blue and sombre grey,
When the seeds of failure grow up along the way,
When love's hurt by the foolishness and the stupid words I say,
When my childish minds oblivious to the air of much decay,
When I think I'm right and insist I have my way,
When I hurt my love ones and I lose their love today,
When my ambition stands before me in the way,
When I fall down on my path because there's a boulder in the way,
When I loose the reason why I'm here and start to sway,
When paradise is lost and I must go away,
When I see the autumn but its really only May,
When I count my chickens and see them fly away,
When I abandon my progression and forget that I must pray,
When I forget that I'm created then I know I've lost my way.

Inspired writing on Sunday, 1st October 2000

This was followed by a vision of a new beginning, the stars brightly shining in the night sky and a total eclipse of the sun.

THE AGES OF MAN

In spring a baby's born,
From its mother it is torn,
She hears that welcome cry
But this baby's born to die.

In spring he grow into a man,
They try to teach him all they can,
But he needs to learn himself
The lessons taught by life itself.

In summer he has reach the stage
Of having grandparents in old age.
They are weak and nearly dead
And he must see what lies ahead.

In summer he may take a wife
And try and lead a normal life.
They may have children to them born
Who one day will their parents scorn.

In autumn he will feel accursed
By what life brought to him on Earth.
He worked so hard for everything
But what earthly pleasure did it bring?

In autumn he retired at last
To find that time was going fast!
He loved his family too much, did he
For there were grandchildren to see.

In winter he can only wait
And consider what was his mistake.
He looks to Heaven, so aware
That he may be not asked in there!

In winter now it's very hard
To make redress for what he barred.
He had tried to lead a goodly life
That was rewarded free from strife.

But now the winters closing in
He will soon pass and with each sin,
Will have to face the reasons why
He made mistakes to passers by.

In Summerland does he avow
Beyond the state of winter now,
To help those of us on Earth
To avoid mistakes and be accursed.

In Summerland it may seem sweet
To those on Earth with swollen feet
Caused as we walk our separate path
Before coming home to Spirit and a bath!

In Summerland this bath is love,
Where everything is quite above
Our expectations made on Earth
There's nothing more to cuss and curse!

Inspired writing on Thursday, 26th October 2000

"Thank you my darling. I will. I am grateful for your guidance and may Spirit be with me to read them well. For that is where they have come from."

"You will be helped my Bear by the poet who wrote them and he will speak through you. So don't be afraid of letting anybody down. Continue to work on the sittings that you have received. You are rightly trying to put the package together to see what they all mean. By careful my Bear and look after yourself."

I said a prayer for a lady who I was aware needed some spiritual guidance and help.

"Well done Bear," I heard Libby say. *"That will help."*

"Thank you my darling. Did I go off my path such a very long way?"

"My Bear, you had to experience the things that you did in order to cleanse and purify yourself for the work ahead. Please don't feel so hurt. Try and be positive and look upon these things as part of a learning process for you. Your path is more important. It is necessary for you to be pure and cleansed for the work that is to come. You have many lessons to learn my Bear, but you will learn them in time. Never fear that you will not be of use to us here in Spirit in the Summerland.

"You have much to do and much to learn. You are progressing well, but you cannot learn everything overnight. Some of the feelings and beliefs that you have are so deep rooted that it will take time for you to be able to pull them up. Some roots that you have put down have shrivelled away but there are still some little bits of the taproot remaining. You must learn to deal with these as you will. At the moment one of your lessons that you are to learn, which you will not like, is jealousy. You are not a jealous person Bear, but you must

learn the lesson of jealousy if you are to help others through this problem. You have taken a big step along this path. You must learn the lesson of true friendship and that is the exchange of love without physical reward. There are opportunities for you to learn this and friends are being sent to you and you must learn to respect their friendship without physical encounters.

"Should a physical affair be necessary for you to accomplish what is needed, then you will be made aware of it, but it will not be there in your short-term plans. So try and put these thoughts out of your head and try and concentrate on the work that is there for you to do.

"Now my Bear, you must concentrate on your driving and think about the evening that you are going to spend sitting in God's Circle. Ask for enlightenment for you both for you both need it – especially you my Bear. I am going now. I shall still be with you and watching over you. So be careful. John and I will give you our love and many will come to help you from the Spirit and from the earth plane. The latter will be guided by Spirit, so heed what they say and learn your lessons well. You can do this my Bear, I know you can. I am proud of you and I love you. God bless you."

I was given an inspired poem called The Great Joy that Spirit Brings.

Then I heard Libby say, *"Well done Bear. It is hard I know. You will get there. Don't belittle yourself my Bear. You are too easily put down. Remember you have many great gifts. You are always working for more and to do better things. That is not wrong. Don't belittle yourself. Take your confidence – build yourself up. You can rely on us. Remember Bear, you have great good in you. Others have told you this as well and I am telling you this now. There is much good in you. Let your confidence increase and don't belittle yourself. Sometimes you are your worst enemy you know Bear. God bless you. Enjoy the circle and give your love to God. "*

In circle that night I was given great confirmation of my path through life and what I must do.

Wednesday, 15th November 2000

I awoke early and refreshed. I continued my typing of last night's notes from the Dictaphone. I had received wonderful confirmation and I felt much better. I knew where I was going and what I had to do. I could now cope with the problem of the broken friendship that I had and I felt much easier in my mind and my stomach.

But today I had some early duties to perform. I went to Halfords and bought a new battery for the Range Rover. I then drove into Wokingham to collect the ballot boxes before continuing on to Camberley for a workshop.

I left at four o'clock to drive up to Nuneham Courtney for my first meditation class. This went quite well but I found it very difficult to meditate with my eyes open!

Note from Brahma Kumaris on Compassion,

I care for the honour of all beings. Being open to the feelings and needs of others allows me to give what's needed at the right time. With true compassion I always empower, never judge or intrude.

When I got back I started typing up the circle notes from the Tuesday evening. The incredible thing about the tape was between my switching on the tape to record the closing prayer and the beginning of the prayer there was very clearly a dog barking! There was no animal in the house. John told me that he had brought Portia, my 'dead' Golden Retriever, to see me!

Thursday, 16th November 2000

Today I got up at six-thirty to be at Maiden Erlegh School for seven-thirty. There I opened the Polling Station at eight o'clock and presided over a Parish by-election until nine o'clock. I then helped with the count afterwards. It all went well and I got back at ten o'clock.

I had stopped reading my book to pray to my Father, which I felt very strongly that it was time that I did. I also felt there was something that was necessary waiting for me. After my prayer I lay back and waited. I soon felt the presence of my beloved very close to me. Then I smelt her.

"I love you my darling," I said.

I heard her say, *"I love you too my Bear."*

I smelt her as I remembered her and then there was the strong aroma of her scent, Fiji. I smelt it very strongly and I breathed in deeply to take in her aroma and to send it deep into my lungs to make it part of me. I do love her so.

I heard her say, *"Now go to sleep my Bear. You have had some very hard days and you need your sleep."*

Then I smelt her again and again breathed the aroma deep into me – deep into my lungs in great love. I do love her so. Our love is spiritual, not earthly. It is so wonderful. So much more wonderful than earthly love can ever be. I thought of her in my mind's eye as she must surely be now, as a white silver light that is so near me. She is unique because her and her spirit are made up of her experiences and therefore she is unique.

There are many friends who tell me that I am not ready for any other relationships because I have not yet got over Libby's going home to Spirit. Whether I am to have these relationships is neither here nor there. What I can't explain to people is that I have this great love of Libby in spiritual form. She's my helper, my guide, my love in spirit. Because of all the wonderful things that have happened, it proves without doubt that she is still alive. She is working with me from Spirit to help me on this earth plane. There is so much that has happened in the thirteen months since she passed and went home. There is so much proof that I have been given. I can't let go of her spiritually. I cannot ignore the proofs that have come to me. People think that they are earthly feelings but they are not, they are spiritual.

Oh why do I find it so difficult to get people to understand? I don't communicate as well as I should. I don't think that they are ready to hear. I don't think they understand. I don't think they know as I know that Libby has passed on to the Spirit World to help me on my path. This she couldn't do if she was here with me. I have no yen to have her bodily here with me because I couldn't do my spiritual work. I am content that she is spiritually with me all the time. She guides me and looks after me. I am the badger and she is the bat in the tree. How wonderful it all is. She makes me feel so good. I have this wonderful relationship with my Creator and the Master Jesus and all my guides and helpers and those who love me in Spirit as well as my beloved and John. How can people understand? What they say privately and behind my back is of no consequence. I know these things are true. I must work to purify myself, to learn to have experience to do God's work when it comes to me in the spring of next year.

Friday, 17th November 2000

I was woken up just before four o'clock. So I made myself a cup of coffee to try and clear my head. I feel that I can be far more rational and the ache inside me is diminishing, but my thoughts remain.

I am seeing Linda Williamson later today for a reading. This was arranged before Tuesday and the messages that I received on the journey up to and in circle. I must reflect on them and see myself in the light of what my Creator, my Master and my beloveds have told me.

In the afternoon I went to see Linda for the reading. I was a quarter of an hour late in leaving because I felt strongly that I had to finish the typing that was on the tape from last night and that I should reuse this tape for this afternoon's sitting. I had only been driving for five minutes when I heard Libby say, *"Bear, drive carefully and don't expect too much from the reading. There is a lot that we can't tell you yet."*

I said, "I understand that my darling, but I would be grateful for some guidance and some confirmation that would make me feel better about my life at the moment. I need some reassurance."

Libby replied, *"You were given a lot of reassurance on Tuesday on the way to and during circle. I came to you last night in love and you know I was with you."*

"Yes, I know my darling, thank you so much for that. It meant a great deal to me. It's more the earthly things that I feel I have problems with at the moment. Spiritually I know my path is there in front of me and Master Jesus is leading me. I am finding it difficult to learn the earthly lessons of the Sanctuary. They are continually in my mind. I forgive all those concerned and I send love and healing, but inside myself I don't feel better. Not yet."

"Well Bear, give it time. You do really expect to learn all these lessons in such a short space of time."

"Yes my darling, because I am so keen to get on with my spiritual work. ".

"We know that Bear, but you must learn patience and trust."

"Yes, I know my darling. I know."

The reading was extremely helpful. Afterwards Linda invited me to attend a Mediumship Development Course in the New Year. I said that I would be delighted to attend. I felt very drawn to meditate at six-thirty. I lay on the bed and played some meditation music.

I saw myself lifted out of my body on a silver cord and I floated out of a window towards the stars. I had previously seen this window in the circle on Tuesday. Without any intense feeling of speed I went rapidly into the stars. I came to a flat square planet, where inside the deep pink square there was a shape of white/silver light. This was the same planet that I had previously seen in that same circle.

As I gently slowed down and went into the mist of light, I found another light. The light was Libby. Together, holding her hand, we went down into the light and I found us standing together on the seashore. The blue sea was gently rolling in. We were standing on sand. Beyond there was shingle and some low cliffs.

We held each other's hands, looking into each other's eyes. We didn't need to speak. We just looked at each other in beautiful, complete love.

Later we walked along the sand with the blue sea on our left, still looking into each other's eyes together – happy, serene full of peace and love.

I looked back at one point and I saw there were no footprints in the sand. I asked Libby, in thought, why there were no footprints.

She thought back, *"We are too light to make footprints in the sand!"*

We were both of white/silver light and we walked with our hands held together, beside us and in front of us along the seashore under the blue sky.

We walked on and on together, just happy and content to be together, until we both knew that it was time for me to return. She came with me on the journey, up through the white/silver light and through the stars until we were outside the window.

Then she stopped and smiled and I floated on through the window with my silver cord and back into my body. I felt so wonderfully relaxed as I lay there on the bed and so happy and moved by this wonderful experience of being together with my beloved. The whole meditation had last just ten minutes.

Later in the evening I went to the ISM Yateley meeting to witness the demonstration of Bill Dean on meditation. I received some inspired poems on the journey back.

Saturday, 18ᵗʰ November 2000

I drove up to Banbury and listened to the tape of my reading with Linda Williamson. I found it extremely comforting. I also listened to my meditation notes of walking on the seashore with Libby yesterday evening. I asked for a healing poem to send to a lady named Sylvia who was ill and I received "For Sylvia".

After I had left the cottage I called in and saw Doreen before visiting Alan in Banbury Hospital. He was feeling very lonely and he didn't relish the prospect of his incapacity. I felt that there was not a lot one could say but I did my best to cheer him up and befriend him. Alan told me that he would bet a thousand pounds to a penny that I would go back to the Sanctuary! He said he didn't like the sound of what's going on there, but we shall see. Ron apparently visits Alan after he has seen his mother, Kathy and Alan was very fearful for the future of the Sanctuary because he tells me that Ron doesn't know what he's playing with. Alan said that he wouldn't be at all surprised if it didn't all blow up.

There was a light drizzle falling as I drove back. The clouds all over the sky were making it grey and there would be no sunset to enjoy that night, but despite this my heart was full. I was at peace. For the first time for some while I was looking forward to the days ahead. I heard Libby say, *"That's good Bear, that's good. You are beginning to understand at last,"* she said. *"I have been very concerned for you in the last few months, but now you are back on track. There are so many possibilities ahead of you that we will have to decide how best you can use your talents for spiritual work."*

I felt that the turmoil I was in yesterday was being sorted out because I could see a great deal more than I could before. Of course there were areas that I did not understand, but I could understand enough to continue on my way with a large amount of hope and understanding.

"You see Bear," I heard Libby say. *"There is so much that you have to go through to prepare you for what lies ahead. With the experiences that you have had, particularly those you have had lately, you will be able to cope with what lies ahead. You know as you drive round Libby Corner you will never forget that, will you my Bear?"*

"No my darling, that will always be Libby's Corner and I shall always think of you as I drive round it!"

"God bless you my Bear," she said chuckling. *"You do know Bear, don't you that we will never give you anything to do that you are not equipped to cope with?"*

"Yes my darling, I do understand that and that gives me a lot of comfort."

"Remember that you were not equipped to cope with the problems at the Sanctuary, so we pulled you out. You are still not equipped to deal with them and we don't want you to be associated with what we feel is going to happen there. So stay away my Bear. Stay away."

"I will my darling. I will. Will I be invited to the Christmas Séance?"

"No my Bear, you won't and even if you were you should not go! It is their loss not yours. You don't need experience from physical phenomena. So for the time being stay away. I know that you would like to write an article about it and in some ways it would complete your experience, but at the moment we think it best if you don't go. Do remember my Bear that we have not told you what you should do and what you should not do. We have only given you advice. I hope that you will remember that you can go through these doors for experience if you want to. That is for you to decide, but you don't have to go through them. That's the important thing to remember."

"Thank you my darling. It does make it easier for me to decide."

"We will deal with these things on a day to day basis. We will take you and guide you daily on what you should do, what you need to do and what care is needed. This next year may seem a long time for you but you will come through it soon. I know that all will be well. You will succeed with us. God bless you Bear. Take care and enjoy the drive through Henley. God bless you."

"God bless you my darling. Thank you for everything that you are doing for me and have done for me. Without you my life would be very different. God bless you."

Sunday, 19th November 2000

Today I took Linda from Barkham to the Barn Owl Conservation Trust at Brockworth near Gloucester. Linda suggested that she would drive down and this was a treat for me. I bought two instant cameras and a model cat for Linda. She was very pleased with it. We had lunch at the Air Balloon near Birdlip and drove on to the BOCT to arrive at one o'clock. We had a coffee there and had a chat about owls in general before seeing some of them in the aviaries.

Soon we met Khan, a magnificent European Eagle Owl, who would fly for us later. He was weighed and prepared before we all drove out to the flying range. Khan was superb. He had a wingspan of some five to six feet, red eyes and beautiful mottled brown plumage. We saw too the beautiful mottled white Barn Owls and later I was given this inspired poem from Spirit.

THE BARN OWL

The Barn Owl's face is white,
As is its front, a lovely sight!
Two eyes that stare straight out at me
Looking perhaps for sympathy.
It flies with a big head and wings
Looking down for certain things
To fill its crop, a vole or mouse
Before returning to its house,
A hollow in some ancient tree
Or a nest box by courtesy of you or me.
Their head and feathers on its back,
There's nothing that this owl does lack,
With beauteous colours made by God
In true magnificence, nothing odd,
Made on a day of true perfection,
But now these owls need our protection.
Man must learn to quell his greed,
And not let his imagination feed
On selfish lines to keep as pets
These freedom loving birds that he neglects.
Man needs to learn of conversation.
He must learn of God's consternation
Of how we treat the creations from His mind
And not through our greed be so unkind.

Tuesday, 21ˢᵗ November 2000

I visited a lady psychic artist in Oxford. She drew me a brilliant picture of a female guide who I call Angela, who was to be very important in my life as her job was to prepare me for my new companion who Libby had shown me clairvoyantly the previous February.

The clairvoyant gave me this picture of Angela, "She is definitely a horsy person. I'm seeing a show jumping ring. She's on horseback and she's wearing a very deep green velvet riding jacket. She's touching her hat with her crop to you. I get the name of Angela.

"There is hunting too because there are hounds as well and I'm getting stables with horses looking over the doors. This is what I call the hunting, shooting and fishing set!"

She continued, "I'm actually getting her saying "Well you wouldn't expect her to be anywhere else would you?" I'm also getting people with the horse rakes and the hay and the straw and so forth, you know, as if your wife is still helping in the stables doing that sort of thing.

"Why am I getting the name of Mayflower? It's almost as if it's the name of a horse. The lady in the picture had blonde hair, grey hair but it would have been blonde, if you know what I mean. She used to wear it in a Chignon at the back – a bun. "That's me before I got a bit more haggard," she's saying. "I was quite a tough old bird."

I said, "She looks lovely. I'd love to know her."

Thursday, 23ʳᵈ November 2000

After I had typed up the notes about my gift of a psychic drawing of Angela, I felt her strong presence. I felt a very distinct coldness about my feet. I closed my eyes and I was told that she was here to help me with decisions about the farm. I asked if she would help me with anything else.

"Yes," she replied, "I will help you with your spiritual development."

"Am I so far off course?" I asked.

"Oh no," she replied, "but you still have a long way to go. You are really doing quite well. However you must continue to meditate. This is important. You will learn a lot from meditation. You see, when you meditate we can teach you a lot. Not just straight forward lessons but also the peace and love that you need to get through your earthly life on a day by day basis. You mustn't let your mind rule your actions. You must take control of your mind and then you will find it easier to 'keep your cool' as they say. All your actions are governed by your mind, so you must be in control of your mind for the sake of yourself and others.

"You need your rest now. Your mind is calmer. That is why you couldn't sleep. Go to bed now and you will rest. There's another day for you tomorrow! Good night, I will come again."

"Thank you. I do appreciate your coming."

Friday, 24th November 2000

I knew that I was spirit in human form. My confidence in myself had to be restored and I needed to be cleansed and purified before I could go on with my work for Spirit. For the moment I had earthly things to address such as where I am going to live as well as getting up to date with all my paperwork and studying. My spiritual friends who were guiding me had told me that many doors would be opened to me in the New Year and that I should do nothing that doesn't feel right. I must not push my way through those doors, but to go through the ones that were clearly open that Spirit would guide me through.

In the meantime I felt that I had completed my search for guidance and enlightenment in spiritual matters because my guides were, as I was told that they would, starting to introduce themselves to me. Recently three spirit guides have done so. Firstly, there is the Egyptian, who will be working with me later. Secondly, there was Brother Bertram with whom I had worked on a trip to Iona in Scotland, who would again be working with me and talking through me. Thirdly, there was Angela who was guiding me and who came and spoke to me last night, but my main guide and doorkeeper didn't make himself known until later. I gave my love and blessings to everybody in Spirit for making these things possible.

As I drove on the sky ahead brightened, although it was still cloudy the rain has stopped. I felt that for me it was a portent of the future. Things were getting better all the time. This I must realise, remember and continue on my upward path, where I knew that Libby was symbolically at my back pushing me upward. There were many others who were helping me and if not only for my sake but also for theirs, I must continue to progress and progress well.

I was now driving round Libby's corner towards the cottage and I felt her presence with me. This was always a special part of the journey. I felt and knew that she had much love for me. I heard her say, *"Get the change over at the cottage done and we will see if we can find some happiness for you."*

"Thank you my beloved. I do feel the need for a little restorative."

"Oh," I heard her say, *"we are using big words now are we!"* She chuckled and so did I.

I felt at that moment that I was a little low in my need for company. I felt that I had no need for the friends around me. This may sound arrogant but it was not meant so. I meant that I didn't feel drawn to go and see them. I felt most definitely that this pathway was for me on my own. I had a feeling of insecurity with this nervous tummy bubbling away.

I said, "Let the change over go well."

I heard Libby say, *"It will Bear, it will."* I was grateful for this. *"You see your path ahead clearly, although you are not enjoying it, but my Bear, sadly this is how things must be for a while. Put your house in order and be ready for the work that is to come. It is only just over a month before the New Year and you have much to do. So get on with it my Bear! You will feel better as you make progress in this direction."*

"Thank you my darling," I said. "It's good to hear from you."

"As you know Bear, I am always here. I'm watching you from above. Remember the badger under the tree and the bat looking down. (This I had been given in circle.) *It is so, never fear. Your Bat is always here."* And I felt her smile as I did.

I thought about the mobile home at the farm that I would camp in and I heard Libby say, *"Have a good clear out Bear. Have a good clear out."*

"I will my darling, even though it may hurt. I will."

"Soon you will be free of these earthly feelings. Go forward my Bear. Go forward. There is much progress for you to make in a short time. Don't sit around waiting for others to come and help you. You must get on with it yourself now. God bless you Bear. God bless you."

"God bless you my darling and thank you for all you are doing for me."

"It is my path Bear. It is my happy path to help you. God bless."

So I went up to the cottage to see the visitors in for one o'clock and as they hadn't arrived at two o'clock I wrote them a note and left. While I was waiting I felt that I should meditate. I received a beautiful teaching from Angela. I was told I would not remember the words afterwards (this was true). However they would be in my heart and they would guide me on my way. After this I felt much more at peace and there was more love and understanding inside of me.

Monday, 11ᵗʰ December 2000

It was another grey December morning outside. We have had some good sunny days, but not this morning. I did the Christmas cards, a job Libby and I always did together and it still hurts. I feel earthly and out of balance today. I am very tired again and don't feel like doing much. I went to bed to sleep at twenty past two because I feel so tired. I heard Libby say, *"You must rest more my Bear."*

"I love you my darling."

"Yes and I love you."

Through the beginning of 2001 I became involved in many spiritual activities that need not be recorded here, but I was very busy and I believe that I progressed well and learned many lessons during this period.

Friday, 11ᵗʰ May 2001

I sat in meditation and heard the word "Michael".

I said, "Hello my friends. Have you come to talk to me in love?"

I heard them say, "Yes, we have."

I received the following message,

"Michael, there are many things for you to do. You will find the way to do them when the time is right. You are being guided to understand new things. You will find that there is enlightenment for you. You will be given love and understanding

because this is your path of progression, but you need much wisdom to think in a spiritual way. Be in tune with the earth and nature. This is important for without this grounding you will be courted by the materialistic world. Your grounding is in Spirit.

"Go to the four winds. Proclaim your love of our Creator. Talk to those who come to you. Be free in your teachings for we will guide you, not only by speaking through you in what you call altered state but you'll know what to say through your subconscious.

"You will find peace, love and enrichment on your path. Beware of boulders because there will be many. Deal with them in love. Speak and give out the word of God. You need not concern yourself with the annoyances. Continue gently on your path and be at peace. God bless you my son."

"God bless you and thank you for coming. Thank you."

Friday, 25ᵗʰ May 2001

As I lay in the hot water of my bath relaxing, I felt that I should pray before completing a meditation.

"Master Jesus, lighter of my path, I thank you for the many wonders of my enlightenment and understandings and these teachings that are leading me to a new wisdom and by helping me to think more clearly of life and how it really is. I understand that I am spirit in an earthly body and that I shall return home and continue my development and that I shall be with my loved ones, friends and guides. Thank you for these revelations. I trust that I may be worthy to give service through you to the Great Divine Spirit, my Creator. Amen."

I then heard, "Michael, yes it is Angela to give you further insight into the World of Spirit. We have been working to prepare you for trance work and you will have noticed that you have experienced at certain times a large amount of what you call 'cobweb effect' on your face. You were told by Linda (Williamson) that this was likely to be a preparation for transfiguration work. This is quite correct and you will become known for transfiguration, but also you have noticed that when you sit where there are great energies about you, that you feel a great tightening – a great pressure inside your head. This too is part of the work of preparation that we are undertaking for you.

"You see Michael there have to be changes made within the physical body that are compatible with your guides and friends who work with you in Spirit. There are, you see, necessities of forming links that are compatible vibrations between your world and ours in Spirit. You are of course spirit, but you are placed on a level of different vibrations and these are much slower and heavier than those of the Spirit World where we exist.

"In order to make contact between the two worlds it is necessary for you to raise your vibrations so that they become brighter and quicker and by the same token, we have to lower our vibrations so that they become heavier and slower. In this way there is a point where we can link. It takes much practice on both sides, but we do everything that we can to make this easier for you because it is more difficult for you on the earth plane. We make alterations within your body so that your mind may automatically link with us and we may talk and work together.

"You will find that in time, when this time is right and it is not so far off, that you will be able to work in trance. You are developing an insatiable desire to listen to the words of Spirit from mediums in trance and you are learning directly from Spirit through the line of communication of many mediums the words that we want you to hear. It is not always the case that those who listen will hear the same words. It is possible for us to direct messages through the medium directly through the minds of the sitters and they will hear what we want them to hear, what is right at that moment in time for them to hear and therefore we are able to send you teachings in this way and you will learn much from the teachings that come directly through the words of Spirit using a trance activated medium.

"You will in time be given this gift yourself. You will be able to be an instrument for Spirit acting as their vessel to link friends in Spirit directly with their friends on the earth plane. They will come to listen. You will need to make the choice as to whether you wish to step aside and be relatively unaware of what you say as we use the vacillates of your earthly body and mind, or whether to stay as we have promised in a state of being able to hear the words and know that you are not saying them.

"You have developed means of recording important things, so that if you choose to step aside and allow us to control your mind and body you will later be able to hear the words that you have spoken. It is a matter of your trust with us. We know that you have said on repeated occasions and I have a strong feeling that you are saying it to me now, that you do trust us. This should be so for we will never let you down. It is only through the actions of certain entities within mankind that there could be any danger for you, but remember that we do protect you. You are protected by our love and the love of Master Jesus and the Divine Spirit. You are also protected by your own love, which is considerable and that you give and receive more.

"There is very little to fear. If you work with us in trance then the method of communication will come more quickly. If you always wish to hear the words that are being said by us through you it will take a little longer. Do not answer me now but think on this. Perhaps when the time is right you may discuss how this work can be brought on safely and more quickly. Because my friend, my son, you <u>are</u> evolving at a very steady rate and we wish to use you as a vessel for communication through the love of the Divine Spirit as soon as you are ready. We know you have great love and enthusiasm for this work and for that we are pleased – we are all pleased.

"Master Jesus and the Divine Spirit are also pleased as are the Masters of the Ascension. You will learn as you continue on your path more about the stages of development within the spiritual vibrations but for the moment it is only necessary for you to glimpse into these areas. It is for you to concentrate on your earthly work and to give your love and trust to us that we will tell you what you need to know when you need to know it.

"Go forth my son and learn of these great things in your studious and loving way for they will be an important part of your enlightenment and understanding. God bless you Michael."

"God bless you Angela. Thank you for your words. I will reflect on them well. I shall look forward to receiving more enlightenment. Thank you my friend."

Tuesday, 17ᵗʰ July 2001

As I was sitting in the bathroom, I was wondering who my doorkeeper was. I thought, "I must ask Angela who my doorkeeper is."

Immediately I heard, "Red Cloud."

"Has he spoken to me?" I thought.

Immediately I heard, "No, but he will."

I thought, "I wonder what tribe he is from."

Immediately I heard, "Lakota Sioux."

Later that morning I went into my little Sanctuary. I was thrilled and delighted that Red Cloud came and spoke to me for the first time. He confirmed he was my doorkeeper and that he came from the Lakota tribe. I was shown a full Indian headdress while Red Cloud was talking.

This afternoon I booked my place on a trip to meet the Council of Elders of the Cherokee at a powwow a hundred miles north of Orlando in Florida. There might be as many as twenty of us going from the United Kingdom, but only twelve had booked so far.

I sat in my circle of one in my Sanctuary at eight-thirty and I had the most wonderful evening with addresses from Red Cloud and Master Jesus. I went to bed at half past eleven – very tired but very happy.

Chapter 9

THE AUGUST

Wednesday, 8th August 2001

After dinner I sat in meditation and received much guidance about the work and my new beloved. Afterwards I was reflecting on what I had been shown. I had seen the face of my new beloved and I thought, "So she will be blonde then. That will be good."

I heard Libby say, *"You will be pleased Bear!"*

I thought, "I am sure I will if Libby has had a hand in organising it."

Thursday, 9th August 2001

I heard Libby say, *"You are coming on well Bear. There is a great deal to happen to you in the next few months and you are being prepared, as you know, for all this. Your earthly jobs are beginning to be sorted out although you still have some to do. So be at peace and rest at this time and get yourself motivated for the work to come. I shall always be with you as you know,"* she continued. *"You will remember at times of special importance that you sense and see that I am there. So have no fear. In all that you do I will be with you and all your guides and love ones and friends are with you too. You only have to think of us and we are there. We are always only a thought away should we not be already there and watching over you.*

"Bless you my Bear. Take care of yourself. You are to do the Divine Creator's work and we are very proud of you. God bless you."

"Thank you my darling. I do love you so very much as you know and I thank you for all that you are doing for me."

"It is not only your progression Bear, but ours also that is involved in all this. We learn from all the lessons and experiences that you have. So whatever you do you are helping us, so there is no need to thank us all the time but it is very nice that you think of it. God bless you."

I was drawn to a very special number plate on the way back on a gold coloured Jaguar. I had no idea what it meant. The registration was E 2000. I heard myself being asked, *"Where did you spend Easter last year?"*

I couldn't immediately recall this particular memory link. When I arrived back, I heard Libby say, *"Well done Bear. Go and look up Easter."*

I went in and looked up Easter 2000. On Easter Saturday, 22nd April 2000, I chaired a Clairvoyant Demonstration in Oxfordshire where Robert Matheson gave me the following message,

"I know that you are very close to your work spiritually and I would say truthfully to you at this moment in time that I see a tunnel with you of light and I feel that you are drawing from that light, at this moment of time, to give what I would call strength and understanding to the earth plane. You have got to wait the time for what I would call the full vision that's coming from that tunnel, but it is there, so they are trying to reassure you that you are not barking up the wrong tree.

"They are bringing the power there for you and the love around you. Also with you I can see a vivid light within the October calendar and I think by then you will have a lot more love around you or a lot more understanding within you, one way or the other.

"They are preparing for you to take to the road and find success. It is more to do with spiritual undertaking than material."

Saturday, 11ᵗʰ August 2001

As I drove up the M40 John came to talk to me.

"Hello Daddy."

"Hello my son. God bless you."

"God bless you Daddy. You are in a very exciting stage of development at the moment, aren't you?"

"Yes John. It is a time of great excitement for me and I am looking forward to the work to come."

"And to meeting your new beloved Daddy."

"Yes John that is so."

"She is a wonderful lady Daddy and she has been chosen specially to work with you. She has been prepared in spiritually and in earthly terms. You will find her a great comfort I know."

"Thank you John. That is good to know. I am very excited at the prospect of meeting this lady."

"We, your beloveds in Spirit Daddy, have been watching over you very carefully and we know that in this period since your beloved Libby passed and came home to us, that you have missed her very much and despite things that we have brought to you to give you company, we knew that you needed more than we could give you at this time. It wasn't the right time and you were not prepared. The time is nearly here and you will at last find happiness and security for your life to come. It is for me to tell you Daddy, that there is much joy here in Spirit at your approaching nuptials. I believe that is the word.

"You may feel that this is a little early to mention this because you have not met the lady yet, but you will and much progress will be made when you two are together. You see Daddy we have been working very hard in helping you by bringing you friendship that will make your life easier. The work to come will demand this because it will keep you very busy indeed.

"There is a great strength of North American Guides, who work and will work with you. It is important that you go to Florida and meet the Elders and talk to them and there is much there for you to learn. Red Cloud is your doorkeeper and he looks after your safety and protects you. Man of the Mountains is another guide with you constantly and he will bring you more teachings so that you may understand the spiritual beliefs and structures that you need to employ from their culture.

"There is also a Chinese influence, which has not been strong yet, but it will become stronger as they take their part in your progression. You will find it very interesting to meet your new beloved's guides for they are very compatible with yours. This has been chosen to be so.

"You will my dear father, progress even more rapidly than you have when your rebirth is complete. It will not be so long now in spiritual terms but you must have patience and keep your enthusiasm in check for this sometimes leads you down the wrong path or should I say a different path from that which we are guiding you on.

"Do not be afeared as to what is happening. You are being well looked after, but you need not worry about anything, save to keep your trust, your beliefs and your love in the hands of Spirit. God bless you now Daddy. I will come to you from time to time but I have other work to do as well. Work, which I believe you would be proud to know of and one day you will. God bless you my dear father. I love you very much and so does your beloved Libby, my mother."

"Thank you John and thank you for coming to talk to me. You give me so much joy and I look forward so much to holding you in my arms in love, when I at last come home to the Spirit World."

"So do I Daddy. So do I."

I felt a bit emotional after this conversation. It was wonderful to hear John speaking to me again and to listen to the glorious words he spoke to me. I loved him so much and all those who worked with me. I was now driving up the M40 with tears in my eyes and full of wondrous Spirit that I had received from all my guides and especially my beloveds, Libby and John.

I reflected on the beautiful gifts that I was given last night as I sat in the Sanctuary at Betty Grove Farm and felt the presence of my new beloved. I could feel it still and I knew that this was no imagination. It really was her there, even though I couldn't see her. The sense was very strong. God bless her and may I make her happy as we work together for the Great Divine Creator.

I was drawn to the number plate of a van towing a trailer that I was passing and the registration letters were LGM. It occurred to me that it was saying, "Let Go Michael".

Thursday, 16ᵗʰ August 2001

I woke up in the night and decided to have a coffee and some biscuits. I started to read On Life After Death by Elisabeth Kübler-Ross. I read the first thirty pages before I turned the light off and prepared for sleep again. I don't propose to discuss her book, only to say that everybody should read it. I learned and confirmed a lot.

What was important was the lesson I learned. I couldn't get to sleep because I was told very clearly that I must get up and write down what I had learned. I had been thinking of my new beloved and just how great it will be to have someone again to share my life with and someone who can help me with my work for the Great Divine through Master Jesus.

I was wrong! It would be good to share my life with somebody again, but not to have someone to help me but for me to have someone to help. I thought about the work that I had been told I was to do. Spirit would talk through me to those that would listen. Maybe it was through my actions that they would stop and listen. Maybe it was through my actions of helping someone with their life that mankind would listen to the words of Spirit. Maybe the new beloved would be a lady who needed the help that I could give her and this would be the work that I was to do.

It didn't matter, at this moment in time, if this was true or not. What did matter and it mattered a lot to me, was that I had learned another great lesson. It was not me who needed help but the help that I could give to others. Perhaps I could hear people saying, "Well, that's a very fundamental truth that you have just learned. You should have known that anyway." Perhaps that was so, but it doesn't matter what other people thought, that was their problem – not mine. I had learned a very important truth and I was very happy about it.

Whether my short comings were for publication I didn't know, but what I did believe was important was that some bereaved people like myself found good excuses for not doing what they didn't want to do. Everybody was different and would have handled things differently. However I could understand people who had occupied themselves in ways that may have seemed lazy or even slovenly. I found that I could now look back and criticise myself. It had always been easier for me to learn about spiritual things rather than get down to the mundane jobs that needed doing. However it was important to have a balance and I was trying to achieve that now.

As the reader of this journal will know, I had been instructed to put my house and myself in order and there were good reasons for this. I had a new beloved to meet and look after. There was also the work that I had been prepared for as she had and I would be ready for this. When the call came I would not be found wanting.

I had just been typing up John's message from the tape that I had found in the car. (See page 279, Saturday, 11ᵗʰ August 2001.) He mentioned my rebirth and shortly afterwards I was drawn to the car with the registration letters of LGM, which it occurred to me stood for "Let Go Michael". I made myself a mug of coffee and lit my pipe and then continued to read On Life After Death by Elisabeth Kübler-Ross from page 75. To my utter amazement she described her rebirth, which couldn't continue until she realised that she had to let go and submit.

I was staggered! I have known some wonderful spiritual guidance but this was very special. We had had a very heavy rainstorm over the early evening and at about half-past seven the rain stopped and the most wonderful rainbow arched itself over the farm. I felt that tonight was going to be special as I was preparing to sit. It certainly was more special that I could have possibly imagined. It was my Rebirth and Baptism in Spirit.

Friday, 17ᵗʰ August 2001

I was awake and up at six-thirty. It was a beautiful morning. There wasn't a cloud in the sky as I busied myself with the preparations to leave for Ayr in Scotland at seven-thirty. I was to attend a weekend conference there, which was entitled A Toe in the Water. At that time I did not know that my attendance there would change my life.

Saturday, 18ᵗʰ August 2001

At nine thirty I took part in a Healing Experiment that was run by Joan Francis Boyle from Hamilton and her assistant Ann Gillis from Glasgow. Joan was very highly qualified in Aura Mastery and had been working publicly with auras since 1987 and using this type of equipment for two and a half years. The idea was to show 'what takes place when healing, in the true sense, was passed over from one person to another'.

My aura was measured before healing on a sensor that measured data of ones bio-energy from points on ones fingertips, up on a screen that showed the aura and the chakras of the healer. Another screen beside the first shows the aura and chakras of the patient. There were also graphs that showed measurements of stress, energy levels, the state of mind, mind body and spirit balance, emotions and a colour wheel. Photographs were taken before, during and after healing.

As I sat at the back of the room waiting and looking around I didn't feel drawn to give healing to anyone in particular. Suddenly a lady walked into the room, stopped and then sat down and I immediately felt drawn to give her healing. It turned out that she was looking for her fiancée, the well-known psychic researcher Montague Keen. She had entered the wrong room but couldn't just walk out again so she sat down politely.

As soon as she sat down, Joan asked if anyone really did need some healing. Veronica's hand shot up into the air. She sat down in the chair, which was to be in front of mine when I was called up. I gave her healing without the laying on of hands and I had my left hand on the measuring equipment and my right hand just behind her back at hip level as I was standing to give healing. Everybody appeared to be very impressed by the data that came out from the technology.

It turned out Veronica told me later, that she had been up all night with Monty, who had been taken ill. She had telephoned a lady called Jenny Eales, who lived in Orpington, Kent. Jenny was a friend of Veronica's and a first rate medium and healer herself. Mustafa, Jenny's four thousand year old Egyptian holy man was her guide and he told Veronica through Jenny what to do and also that Monty would be alright by the morning. Of course Veronica, who was not a well woman herself, had been up all night with her fiancé and was herself now in pretty poor shape. No wonder Spirit directed her to that room for healing.

There was another reason because her guide directed her to give me one of Jenny's cards with the words, "You must meet this lady." I was so excited about my gift of healing, for which Veronica was most grateful, that I forgot all about the card and the clairvoyant medium from Kent.

Sunday, 19ᵗʰ August 2001

I sat in the Trance Experiment this morning at half past nine. I sat wired up with the equipment measuring five different types of reactions in my body. These included brainwave activity, pulse, blood pressure, temperature and breathing rate. The reading showed that I had been reacting in a similar way to other trance mediums. It is highly likely that my communicator had spoken through me in trance at a sufficient level of Beta and Theta cycles that the researchers clearly believed that I was working as a trance medium. Both these experiments, the healing yesterday and the trance today were very exciting to me. Although I went into both with complete confidence in the Spirit World and all my guides nevertheless I had been proved to have been given these wonderful gifts.

During the Trance Experiment my Theta cycles had gone from six to twenty. Trish Robertson, who was running my session, told me that this was high and the higher they were the deeper the trance. As I had always heard the words or a phrase individually I had always assumed that I was not in deep trance, but in a light trance or altered state.

After this experiment, a lady who worked with hypnosis at Edinburgh University had said in answer to a question from Trish that with twenty cycles of Theta brain wave, she would have expected me to be comatose – sufficiently deep for a surgical operation to be performed on me without me feeling a thing! Then I remembered what I had been told by Spirit. "You will always hear the words to prove to you that you are not saying them." Therefore my trance has been developed for some time and I hadn't recognised it because often other trance mediums don't remember anything and are taken completely out of the equation. Spirit had also told me that my trance would be developed naturally and not forced. Bless them. They have developed it so naturally that I wasn't aware fully of what had happened!

There was no doubt in my mind at all that the Baptism in Spirit that I had received in my circle on Thursday evening was a very special event. Three days on I was still feeling very good indeed, cleared of many weights that were weighing me down, clear of mind and knowing that great gifts have been given to me and of these two had been proved scientifically at Paisley University, Ayr in Scotland.

Using me as an instrument, I had given healing without the laying on of hands or touching the patient in any way. The lady received great benefit from it and the measurements and photographs from the equipment proved that I was giving healing, because my body was in a state of being acceptable to do this work. The facilities and organisation at Ayr had been first class and I considered it was the best-run spiritual event that I had attended and certainly it turned out to me to be the most exciting.

I drove back to Betty Grove Farm with the knowledge that the work that has been done in the Sanctuary there had been successful and I looked forward to further work with Spirit as I sat there in the evenings. I arrived at the halfway point after two hundred miles and I began to feel a little weary after the excitement and shortage of sleep over the weekend, but suddenly I was drawn to a number plate, which was an L-registered car with the letters TCM. This was yet another spiritual message and I was given the words "Lots To Come Michael."

Monday, 20ᵗʰ August 2001
I arrived back safely in Berkshire in the early hours of the morning and quite out of character, instead of having a large whisky and going to bed thanking God for getting me safely home, I found myself unpacking my suitcase! The reason soon became clear. I found the card of the clairvoyant medium that I had been given and told to see. I placed it on my desk and finally went to bed.

As soon as I walked in the room later that morning I was drawn to that card on my desk! It kept coming into vision. I was on a spiritual high as I had been proven to have the gifts of healing and trance mediumship. I didn't need to see a medium.

"Oh yes you do," I heard Red Cloud say.

"I don't need a sitting! I am on cloud nine with my spiritual gifts," I retorted.

"You need to see this one," said Red Cloud firmly.

"Well even if I do phone her, she probably won't be there," I replied pressing the numbers on the telephone. "Hello..."

Well Jenny had a cancellation for Wednesday at one o'clock...

Wednesday, 22ⁿᵈ August 2001

I didn't feel until now that I had needed a sitting, but suddenly I was very excited about meeting Jenny Eales at one o'clock and talking to Mustafa. So much had happened lately that he had much proof that he could give me, but what was important was that I received some further confirmation about my spiritual path. I needed no proof of what I have been told but only for him to prove to me that he is genuine.

I had been told by Veronica, to whom I had given healing at Ayr last weekend that she recently had had a sitting with Jenny, which was very accurate and 'I <u>must</u> have a sitting with her'. Her guide was Mustafa, who looked about thirty-six and said he had lived in Egypt four thousand years ago. His head was shaven and he had a small face. He was apparently quite knowledgeable.

Here are the relevant parts of the excellent sitting that I had with Jenny's wonderful guide. Mustafa said,

"You were very aggressive and heartbroken in the past. You have gone through the mill and back two or three times at least. Now you are beginning to open up to a new and involved, but exciting, phase in your life.

"On the surface you are not too sure of your direction just yet. We in Spirit need to work a little harder with you in order to prepare you for the next event and also to protect you from any outside influences, which can upset this vital/delicate apple cart.

"Your own mediumship had taken a downward fall in the past, but we are now adjusting you nicely in order for you to expand your knowledge and versatility. We have in the pipeline several guides, which we are trying out for you right now.

"Trance is *comme ci comme ça*, but we have developed a new technique, which now allows it to flow easily from you. We will continue to persevere with you and develop it further – it needs to be finely tuned only – the basics are already in place.

"A mammoth coloured gentleman, of African qualities, but highly spiritual, comes in and out just now. He is not fully in just yet. There is another guide waiting in the wings for further development to work along side you for rescue work. His name is Mawi. He is sensitive and courageous in his workings of Spirit. You will notice the difference when he works with you, as you will feel instinctively lighter as if being suspended from your chair.

"Your clairvoyance is almost second to none and I'm sure you are aware of that from me.

"Your healing ability, which fluctuated in the past, is now also free flowing. You need to keep little cards, for payment healing, for patients. You need to consider this now. A form of advertising should also be directed at the public at large. Your North American Indian guide is quite impatient now to get you settled, but up and running at the same time.

"This Indian guide has a tomahawk and he prances around a lot. When you get itchy tingling feet, underneath the arch so to speak, this is him working, or wanting to work, with you. He is a man in his thirties or forties. He is a brave man also. He works highly tuned and likes natural music, i.e. the rustle of the trees in the wind.

"This man/guide will turn your life around. Right now he is working out a game plan, so that you become much more settled and finally at peace in your mind and, of course, soul.

"You are a most sensitive of sensitives and have been hurt not only from the earth plane, but from above also.

"You have a mother in Spirit. You didn't always see eye to eye – a drift there. She cut you up verbally many times. She had nerves of steel and was a formidable lady. Although she is passed to Spirit, there is still pain from her to you. You still hurt inside.

"Your own life, although it appears to be dragging on its feet, is levelling off nicely and beginning to climb successfully. So pour all your troubles into the rubbish bin and just leave the rest to us.

"There is a male child, a son, whose tragic death affected you. Your mind, half of it was affected, grieving, about eight years later.

"You are stuck in your life at the moment, still in the doldrums, but equally catching up to getting far better than you once were. All new beginnings to open up and for you, dear sir, to become yourself – your sunny self once more.

"Your relationship with your wife is going down. Your wife was always charitable to you, a heart of gold always. She still prays for your forgiveness, regarding her early passing, but she is now one contented lady and full of smiles not only for you, but also for others. She oozes charm and perpetual warmth. You know instinctively when she is around.

"Marrows, something to give you pleasure once again. You are a keen grower. Again take your time.

"Your finances are low, but coming up. You will have more money in your pocket after April 2002 to September and next year. A final deal is to be sorted. The finances – there is a cut off point – and there will be no more after that and then a new deal is to come in whereby you can produce again. We need for you to be up and running smoothly, but also securely.

"You read many books, but don't look at them too closely, as your own guides are your wisdom behind you. Work – you can take it or leave it. Leave it to us to prepare you further.

"You need to meet and fall in love again – dare I say it, you are wasting away. Give us time to bring in a special lady to you and see just how you handle her. She is not a million miles away from you. Allow us to set the reins in motion and bring her forth into your life.

"Go in peace."

It was an excellent sitting and although there are a few items that I have taken out because they are not relevant to this story all was of the highest quality. The only thing that I couldn't take was the name of Marion. Jenny had asked me if I knew anyone in Spirit called Marion and I had to say I didn't. Jenny and I said goodbye and as I left I was drawn to the name of her road. It was Sidmouth Road. Now here was a Spirit joke. Angela had told me that my new companion would come from Devonshire. Sidmouth was and still is a holiday resort in Devonshire. Now Jenny Eales lived on a crossroads. I was then drawn to the name of the other road. It was Marion Crescent!

I was clearly told, "This was the cross on the map. You won't understand it yet but this is where you are meant to be."

I was confused! It felt a little bit like coming out of deep trance sometimes – still a little muzzy. I drove home carefully, pondering on the sitting.

Thursday, 23rd August 2001

I spoke to Veronica and Monty tonight. Monty asked me if I was going to the Society for Psychical Research Conference at Cambridge next month and told me about it. I knew I was meant to go. I would go. Veronica told me that Jenny has spoken well of me and that she too would be at the conference. I said that I had been impressed by her sitting through Mustafa. Veronica said that she would very much appreciate being telephoned and told this as it would boost her confidence.

After my meditation I telephoned Jenny. We had had many life experiences in common and without listing them here I feel that she is another person who has deliberately been brought into my life by the Spirit World. Whatever happens I can learn a lot from her and I hope we shall have more time together discussing our work and knowledge of the Spirit World and the Creator's Kingdom.

Jenny said that she was feeling very tired and would I send her healing. I went into the Sanctuary and asked the workers with the gold and silver healing rays to send Jenny healing and would they do it in such a way that she knew that it came through me. This would be good evidence and also it will improve my confidence.

I had been very interested that I had been told that my new beloved would come from Devonshire. Jenny lived in Sidmouth Road and during the reading I was given the name of Marion – the next road to Jenny's road was Marion Crescent. Was this just coincidence? I had learned that there was no such thing in the World of Spirit. So watch this space!

Friday, 24th August 2001

Libby also said that 23rd August would seem like any other day, but that in retrospect it would be seen to be very important. Well, if it was what I felt it was, then I understand

and concurred. On 22nd August I didn't feel it was Jenny who was intended for me, but after our conversation on the telephone I was not so sure! Mustafa said that the new love in my life was not a million miles away! She wasn't. My guides have told me that it was very soon and sooner than I thought. Just before going to bed I was moved to reflect on what the Master had told me in last night's sitting.

"There is much for you to do, my son and as we have promised, you will not be alone. God blesses you for your work, for your love and for your enthusiasm. <u>So, my friend it is not surprising that we will bring earthly love into your heart again.</u> Your beloved, who is with us, is joyful that you shall not be alone and shall enjoy the earthly pleasures of each other and <u>you will live your earthly lives together, as an open advertisement of the truth of goodness, love and life.</u>

"<u>Soon my son</u>... soon, relax and be at peace, for we will not let you down because you work with us."

As I went to bed I accidentally touched the wind chimes and they rang. I heard a voice say, "Wedding bells?" All evening I have heard "Ask her out to dinner"! I telephoned Jenny and asked her if she ever did crazy and unpredictable things. If she did, I told her answerphone, would she call me back? Shortly, she telephoned back and said that she did sometimes, so I asked her out to dinner and to my great pleasure she said that she would like that. So as I said earlier, watch this space...

I was just thinking that it was a shame that Linda, a friend of mine who lost her husband at Christmas, would be in America so that I couldn't stay with her before and after the Society for Psychical Research Conference at Cambridge in September. Then a thought flashed across my mind. "Offer to drive Jenny up to Cambridge!" I am a Dumbo. I hadn't thought of that, but clearly Spirit had.

Tuesday, 28ᵗʰ August 2001

I arrived back at Betty Grove Farm after attending a spiritual weekend in Paignton in Devonshire. There was also a message from Jenny Eales, who gave me the reading last week to say that she had booked a table for us to have dinner together on Tuesday, 4ᵗʰ September. Jenny lived at Orpington and my birth certificate registers my birth at Chislehurst only a few miles away.

Veronica and I had thought that as Jenny was travelling up with them to Cambridge and I felt that I was told to ask her if I could take her to Cambridge next month that we could all travel up together. It would be wonderful to have my new friends, Veronica and Monty and Jenny with me. I felt so close to them that I knew that I must take these new friends as a gift and feel the wonders of the Spirit World at work. God bless them.

I miss a beloved very much at this time to share my excitement at these wondrous revelations that I am experiencing. I greatly look forward with excitement to sitting with my Spirit friends, the loved ones and the beloveds. However I must relearn patience. I am so excited by all the proofs and wonders that are happening to me at the moment.

I was alone, in earthly terms, but I had so many wonderful loved ones and beloveds around me. I want to shout what has happened from the roof tops or at least share them with an earthly beloved, but I shall wait and have patience and joy by myself. I will talk to those who come to me tonight at eight thirty in my Sanctuary and not before because I have, I know, earthly work to do, which was set aside for this week.

One thing that occurred to me at this time was that since my darling Libby went home to the World of Spirit before me my life has never been dull! Since Thursday, 16th August of this year my life direction in earthly terms and my very being have changed so dramatically. What was so especially wonderful was that it all made sense, even when I got it wrong it was made to be more understandable and my enlightenment increased to give the wisdom that I needed to think clearly enough to understand great revelations about the true universe and beyond. For example I was just beginning to understand the real God, who was within and not without.

Jenny and I spoke for an hour tonight on the telephone. I am beginning to feel a strong attachment towards her. I will say no more.

Wednesday, 29th August 2001

Jenny telephoned me at one point in the morning to ask if I had astral travelled during the night. I said I didn't know but I had slept very soundly.

"Would you ask your guides?" she said.

"I certainly will ask them tonight."

Apparently Jenny had experienced my breath on the sensitive area below her neck at the top of her spine. She had clearly seen my face and this morning she was completely recharged in every cell of her body.

"I haven't felt so alive for ages," she said.

I said that I would ask my guides tonight, but while I was looking for a file I found myself in the Sanctuary. I heard Angela say, "Of course you were there. Didn't you ask for proof?"

Thursday, 30ᵗʰ August 2001

Last night Angela's message about Jenny and I moved me greatly and I have put her words and some of my own in an envelope, only to be opened by Jenny should I ever hurt her. I pray that she will never read it.

I had been very happy about my meeting with Jenny and our telephone conversations. However, because she was giving a clairvoyance demonstration tonight, we had agreed that I would not telephone her until tomorrow evening. As I was typing up my Sanctuary notes I was finding that there was a new lesson that I have to learn. I will be disciplined and not telephone her until Friday evening, but I was finding it difficult.

This was not just that I wished I could talk to her and I missed her laugh and her company, but I would give my eye teeth to know that she was safely back home. I was realising a forgotten truth in the realms of courtship and falling in love. There is also a painful side and a responsibility. It was at eleven fifty that evening that I suddenly realised that I sensed and smelt the presence of Jenny right there with me to my front right. It was the first time that I had enjoyed this treat.

When I first started out on my known path in the pursuit of spiritual knowledge, I questioned everything! Rarely could I prove anything and then suddenly one day I realised that I no longer believed my wife was in Spirit. **I knew**.

That for me at least was a quantum leap. **I knew**.

The more I put my trust and faith on the line the more **I knew**.

Friday, 31ˢᵗ August 2001

I did telephone Jenny to hear if she was safely home after her clairvoyance demonstration last night, but I could only leave a message on her answerphone. Then I had a sudden memory flash. The last time I had spoken to Jenny, which was Wednesday evening, I had said, referring to the out of body healing, it's your turn to come to me! (Joke!) My goodness she did just that. Last night she came here at eleven fifty and I know that that was her presence. Wow!

Jenny telephoned me back. So she was safely home and last night's clairvoyance demonstration was brilliant she said. Last night at eleven-fifty she was relaxing in bed looking up Capricorns in an astrology book, so there was a link there.

She said, "You missed me yesterday. You wanted to speak to me?"

This was absolutely right. It was good being linked to a medium – unless of course you're up to no good! That would never apply to Jenny. I could only be up to good with her in my life. She also told me that I should have somebody to look after me while I was in trance and to give me healing afterwards. I said I was open to offers and she laughed. We will talk about it again tonight.

I felt that I was being told to send a card to Jenny. I looked around the card display in a local shop. At first I couldn't find it and then there it was in front of me. I was just turning away when it caught my eye. It was of a bear standing amongst some flowers, looking up at a pink butterfly and his balloon floating away. The words were 'Thinking of You'. The rhyme came easily into my mind so that was probably heaven sent too!

THE CARD

I saw this card and thought of you,
The butterfly is pink, but I am blue.
Free Spirit, you know what is best
I'm amply filled, but very blessed.

I know one day the bells will chime
And then I will have made you mine.
All I want to do is give you love,
With directions from the ones above.

They know the road that we should take.
We hesitate when we're awake,
But in the night, I came to you
With love and a healing breath or two.

When I said, "It is your turn
To come to me before the morn."
Your presence came to me, I know.
Will you marry me before the snow?

I know that we must surely wait
Until with certainty we mate,
But I will wait until you're ready
And I can be your loving teddy.

From a loving bear called Michael.

Saturday, 1st September 2001

As I was driving back from taking a friend to Gatwick Airport I had several pieces of confirmation. First there was the sight of two silver streamers (maybe vapour trails, but it didn't matter) falling to earth but getting closer together. They did not meet or join together because Jenny and I are not yet joined together, but we are getting closer.

I was drawn to the registration letters of the car in front of me. It was GOX. Oh there's nothing in that one, I thought to myself. Then a flash – go kiss, it was alright to kiss Jenny. That was most wonderful – yes! I asked Mustafa, Jenny's wonderful guide, to help me to look after Jenny and never hurt her in any way. He answered me later, when I was on the telephone to Jenny, with the words, "It's all going to be alright. Don't panic." God bless him.

On the way back from Gatwick I felt that if I approached a certain traffic light I would go over on green if everything were alright. I got within sight of the traffic light and it was green, so I found myself thinking that it would never stay green until I got through it, but it did and it was green and God bless them!

When I got back Jenny telephoned me to thank me for a tape I had sent her. It had amused her, but she also told me that our communications about unconditional love were incomplete. She was at a very low emotional level and was completely exhausted. She was worn out. She wanted me to know what I was taking on. I asked her to ask Mustafa when she could have some time to recharge her batteries for further work by having a holiday. Jenny consulted her diary and said that it couldn't be before November. We agreed to a holiday between the beginning of November and my trip to Florida to the Cherokee Powwow on Tuesday, 20th November.

Jenny told me that she had known of somebody coming into her life to help her about a year ago, but she wasn't emotionally ready and so it was put off. Now Jenny had only told three people about the man to come into her life. They were Veronica, Montague and another friend and for the time being we were going to keep it that way. I had told my friends about it but that is different. Jenny and I understand that she didn't want the pressure of people saying, "Is this it? Is it going alright?"

You can imagine that she can do without that pressure. She gives and it is now her turn to receive and I will teach her that if I may and I will try and protect her from all things that could possibly bring her unhappiness and hurt. I was now just beginning to appreciate what I had been told about the responsibilities that were being placed upon me. I thought that these were about my work and certainly my work includes Jenny and she was now my responsibility. I was overwhelmed by thoughts of Jenny before retiring to bed and was inspired to produce these poems.

THE PINK FLOWER

Wear a pink flower for me to let me know you care,
That symbolic little gesture to show your love's still there.
If ever you have no pink flower, then take my heart instead
And wear that, my sweetest darling, for our love is never dead.

JENNY

Just as perfect as a soul can be
Entrancing as the beauteous leafy tree
Naked as the glorious flowers of spring
Natural as the bubbling waters sing
Youthful, lithe and loving as the humble bee

There's nothing as sweet as Jenny, nor will there ever be.

MICHAEL

Michael, may he to Jenny be,
In love with her through all eternity.
Creating for her gifts of love,

Housed in golden wrappings from above.
All coated with the silver strand of life
Eternally given free of thanks,
Love of no boundary or banks.

TOMORROW IS ANOTHER DAY

If I lived a million miles away
I'd always find the words to say,
Sleep well my love, tomorrow is another day,
And I will see you then, hip-hip-hurray!

A Sonnet called
JENNY

Jenny, by any other name is fair.
She gives until the cupboard's almost bare.
She takes the punishment for others on herself,
And smiles through the agony of pain itself.
She gets her guidance from her guide above
And gives to everyone she meets, the hand of love.
Compassion is always in her eyes,
It's only when alone, she cries.
She asks for nothing for herself.
Even when there's nothing left upon the shelf.
Now she lives her saintly life alone, through love,
Never taking, for she's unique – a dove.
But there's one who's come to support her every bone
So that Jenny from now on, will never stand alone.

Sleep well sweetheart.

Sunday, 2nd September 2001

It's a quarter to one and after sending an email to Jenny with the poems I went to bed.

Later I took Jenny to a hall near Maidstone for her clairvoyant demonstration this evening. It was the first time I had seen her work on the 'platform' and I must say that I was very impressed with her and her guide Mustafa. However halfway through I knew that I had to go outside. I hesitated because I didn't want to appear rude to Jenny, but it was made very clear that I should go. I walked through the crematorium nearby reading the messages on the tombstones and thinking how sad it was that they didn't know the truth of everlasting life.

I felt Libby there at the far end and I walked towards her and she told me that she was going to withdraw more from me although she would always be with me in spirit. Because now I had found the person who was to take my earthly love and she would not be watching as we were together and made love.

Monday, 3rd September 2001

At one thirty this morning I left Jenny and drove back from Orpington to Betty Grove Farm. I left her in the pouring rain, but I knew that everything that I had been promised was true and that Libby had given me the greatest present that a woman can give to the man she loves – the love of another woman.

THE POURING RAIN

**I left her in the pouring rain
Outside her door from whence she came
But nothing could dampen my joy at heart
Where my returnéd love did start.**

Her lips as sweet as honey dew
Meet mine and quickly threw
My heart beat into realms anew
And made my balanced view askew.

She knew I loved her from the start
There's nothing false inside her heart
It was so clear we'd both be true
But I had to say those words that I love you.

She knew of course that this was so
She couldn't fail to see the glow
Inside my heart and through my eyes
That nothing known to man nor woman could disguise.

And so I left her in the early morn
Where confirmation of our love was born
It will proceed at steady pace
And so, I know we need not race.

It is truly love in which we're bound
Blessed by Spirit so profound
Was put in place so long ago
We waited and found this was so.

Both of us are truly blessed
With such a gift to manifest
Clearly in each other's eyes
Where love without condition lies.

Sleep well my love, for now it is another day
And on the morrow will again hold sway
And share together a few more precious hours
Bedecked by all the colours of the flowers.

When we're together the petals are so sweet
And they will keep us healed until it's time again to meet.
They wrap us in a cloak of love to show
We're surrounded and protected by God's rainbow.

But with all these colours, when we stop to think,
The greatest one of all is pink.
It is surely manufactured in the heart
By letting unconditional love simply play its part.

We have no need of promises, to swear that we'll be true
It is already written in the records of the few,
Who are blessed by their Creator, who will raise them
high above
By giving to His children His unconditional love.

Thank you my darling Jenny, for all you give to me
I thought that it was to be my job to always give to thee
But you my darling Jenny give me the opportunity To
look into the future of what is writ for you and me.

I see that we will spend our life in perfect harmony
I see that we will find there also much tranquillity
But I also know that I have a great responsibility

As you entrust your delicate heart to me
I will with joy accept it through serendipity.

I woke up at a quarter past eleven and made straight for the coffee! I checked my email just in case there was another piece of magic, but no. I was then advised that I should check my answerphone and so I did. Unbelievably there was a message from my love asking me if I would keep 19th and 20th January free. She said that she would explain later. Oh, such joy my life is full again.

I telephoned Veronica, who was exhausted after entertaining friends from Amsterdam over the weekend. I thanked her for bringing Jenny and I together and she told me that she knew she had to in Ayr. She had looked everywhere for me on the last day and finally saw me out of the corner of her eye talking to somebody outside. Veronica said also that she had forecast the flowers arriving when she was talking to Jenny at nine o'clock on the morning of Wednesday, 29th August. She had told Jenny that she would not be alone at their Wedding on 23rd September and promptly asked me to come to the wedding with her. This got more wonderful every moment.

I have decided to ask Jenny to marry me at the wedding of Veronica Ford and Montague Keen on Sunday, 23rd September 2001. This will be a month after I knew that Jenny was my Heaven Sent Lady of Love. Jenny can have the longest engagement that she may wish to have, but I want to put a ring on her finger as a symbolic statement that our lives were settled now that we were together and our love was there for all to see.

Last night with Jenny was so wonderful. It was like watching and feeling your life on a video. You have seen it before and you know the outcome but you have to watch the bits that come in order. The fast forward was not an option. You just sit and enjoy the moment without the slightest concern that the ending would be different from the one you knew.

I went into my Sanctuary and thanked the Great Creator for the wonderful gift of Jenny and then asked for love, healing and energy to be given to Veronica. After I had sat down again at my desk I was told that I should send healing to her and so I did. I felt my warm hands tingle as I sat for sometime. I have no idea how long.

I was going into Wokingham this afternoon to buy a book of love poems to say thank you to Veronica for introducing Jenny into my life, but my car keys had disappeared. I also had discovered that the second poem that I put on tape on the way home last night is not there either! Jenny and I had a chat this afternoon. Oh the wonder of it all. She has asked me if it would be alright to change the booking of a single room for a double room for Veronica and Monty's wedding weekend on the 23ʳᵈ. I was pleased to say that that would be fine with me.

We are planning to spend Christmas together and she has my birthday on 27ᵗʰ clear for us to be together. Jenny has confirmed that she would be able to stay with me at my mother's cottage in Shenington, Oxfordshire from Saturday, 29ᵗʰ December 2001 to Saturday, 5ᵗʰ January 2002. I had been invited to accompany Jenny to Husbands Bosworth in Leicestershire for a 25ᵗʰ Wedding Anniversary Party weekend. Next June we are to go to Toronto for the 27ᵗʰ World Congress of the International Spiritualist Federation.

I sat in my Sanctuary this evening and thanked my Creator for Jenny. As Angela was talking to me there was a very clear bird's call of a Jenny Wren. That was wonderful and very special and I thanked my friends for it.

Tuesday, 4ᵗʰ September 2001

In the early hours I wrote down a poem for Jenny called Visualisation. It was personal and not to be reproduced in these pages. It was about a visualisation that I had about her lying in bed asleep. She telephoned me early this morning to ask if I was having thoughts about her at one o'clock this morning. I was of course and she felt them. I read her the poem so she knew what I was thinking. This is yet another piece of clear evidence that we were brought together spiritually. I know this to be a fact. Jenny knows this to be a fact. Our guides and loved ones in the Spirit World know that this was a fact. We do not need the world to know that it was a fact – but they will!

I must record that I never thought that it was possible to love someone as much as I loved Libby, but now there is Jenny. In case anybody thinks that this is unfair or disrespectful to Libby they are wrong. It is the greatest compliment to her for she has brought it all about. God bless her.

I left Betty Grove Farm at five o'clock to drive to Orpington, where I was to collect Jenny and take her out to dinner tonight. This was actually our first date. It will be the third time that we have met and it was wonderful that we both knew that this was it! It was what we had been waiting for and what we had been told to expect. We had spent much time on the telephone, sending and receiving emails and in spiritual terms I had visited her and she had visited me.

There was absolutely no doubt that we were going to marry and live our lives in peace and love and harmony, working for the Great Divine as an advertisement as to how mankind should live together and it was going to be wonderful, absolutely wonderful. Jenny was very pleased with the carnations that I had sent to her. They were of course pink carnations, her favourite flower and colour. There were twenty-two as we met on the twenty second. I had missed this but Spirit hadn't.

She said, "Oh you have been busy today!"

"No," I replied, "I ordered those last week to be delivered today for our first date."

I could, of course only speak from my point of view but Libby had chosen a lady for me to live and work with and her choice could not have been more perfect. I had a long telephone conversation with Veronica this afternoon. She was still not well and needs more absent healing, which Jenny and I will give her together from Orpington. Veronica had told me that Jenny was on cloud nine. I didn't know what number cloud I was on but it was pretty high!

As I drove on there was very clearly a very large turtle in the clouds above with the message that this was the speed I was being told to go at. God bless them. If they told me to go backwards I'd go backwards!

"I believe in you. You're the one who made my dreams come true."

We had a splendid dinner together at Guests Restaurant in Hayes and we were very happy together. Jenny drove my Green Goddess home, effortlessly and well. Tonight we slept together. It was wonderful.

Wednesday, 5th September 2001
This morning I reflected on the wonderment and love that we have for each other. It was very, very special of course. Alastair, Jenny's son and his girl friend didn't appear to have a problem with us at all. I was delighted and very happy this wonderful Wednesday morning.

Sunday, 9th September 2001
I had been invited to join Jenny at Husbands Bosworth, where she was staying with friends. I arrived at twelve thirty and I enjoyed meeting them. We had a late lunch and then sat in circle together. I followed Jenny down the M1 and round the M25 back to Orpington.

Tuesday, 11th September 2001
I took the diamond engagement ring into a Banbury jeweller for cleaning and checking.

Friday, 14th September 2001

Jenny and I drove up to collect Veronica and Monty from Totteridge and then we all drove up to Cambridge for the Society for Psychical Research Annual Conference. We stayed in a Bed and Breakfast nearby where we made love and enjoyed each other. We walked into Clare College each morning to attend the conference.

Saturday, 15th September 2001

We spent some time walking through Cambridge and its gardens, taking photographs and enjoying each other's company. The conference was worthwhile and we enjoyed the whole weekend.

Thursday, 20th September 2001

I collected the ring I had taken into the Banbury jeweller for cleaning and checking of the settings prior to proposing to Jenny. I am now ready for the weekend.

Friday, 21st September 2001

After packing and domestic tasks we drove to the hotel at Elstree in North London, where the wedding of Veronica Ford to Montague Keen was to take place. In the evening I took Jenny to the Hen Night at Totteridge, while I went with Montague and his neighbour and relative, called Geoffrey, for an Italian meal at Alfresco's in Whetstone. It was a lovely enjoyable evening and later we joined the ladies for liqueurs. Then we returned to Elstree.

Saturday, 22nd September 2001

Jenny and I drove up to the Rugby Independent Spiritualist Church for a demonstration of healing by members of the Harry Edwards Sanctuary at Shere in Surrey.

Ray Branch and his wife Joan were extremely good and gave a superb example of spiritual healing done at the highest level.

Sunday, 23rd September 2001

We swam in the hotel pool and then had a Jacuzzi, sauna and a shower before getting ready for the wedding. Everything went well. During the bridegroom's speech I was given a thirty-second slot to prove that Veronica was a matchmaker by my proposing to Jenny. I quote here from the video tape of the occasion.

Montague Keen, "She is also a match maker and for this purpose I will give a demonstration of people that have not heard of each other, have not known each other even a few weeks ago are already on the point of matrimony. If you do not believe me I shall call on Michael Ayers to prove it. Michael, you have thirty seconds from now."

"Mr and Mrs. Keen, Ladies and Gentlemen, the bridegroom as you heard has given me thirty seconds to prove without doubt that his wonderful wife is a match maker *par excellence*. Only last month up in Ayr in Scotland, I was told that I had to go and meet a certain young lady and on 22nd August I met a very charming, very lovely and very talented medium called Jenny. Stand up Jenny.

"This Ladies and Gentlemen is Jenny. My proof Ladies and Gentlemen comes in three parts. Firstly, Jenny, will you take my unconditional love?"

"Yes, darling," said Jenny.
"Secondly, will you take my name?"
"Yes," said Jenny.

> **"And thirdly, will you wear this for
> me? Whichever finger it goes on."**
> **"That one," said Jenny quickly. "Oh
> my goodness."**
> **"Will you marry me Jenny? Will you
> be my wife?"**
> **"Yes," said my beloved Jenny and
> this was followed by wonderful applause
> while we kissed.**
> **"Well done, Michael," said Montague.**
> **"Well, that's proof."**

"Oh goodness," said Jenny and I was extremely happy with my new fiancée.

We received many congratulations and good wishes. Afterwards, as Jenny went upstairs to change for the dancing, Libby came and referring to the ring said to her, *"I wanted you to have that."* We danced and enjoyed the evening, but, not surprisingly, were tired and ready for bed by the end of the proceedings.

Tuesday, 25ᵗʰ September 2001

I felt a bit better after the night's sleep and so I got up at about seven thirty and made us some lemon tea. I was reflecting on the wonders of Jenny in the bathroom when I heard Libby say, *"I wouldn't have sent you anybody less. You deserve her. Handle her gently, look after her and use her well."*

Wednesday, 26ᵗʰ September 2001

Jenny was beginning to show definite signs, as Mustafa has predicted, of being on a higher cloud than nine.

Friday, 28ᵗʰ September 2001

This morning Jenny told me that she loved me very much and that it was beginning to hurt. She didn't ever want to share me as her lover and husband. I know the feeling well. It was my turn to try and keep my feet on the ground and help her through this exquisite pain of true love. I had experienced this so much from so early in our relationship. As sensitives we felt emotions so much more strongly and love was no exception. We were unable to play at it. It was total, complete and demanding. We wished for no cure. We enjoyed every pain of ecstasy. We couldn't think clearly, we stumbled, we forgot but never the love. We could not give our full attention to anything else. We always wanted more than we had of each other. A kiss needed to be longer, a caress a little lighter and then much stronger, a continued desire of taking your loved one and incorporating the both into a single being of absolute love.

Saturday, 29ᵗʰ September 2001

We left at eight o'clock and drove round the M25 in heavy rain and spray, arriving at Honeysuckle Cottage at about twenty minutes past ten. The visitors had left everything in very good order and so there was time to show Jenny round. She loved the cottage, my mother's home and we were looking forward to spending seven days and nights there over the New Year period. After lunch at the Bell Inn I drove us to Chipping Campden and we walked through the town and its beautiful church and church yard. We were so very much in love and Jenny announced in St John's Church that we had to get married in church.

We then drove to the Rollright Stones and after asking if we could enter, we stood in the centre and enjoyed the energies and atmosphere. Then Jenny suggested that we walked round the circle of stones and tried to pick up messages or energies that might be available to us. At each stone Jenny was given a message and afterwards we tried to put down all that we had been told. Those that we could remember are recorded. The messages we received from the stones were wonderful. We stood together in the centre of this stone circle and I gave our thanks for being allowed to come in and also for the messages. We left with a final word of thanks and our intention to return together.

After driving home to Orpington, Jenny told me that she would not be able to live without me and I know that I couldn't live without her. We are deeply and totally in love and enjoying every second of it so we had dinner and went to bed.

Sunday, 30th September 2001

What a wonderful day! It was raining most of the time but we got up for meals and spent the rest of the time in bed. Jenny told me this morning that I am a young spirit with much purity.

Before closing this month's chapter, I felt that it was only right to record what Jenny and I felt and discussed together. We were totally at peace and in harmony because we knew that our meeting and relationship was Spirit sent. We loved each other madly. What more could we ask for? We were two sensitives in love and our lovemaking had taken us into higher realms than either of us have ever experienced or reached before. I loved and adored Jenny. I loved her mind, her body and her spirituality with a hunger and thirst that I had not experienced before. This was not a reflection on anybody else that I had loved, because it had never been on such a footing of spiritual enlightenment before.

It was a great passion, which had only an equal in my desire for spiritual food and drink. I was doubly blessed and thanked my Creator for the two greatest gifts that it is surely possible to receive and when the time was right we should work for the Great Divine through our guides and loved ones. Spirit was our guide and mentor and we were privileged to have been chosen for each other and for the work to come.

Chapter 10

THE PREPARATION

Mustafa told us in a sitting, **"A love match seen by no other for quite some time, you are indeed both truly blessed and we in Spirit are more than happy for the pair of you. We know that you two will have a very full and enchanting life together, full of laughs, disagreements on facts, but not between yourselves only on outside influence. This I must stress only. You have both of you a rare compatibility and this will become more apparent as the months and years go by.**

"Your home will have magnificent splendour, both inside and out. We know that this will be your final resting-place and therefore it has to be just right. We will instruct Michael to find it and he will be over the moon with its location. You Jenny will have to get used to it as it will be a little off the beaten track but not in the middle of nowhere. So just wait patiently for that time approaching. We will instruct Michael through his own mediumship so be aware to link in with us for the relative

direction and information given. You, dear sir will be over the moon.

"A price comparable to both your pockets with sufficient money to extract for your immediate needs. There will be sufficient funds for the pair of you. So if you do feel like spending a little more than usual, we do not wish you both to concern yourselves as all will be replenished in the right time."

Thursday, 4th October 2001

Jenny drove us up to the Society for Psychical Research lecture at Kensington, London for a lecture given by Montague Keen. We had supper at Dino's and we gave a lift to Marion Ellison to collect her car from Beckenham station. She was the wife of the late Professor Arthur J. Ellison, who was a distinguished voice in paranormal research and twice President of the SPR.

In Beckenham Road, while it was dark and pouring with rain, the near side tyre touched a piece of jutting out curb stone and sent us on a collision course with an oncoming car. Jenny and I were taken to Bromley Hospital and the others to Lewisham Hospital.

Discussing the accident later, Jenny and I both experienced a gap in time from seeing the car that was to hit us until after the impact. The accident was foreseen by the Spirit World but we were not meant to die in it and were saved by an angel, who took us out of body just before impact.

Jenny lost her sight temporarily and also received a badly bruised sternum and a broken right wrist. She was treated for shock. Later an X-ray showed a broken left wrist and also the scaphoid bone as well. I had badly bruised ribs. I was treated for shock by the roadside after I felt sick and nearly fainted and in the ambulance they put me on oxygen until about two o'clock that morning. Jenny was kept in overnight for further X-rays and I was sent home by taxi, arriving back at three in the morning.

Friday, 5ᵗʰ October 2001

I typed up the journal and felt weak and unhappy that I wasn't with Jenny. It is our first real trial. Jenny had never had an accident in her car before and I had never had treatment before being rushed to hospital. We had planned to go to the Lake District later today but that will have to be put on pause. It was also the first time we have been parted overnight since our love grew into a mad passion and we would miss each other greatly.

I woke up at eight fifteen. I lay for sometime on the bed trying to work out the best way to get up with the minimum of pain! I cancelled Jenny's appointment, the only one in her diary for today fortunately and then telephoned Veronica with the news. She would find out what happened to Marion. Sadly I still had my cough after the head cold and that doesn't make my bruised ribs anymore comfortable. I still felt rather shocked and I wanted to be with Jenny but I had to wait for her call from the hospital to say that I could come to her and bring her home.

What a leveller! We had been so happy together and now the cloud of last night filled my mind. Libby had come and spoken to me in the hospital and she explained that it was simply an accident. There were no fatalistic reasons for it – simply an accident. In other words there was no blame. I didn't know what to do with myself. I just sat in front of the computer drinking lemon tea. At last Jenny telephoned to say that I could come and collect her from the hospital. Alastair, her son, came with me and my poor darling Jenny looked so white and drawn. At least we were alive and only bruised except that Jenny had a broken wrist. However the bruising was very deep and we were told it would take two weeks to come out!

I was able to help Jenny in some ways such as putting the toothpaste on the toothbrush for her, washing her in the shower but we managed to cook the dinner between us and I could wash up. In general Jenny was better off lying down and I was better off standing up! Her injuries were to the left hand side and mine were to the right.

Wednesday, 10ᵗʰ October 2001

In our sitting today Mustafa told us, **"The crash came at an unfortunate time for the pair of you. It really wasn't there to strengthen the pair of you as this was already intact, but it had to happen anyway. The reasons were a cleansing of the past and the final shutting off of both your doors so that you have your own cementing blocks and this is what was required.**

"This cementing will hold you up for all time and no one now can judge or pull you apart ever. The dye and bond is now cast permanently and this is why we needed this ordeal to bring you both as a united force – impregnable for all time with this common bond, which has not shaken you but strengthened your resolve together. No amount of force now can ever tear you two apart. The cement/bond is solid and secure.

"We have adjusted the pain barrier so that you can manage for a time. Never forget you both are in a great need of rest

and recuperation. The holiday romance
will be the blessing on you both from us in
Spirit and also from Libby herself. She
above all wanted this break away for you
both. You will be perfectly happy together
as she smiles lovingly on.

"No faults just romance – please be
careful of the good food. Camels – perhaps
leave to another time. I think it would be
wiser."

Friday, 12ᵗʰ October 2001

Neither of us slept well but the pain was beginning to
diminish at last. I got up at six o'clock with a cough that was
disturbing Jenny and outside the window we could hear a
Jenny Wren singing. There was a great deal to be done before
we could go to Lanzarote for our first romantic holiday, but
we would do things together and so everything was more of
a joy and less of a chore.

I took Jenny back to Bromley Hospital for her visit to
the Fracture Clinic. The news was encouraging and the
specialist was pleased with the amount of grip she could
achieve. The splint and the sling had been dispensed with
and Jenny now had a wrist brace. A further visit was planned
for five weeks time after we return from holiday in Lanzarote.

Saturday, 20ᵗʰ October 2001

I joined The International Spiritualist Federation
today and sent off my application to attend the
ISF 27ᵗʰ World Congress in Toronto, Canada next June with
Jenny as my wife.

Sunday, 21ˢᵗ October 2001

My healing guide, a wonderful North American Indian Chief, gave Jenny healing using me as his instrument. I could feel the gentle power and warmth through my hands. I could only hear clairaudiently very faint instructions and I asked if they could be made louder. I was told that they would be in time, but I was only at the beginning and this would take time.

I moved forward and took Jenny's hands and wrists for healing warmth and later under her left breast. I felt the power and I was asked to go deeper and felt I was taken into light trance.

Afterwards I said, "Thank you my friend."

My guide replied, **"You don't have to thank me. It is enough that you use me. We will work much together and we will develop you so that we can use you as a trance healer. You will never be taken right out and will always know what we are doing through you. You will, my friend, develop into a well-known healer as well as working to bring the words of Spirit to those who will listen. Yes, you will travel all over the world with your beloved Jenny and be assured that your beloved in Spirit, Libby, will always be with you. You are both very close and it is a measure of your love that she is and will work with both Jenny and yourself over many years of your time.**

"We, in Spirit, are overjoyed with the way that you and Jenny are cementing yourselves into one unit as you develop

**your gifts and patiently build up your
strength for the great amount of work that
is before you. Worry not about the hows
and the wherefores, we will take care of
that. It is enough that you allow this work
to be done through you. Enjoy each other
and you will be given all you need to
complete the tasks ahead of you.**

**"Go in peace and rest as much as you
are able. We will work out the nuts and
bolts for you to work as a smooth well oiled
machine together. God bless you both. Be
at peace."**

"Thank you my friend and take our love and blessings."

It rained all day today and Jenny and I have busied
ourselves making new appointments for Jenny's clients who
had to be put off because of the accident. I was typing out a
sitting that Mustafa had given to Jenny about her son Alastair
and as I emptied the ashtray I reflected that it belonged
formerly to Jenny's father.

I heard him say,

**"I am pleased for you to have it. You
will I know look after my little darling girl
rather well and I know that you will love
her and take care of her always. You are a
good man and I know you have been chosen
with great care to look after each other.**

**"You see I have spoken with Libby.
Yes, I also know that she is your inspiration,
Michael. She has worked very hard to see
you settled and now you are. It is
imperative that you and my little Jenny**

work well together. There is far more at stake than either of you can possibly think. One day you will both see how important it is that you form together a great working and loving relationship.

"I can only sit back and watch. Greater loved ones than me have it all in hand and you are both well guided. So go on your way my son, for you are indeed my son now that you are at one with my little Jenny, Michael.

"I give you my love and I will see that whatever I can do for you both is done. May God bless you and guide you together in complete love on Earth that I never truly found. Be at peace together."

I had finished typing and I thought of John.

"I love you John," I thought.

"I know you do Daddy. We'll talk when you are rested."

At bedtime Jenny gave me healing on my right side. I asked her where Sister Charlotte, her healing nun, lived on Earth. She told me that she lived in France although she didn't know where.

Sister Charlotte told me she came from Lourdes. She spent much time on her knees and also stretched out on the cold stones. That was where she learned her basic skills of healing. She told me that if we went there she would be happy to show us around. Jenny said that she was a nursing nun and had a beautiful face full of peace. I thought it must be easier within a nunnery to be at peace. Sister Charlotte told me that this wasn't necessarily so because there were different sorts of worries. Her healing was very effective and I felt much less pain in the night. I came downstairs to type these notes and she told me in answer to my thought that she lived there about two hundred years ago in our time scale.

"Healing must have been quite different?" I asked.

"Yes," she said. "We used God's herbs that he had sent us."

I thanked her and went back to bed.

Monday, 22nd October 2001

I am having to learn to be patient and allow Spirit to work things out in their own way as to what is best for me and not keep pushing for the action. Yesterday I received three messages without asking for them. Firstly, from my High Indian Chief, who is my healing guide. Secondly, from Jenny's father and thirdly, from Jenny's healing guide Sister Charlotte. Patience is its own reward. I am delighted to be so honoured.

Friday, 26th October 2001

Tonight Jenny leant me a book. It was called Bury My Heart at Wounded Knee by Dee Brown. It was all about the downfall of the Native American Indians and has a picture of Red Cloud and a chapter entitled Red Cloud's War. I was to take it to Lanzarote to read. It was perfect study for my trip to meet the Elders in Florida. I was very excited. I knew that it was Spirit sent and I will study it well.

Monday, 29th October 2001

It is dawn – six o'clock. An hour or so ago I was woken with a strong desire to caress Jenny. Together we made love but it was not to be an act of earthly fulfilment. It was spiritual. Afterwards Jenny told me that our souls touched. Jenny touched with the Divine. It was like two cells meeting. It was purity. She said she felt complete.

Wednesday, 31ˢᵗ October 2001

I don't propose to change my mind and give details of our love making, but the highs that we reached were certainly not down to me alone. We made wonderful meaningful love and I just need to record an example from this morning.

At one point Jenny said, "You are like a maestro conducting an orchestra. You know exactly what to do with my body."

Now I knew that when I made love I was not alone because I had a guide with me who, I had now proved to myself, gave me guidance as to what would give Jenny the most pleasure. This morning was a case in point.

"Put her arms down beside her," I heard.

"What good will that do," I thought. "It can't make any difference, but then they are usually right!"

As soon as I had done this a great sigh of pleasure escaped from Jenny's lips. I knew we were blessed and now I knew for certain that I was guided at certain points, usually later on in the experience and sometimes as to when to approach Jenny during the night. When I did as I was bid she was already on a sensitive high and our lovemaking took off as if all the groundwork had been done and we were completely ready and yearning for each other. A second before we touched we had no idea what wonders were so close by.

Later, much later, four years on in time, I read about Sacred Marriage and the joys and wonders of two spiritual people in love and perfect harmony reaching out towards God in the fulfilment of his love.

Thursday, 1ˢᵗ November 2001

The first day of our holiday is here at last. The alarm went off at six o'clock and we left Orpington at about half past seven for Gatwick Airport. We caught the eleven o'clock flight and arrived at Arrecife at ten past three in the afternoon.

At five o'clock I was looking out over the white washed buildings with green shutters, the landmarks of Lanzarote and the palm trees looking east beyond the sea towards Africa and the Sahara Desert. We found sand on our balcony that had been blown there from the desert on the easterly wind. We dined on the balcony eating sardine sandwiches and drinking local red wine. It was a wonderful romantic evening of love.

Wednesday, 14ᵗʰ November 2001

We hired a little manual VW Polo and I drove Jenny around the island. The weather started with a beautiful blue sky with small white puffy clouds and the sea was also blue and inviting. The temperature outside the hotel was a pleasant twenty-five degrees centigrade but it felt cooler because of the gentle wind coming off the island.

We drove north up the centre of the island to see the breathtaking views from the Mirador del Rio, where we had lunch. When Jenny and I left the entrance, I had a very strong conviction that when Jenny and I married I was to be released from my vow to always wear Libby's wedding ring in her memory, which I had made at her passing and still wore the wedding ring with my signet ring. It was so strong and overwhelming that I know that it came from Libby. So on my wedding day next spring I shall take off Libby's ring and wear a wedding ring for Jenny. The feeling that I was given, which came from absolutely nowhere, was a complete and utter conviction that when Jenny and I married I was to know that she and I were married as if for the one and only time. We were living in the now and this union was all that mattered.

This was the second time that I had driven a left-hand car in Spain. The first was on honeymoon with Libby, some eighteen years ago when I drove from Valencia towards a villa near Alicante and now with Jenny on our first holiday together, which to us is our first honeymoon.

Thursday, 15th November 2001

We awoke together at about eight o'clock and not surprisingly we made love on our last morning here.

Jenny then told me, **"During the night I had this dream where I saw Alastair in a wedding outfit of a grey suit with tails and he was smiling nicely and he shook hands with Michael, who was also smiling. The mood was sober and in order. So although things are in place they are not sorted out yet and there is perhaps urgency now to get arrangements at least sorted out. What was wonderful for me to see Alastair and Michael both happy. That certainly means a lot to me."**

We had a smooth journey back to our home in Orpington.

Friday, 16th November 2001

Our first appointment this morning was at the fracture clinic of Bromley Hospital. We were told that the right hand breakage was healing nicely but, after X-ray, it was discovered that there was a broken bone in the left hand. My poor Jenny now has her left wrist in plaster but is able to do the basic necessities of life.

Sunday, 18ᵗʰ November 2001

Jenny cooked a wonderful roast beef and Yorkshire pudding dinner and as we discussed our pending wedding arrangements, we decided that the proceedings could well be conducted at Stansted Hall in Essex. Jenny told me that there was a wonderful chapel at Stansted, where she had always wanted to be married. So now it was decided, we will be married in March at Stansted Hall, within a few miles of where I used to live at Great Easton.

Monday, 19ᵗʰ November 2001

I came downstairs and Jenny was having a sitting with Mustafa.

He said, **"We are very pleased with how you are both progressing.**

"To say that Michael's departure from your heart and mind for a while will be short term devastating. He too will feel abandoned, but not for long as he will see the excitement before him on his vast learning trip. He will indeed feel the wrench from your side and ache with long felt passion for you. However his time will pass as he busies himself to gain this vast knowledge set before him. He will understand that the break is necessary for the pair of you as he works long and hard into the night thinking of your return together. He will see his passion curb slightly and be enthused to come back quickly by your side.

"A spring wedding has been forecast and it will take place quite rapidly. All are

waiting to set matters into motion and bring about a speedy successful outcome. Do not be worried ever about monetary matters as we always provide enough for both your needs.

"Yes, an expensive time to come, but the finances will prove fruitful enough as a tiny amount will be released from nowhere, which will see all those bills settled in full, enough to go around and a bit more besides. Jenny will have her hands full as usual, with Michael's health recovering further. He will be determined to make both your dreams come true and both will be ecstatically happy – no problems there.

"The trip to America will be more than successful on a spiritual basis. Please watch your pockets there. An orange glow of spiritual warmth and upliftment will overtake Michael and he will feel as if floating, so called elevated and one of his lady guides will assist there, yes, I said lady guides.

"A fork-symbol making with the left hand and a tiny booklet inscribed will be given to Michael to keep – a form of souvenir. Also a pendant – round on a turquoise beaded necklace, he will purchase as he will be drawn to it naturally."

We went to bed very tired but I was woken up at four-thirty to go to the bathroom. On my return to bed I was told to get in facing Jenny and I was to put my hand out and touch her. My thoughts were "No we are both to tired to make love and it is a busy day tomorrow".

However the feeling was very strong that I should do this so, still feeling very sleepy I touched Jenny's tummy. She told me later that Spirit had woken her up too. She was on fire! Her body was very hot and utterly turned on. We were guided in a fantastic love making session lasting for half an hour. We were both too exhausted to fully climax but the sensations and feeling were extraordinary. We were so aroused afterwards we couldn't get off to sleep for a while.

Tuesday, 20th November 2001

At eleven o'clock this morning, after being checked in by a lady, whose birthday was the same as mine and Libby's, I was sitting in an Airbus A330 aeroplane at Gatwick Airport for the flight to Pittsburgh. From there onto Orlando, where I was to be taken with seventeen others, to visit the North American Indians at Chambers Farm, Orange Springs, Marion Country, Florida.

My adventures and spiritual experiences there would fill another chapter. As we haven't the space in this little book it will have to wait perhaps for another occasion, but it has to be said that Libby was with me. I missed Jenny desperately and I learned a lot about the spirituality of the First Nation Americans, whose hospitality was outstandingly generous. While I was there I did purchase the turquoise beaded necklace that I was attracted to without having made any conscious effort to fulfil the forecast.

Sunday, 25th November 2001

Everybody was up by half past seven. I reluctantly joined them. There were some presentations made to us including a Thunder Warrior shirt, a scroll, some sage and an American flag.

After breakfast the British contingent went to the east gate of the arena just before nine o'clock for the Raising of the American Flag Ceremony. By nine fifteen I reflected that the sun was shining pleasantly and there wasn't a cloud in the sky as I stood under the oak trees bedecked in the Spanish moss that was hanging down from them. I sat in camp, ready to leave at eleven o'clock for Orlando Airport. It was a time of photographs, farewells and although it was a great experience, a very great experience, I was very much looking forward to touching base at home and being with my beloved Jenny again. I had missed her greatly but as there was so much to do my mind was kept occupied most of the time. After sleeping in a tepee for the week, I was looking forward to hot water and a comfortable bed and feeling the warmth of my beloved next to me and exchanging love with her.

At twenty-two minutes past two I was at Orlando Airport, having survived the problem of the truck belonging to a man called Squirrel breaking down at the gas station at twelve noon! We all had to squeeze into the remaining vehicles and we arrived safely and checked in. It was a beautifully sunny day in Orlando, Florida. I found a washroom and had a good all over wash. It was wonderful to have hot water again.

I missed Jenny very much. The activities of the week had taken my mind off her a little bit but I couldn't wait to be in her arms again and feel safe and secure in our new life together. I had some Cuban coffee and some pastries that were excellent before checking through to the departure lounge and I was feeling good for the journey home. As I prepared to board Flight 334 at Orlando for Pittsburgh I reflected on some words to write for Jenny on the flight home.

I WILL NEVER GO AWAY

Jenny, I love you,
you know that this is true.
Jenny I love you,
I'm coming back to you.
This week has seemed a lifetime;
I've been so far away
When I come back to you
I promise that I'll stay.
I can't abide the separation
and what we've both been through
The next time I'm invited,
I'll tag along with you.
Wherever you want to lead me,
I'll be happy at your side
Our souls are too close to part;
it's with you that I abide.
So know my sweetest Jenny,
I will never go away…

An hour after scheduled take-off time, we were still sitting in the plane at Orlando, waiting for clearance to leave. This meant that we should miss our connection at Philadelphia, so goodness knows when I shall see my darling Jenny. At seven o'clock all international passengers were ushered off the plane and during the next couple of hours the usual airport wrangling and chaos reigned. Eventually at nine o'clock we arrived at the Hilton Garden Inn, a five-minute coach ride from Orlando Airport. There were rumours of a snow storm in Pittsburgh!

I had a very pleasant room but it was of very little cheer without Jenny, but the large double bed was much more comfortable than I had been used to recently as I had been sleeping on the ground in a tepee. However the hot, clean shower was wonderful and I shaved for the first time in a week.

I felt better after a meal and back in the hotel I managed to get through on the telephone to Jenny with the bad news that I was delayed twenty-four hours. It was five o'clock in the morning for her in England. She was devastated of course as I was. She telephoned me back and we spoke for an hour. It was so wonderful to talk to her, to share things with her and to know in concrete terms what I already knew – that she loved me as much as I love her.

Tuesday, 27ᵗʰ November 2001

At seven twenty-five I could still see the stars out of the window. They were still plainly visible but due east I saw the lightening of the sky and I knew that we were flying into the sunrise. Below me I could see the tops of the white clouds and the sun that I had seen set in Pittsburgh was now rising in England to greet the day, the moment when Jenny and I were together again after what now seems a very, very long time.

The extra twenty-five hours delay in getting back to England had indeed stretched the time we have been apart almost to breaking point. I could imagine just how excited Jenny would be at this moment. She would be driving on the M25 or maybe she had already arrived at Gatwick. Wherever she was I knew that she loved me and was waiting passionately to welcome me back to England and into her arms again.

We landed in sunshine at Gatwick at eight forty-one so the flight time was six hours and sixteen minutes. It was two degrees below and calm. As we taxied to the terminal I couldn't help wondering if my dream of being met by a beautiful and wonderful lady would turn into a reality. I thought that I would need to rub my eyes and pinch myself to find out. It was wonderful to be back in England. All I wanted now was my beloved and I could be happy, happy, happy.

Jenny was there at Gatwick Airport waiting for me. She was dressed as a squaw in an Indian coat and two feathers. We held each other lovingly and could have devoured each other. All we wanted was to get home and make love together.

Jenny had changed. She was bright eyed and free. Her past had dissolved away and she was only there for us. Nothing could touch us. We were free of the past and lived in the now. We worked for the Great Divine from whom all love came and we were totally and completely in love with each other in a way that was impossible before we met.

We had been in training during the previous years of our lives for each other and now we were the perfect couple. We are totally complimentary. We dovetailed in every way. We were complete together and devastated apart. We should never leave each other again. We could not face the pain of parting and being apart because the more our love grew, the more our souls become one, the more devastating the parting.

Thursday, 29th November 2001

Today Jenny and I have been together for one hundred days. I got up at eight o'clock to make some lemon tea and to type up a little something as a celebration poem.

ONE HUNDRED DAYS MY LOVE

Congratulations! Our love is a hundred days old today. It is another milestone accomplished and another cause for celebration. So kiss me my love and say that it is as wonderful for you as it is wonderful for me to be blessed with the gift of living our lives in total harmony.

Together we are blessed by the Great
Divine Spirit, who made us, raised us and
brought us together.

NOW IT IS ONE HUNDRED DAYS TOGETHER

Within my heart a light burns bright for thee.
And it will burn there throughout eternity.
You have aroused my honour and my deep respect
Before, somehow existed I, but wallowed in neglect.
You brought out the sunshine and showed me how to
love,
Before I just played at it. It wasn't gifted from above.
I didn't have the grace and depth, now engrained into
my heart
As I wonder at the miracle that set you and I apart
In ecstasy of loving, making love and being love.
We rejoice in all the wonder of fitting like a glove.
So come my gracious darling, the wonder of my life,
A hundred days of loving, of being as man and wife,
Is just a blinking of an eye throughout the time that's
been set by
Remember that our love is built to last throughout all
eternity.

Friday, 30ᵗʰ November 2001
    We sat up in bed drinking lemon tea and looking at the
brochure for our Honeymoon in Egypt, when Mustafa said to
Jenny, "We are delighted you are going."
    I am delighted that we were going too. Independently
Jenny and I had always wanted to go to Egypt, because we
both have a natural fascination with its history and culture.
Neither of us had been there and it will be a fitting place for

our honeymoon. We have fixed the wedding day as Saturday, 30th March 2002 at Stansted Hall, Essex. So now we have the wedding and the honeymoon in sight at last.

Mustafa gave us an evening sitting and everything was on track and this is some of what he told us, **"You are on the right track both of you. See what is more convenient March or April. We prefer March if at all possible. We know that the finances will be tight but we did promise much funds coming in. It will give Jenny much needed revenue and the necessary time to re-adjust further. We know Michael that you are already there and waiting. Jenny still needs catching up time, so allow her this.**

"We are all delighted as to how things are progressing right across the board. Jenny has done very well with leaving her past behind her now and this we commend her courage. She stood strong in the face of adversity. So again well done.

"So hold your course – all to be settled quite nicely very soon. A golden glow over the pair of you from now on – and please be very pleased."

Chapter 11

THE WEDDING

Friday, 8th March 2002

We went to Bluewater today and bought the wedding rings. That was a relief. The interesting thing, bearing in mind that co-incidences didn't exist, was that both rings cost the same amount of money. This to me was a clear indication of the equality of our partnership in spiritual and earthly terms. We had been told that we would work together as equals and for me this was a clear reminder of the equality of our relationship when viewed from all angles.

Sunday, 10th March 2002

I thought of Libby. I knocked out my pipe and the embers formed a perfect triangle on the patio, each side was the same size and brightness. I knew it was symbolic of the triangle formed by Libby, Jenny and myself. I thanked her for her love and the love, which I knew she would continue to give to me. I gave her my spiritual love. I thanked her for giving me Jenny and for giving Jenny her love.

She said, *"I love you Bear and I always will."*

I felt her presence and as she left I felt, rather than saw, her white silvery light as she departed from me. I knew that I was to tell Jenny about this because our love was one together.

Saturday, 23ʳᵈ March 2002

A sitting with Mustafa in which he told us, **"You two indeed can count your blessings as we want the very best for the pair of you and all is coming just at the right time. A great bunch of people at the wedding and all including Alastair will enjoy it. His speech will be minimal, not much to say at all, but that's okay. He needs to build up his confidence there."**

Friday, 29ᵗʰ March 2002

After making love this morning we busied ourselves getting packed and re-writing speeches. The bouquets and buttonholes arrived. The buttonholes arrived in a box marked "Class I EGYPTIAN PRODUCE". Thank you Mustafa for your love and support.

I was shown a twig, just outside the house shaped as a wishbone and I knew that it was for good luck. Alastair started the wedding video by seeing us out of the house and into the car. We, that is Jenny, Alastair and I, left for Stansted Hall. It was a pleasant drive up in the sunshine and we managed to get our cases unpacked and to have a good walk round the gardens. Kathy, our Maid of Honour, soon joined us from Ashbourne in Derbyshire and we dined in a four hundred-year-old tithe barn just along the road from Stansted Hall. We had the whole barn to ourselves and enjoyed a good meal and each other's company.

Saturday, 30ᵗʰ March 2002

Jenny and I slept well and prepared the last minute tasks before she came down the aisle looking so beautiful and loving. We were so happy all through the ceremony that Steven Upton conducted.

The music was played wonderfully by Ron Holding. Montague gave a beautiful reading followed by Steven's excellent address.

The sun shone and everybody was happy. The food and wine flowed, the speeches were all good and everybody, as Mustafa had predicted was very happy and they all enjoyed themselves. It was all too wonderful for words. Jenny and I were married and for us it was a perfect day – everything was perfect and we enjoyed every minute. There were no nerves between us and we knew what we wanted and everything was provided.

We knew that in the Sanctuary where the ceremony took place were Libby, my mother and Jenny's mother and father. We also knew that many more came from Spirit. I was blessed in being shown from just outside the great hall, looking up the huge landscaped lawn, a vast number of spirit people in an arc across the lawn and as high as the great trees, some five feet off the ground. They were beautiful and smiling and full of joy and love and peace.

Sunday, 31ˢᵗ March 2002

We woke up early in the four-poster bed and made love. After breakfast with our friends who had stayed the night, we packed and left for Orpington. Alastair went to visit his father and grandmother to celebrate her 80ᵗʰ birthday and stay the night. We felt compelled to make love again. We were so ready and we both came to the biggest orgasm I had ever known. God bless our loving guides. The biggest and the best coming together saved for the first day of our married life at home in Orpington.

After dinner I was having a pipe in the garden when I thought I should remind Jenny to thank Mustafa for all the wonders of our wedding day. I felt I should thank him myself and so I did. Mustafa said that soon Jenny and I should start to work together. He was pleased that everything had gone so well and told me that we would enjoy ourselves in Egypt. He told me he would be looking over us.

Monday, 1ˢᵗ April 2002

We woke up early to get ready to leave the house at eleven-fifteen to drive to Heathrow to catch the quarter past three flight to Luxor in Egypt and start the holiday part of our honeymoon. We had excellent seats in the second row upstairs of this Boeing 747. Jenny had fallen into conversation with a lady who was attending a healing conference in Luxor and who was in need of healing and advice for herself. Jenny supplied both these and on our return to England received a letter from the lady thanking her for the healing and confirming the good advice give by Mustafa through Jenny.

We got through Passport Control and Immigration very quickly and we soon found the representative and we were taken to the minibus for transportation to the boat. We were kept waiting an hour and fifty minutes before everybody had arrived and we could start our journey. We were the first in the mini-bus but the last to be dropped off. By the time we had unpacked and eaten the sandwiches that had been thoughtfully left for us, it was half past one in the morning. Jenny and I saw a spirit light that sparkled in front of us in the cabin. It was good to know that we were in such good company. We felt very happy and relaxed that we were here at last and that we were protected by the World of Spirit.

I was convinced that we would have a wonderful week here on our chosen cruise and a second week by the Red Sea and followed by a stay in Cairo. While Jenny was in the bathroom Mustafa welcomed us to Egypt and told us how well we had done on the journey. I felt the great warmth of his love for us both. So, very tired but glad to be safely here in Egypt, we settled down for a few hours sleep.

Tuesday, 2ⁿᵈ April 2002

We were woken up by an early morning call at seven-thirty and we could see out of the porthole the River Nile swirling by us and on the other bank there were various kinds of palm trees and some small mountains. I was to discover later that beyond them was the Valley of the Kings.

The sun was of course shining as we left to visit Luxor Museum and after lunch the Temples of Karnak and Luxor. At seven o'clock that evening we left the boat again to see the Sound and Light display at the Karnak Temple. This was very significant for us because just after it had started Mustafa came to us and Jenny felt him very strongly with her.

As we held hands, he told us that we would be together for all time. What wonderful, wonderful words they were. Clairvoyantly he showed himself to me and he was smiling. I felt very strongly that he was inviting us to enjoy our visit and that we certainly did.

And so we were set for our new life as Mr and Mrs. Ayers with our honeymoon in Egypt and later the new home was to be brought to us, but all that as they say is another story. God bless you all and I hope you enjoyed reading these words, every one of which is true.

BIBLIOGRAPHY

Borgia, Anthony. *Life in the World Unseen.*
M.A.P. Inc. 1983. ISBN 0-9636435-0-9
Borgia, Anthony. *More about Life in the World Unseen.*
M.A.P. Inc. 2000. ISBN 0-9636435-2-5
Borgia, Anthony. *Here and Hereafter.*
M.A.P. Inc. 2000. ISBN 0-9636435-3-3
Borgia, Anthony. *More Light.*
Two Worlds. 1995. ISBN 0-947823-43-3
Borgia, Anthony. *Heaven and Hell.*
Two Worlds. 1995. ISBN 0-947823-41-7
Borgia, Anthony. *Facts.*
Two Worlds. 1995. ISBN 0-947823-42-5
Findlay Arthur. *On the Edge of the Etheric.*
1992. ISBN 0-947823-05-0
Findlay Arthur. *The Rock of Truth.*
1999. ISBN 0-902036-07-6
Findlay Arthur. *The Unfolding Universe.*
1999. ISBN 0-902036-20-3
Findlay Arthur. *The Torch of Knowledge.*
1996. ISBN 0-902-036-09-2
Findlay Arthur. *The Psychic Stream.*
1992. ISBN 0-947823-31-X
Findlay Arthur. *The Curse of Ignorance Volume 1.*
1993. ISBN 0-947823-33-6
Findlay Arthur. *The Curse of Ignorance Volume II.*
1993. ISBN 0-947823-34-4

Kardec Allan. *The Book on Mediums.*
Weiser. 1998. ISBN 0-87728-382-6
Kardec Allen. *The Spirit's Book.*
1989. ISBN 0-914732-25-0
Kennedy. David. *A Venture in Immortality.*
Colin Smythe Limited. 1987. ISBN 0-86140-284-7
Kübler-Ross, Elisabeth. *On Life After Death.*
Celestial Arts. 1991. ISBEN 0-89087-653-3
Lewis C. S. *A Grief Observed.*
Faber and Faber. 1966. ISBN 0-571-06624-0
More, Thomas. *Soul Mates.*
Element Books Ltd. 1994. ISBN 1-85230-522-3
Polge, Carol. *Living Images.*
The Aquarian Press. 1991. ISBN 1-85538-084-6
Redfield James. *The Tenth Vision - Holding the Vision.*
Warner Books. 1996. ISBN 0-446-51908-1
Redfield, James. *The Celestine Prophesy.*
Bantam Books. 1994. ISBN 0-553-40902-6
Sherwood, Jane. *Past-Mortum Journal.*
C. W. Daniel. 1991. ISBN 0-85207-253-8
Swain, Jasper. *On the Death of my Son.*
The Aquarian Press. 1989. ISBN 0-85030-788-0
Taylor Allegra. *Healing Hands.*
Tuttle. 1993. ISBN 0-8048-1832-0

(Please note that these are the editions that I have and other editions of other dates may he available.)

FILMS & VIDEOS

Field of Dreams
Message in A Bottle
I'll be Home for Christmas
Truly, Madly, Deeply

Lightning Source UK Ltd.
Milton Keynes UK
UKOW05f0040281216
290897UK00001B/191/P